D0365026

CRUSADERS

*Voices from the
Abortion Front*

CRUSADERS

Voices from the Abortion Front

by Marian Faux

A Birch Lane Press Book
Published by Carol Publishing Group

363.46
FAU
c.1

MADISON COUNTY
Canton Public Library System
Canton, Miss. 39046

Copyright © 1990 by Marian Faux

A Birch Lane Press Book
Published by Carol Publishing Group

Editorial Offices
600 Madison Avenue
New York, NY 10022

Sales & Distribution Offices
120 Enterprise Avenue
Secaucus, NJ 07094

In Canada: Musson Book Company
A division of General Publishing Co. Limited
Don Mills, Ontario

All rights reserved. No part of this book
may be reproduced in any form, except by
a newspaper or magazine reviewer who
wishes to quote brief passages in
connection with a review.

Queries regarding rights and permissions
should be addressed to: Carol Publishing Group,
600 Madison Avenue, New York, NY 10022

Manufactured in the United States of America
10 9 8 7 6 5 4 3 2 1

Library of Congress Cataloging-in-Publication Data

Faux, Marian.
        Crusaders : voices from the abortion front.
        p.   cm.
        "A Birch Lane Press book."
        Includes index.
        ISBN 1-55972-020-4 : $19.95
        1. Pro-choice movement--United States--Case studies.
    2. Pro-life movement--United States--Case studies. 3. Social
    reformers--United States--Case studies. 4. Abortion--Moral
    and ethical aspects. I. Title.
    HQ767.5.U5F38   1990
    363.4'6--dc20   90-2228
                                                 CIP

Carol Publishing Group books are available at special discounts
for bulk purchases, for sales promotions, fund raising, or
educational purposes. Special editions can also be created to
specifications. For details contact: Special Sales Department,
Carol Publishing Group, 120 Enterprise Ave., Secaucus, NJ 07094

FOR SADIE WALSH

| Acknowledgments

As is always the case with a work of nonfiction, I was aided in the writing of this book by many persons. I am most indebted to the subjects of this book, who graciously shared their lives with me: Frank Susman, B. J. Isaacson-Jones and the women of Reproductive Health Services, Randall Terry, "Moira," Vernice Miller, and Frances Kissling. Without them, there would have been no book. I am especially grateful to the women of Reproductive Health Services, who spent many hours talking with me, gave me free rein in their clinic, and did whatever they could to facilitate my work. They led me to see abortion as the provacative, multidimensional, complex issue that it is.

I am deeply appreciative to the following persons for the insightful interviews and invaluable information they provided: Judith Widdicombe, founder and former director of Reproductive Health Services; Roger Evans, co-counsel on the Webster case and chief litigator for Planned Parenthood; Carol Sobel and Betty Ann Downing of the ACLU Foundation of Southern California; Carol Tice, a West Coast pro-choice activist who also writes about women's issues; Marie Bass and Joanne Howes of Reproductive Health Technologies, for information about RU 486; Lynne Randall, of the Feminist Women's Health Center in Atlanta, and Carol Downer, of the Feminist Women's Health Center in Los Angeles, two pioneers in the field of abortion services who shared their professional histories and that of the abortion-rights movement with me; Rev. James Burtchaell of Notre Dame for talking with me about the history of the pro-life movement; Mrs. Yancy at the Los Angeles Municipal Court; Toni House and Priscilla Goodwin at the Supreme Court;

Sergeant Carl Pyrdum for sharing his fascinating perspective on Operation Rescue; and Jesse Lee, Mark Lucas, Linda Sclafani, and Barbara Magera for penetrating interviews about Randall Terry.

Special thanks to dramaturg Susan Mason, who, in addition to doing research for which she was thoroughly overqualified, also shared with me her professional analyses of several persons in the book; and to clinical psychologist Marie M. Burnett, for her invaluable insights.

I owe a special debt to Carolyn Childers, a pro-choice activist who spent hours talking with me about the West Coast clinic defenders, whom she helped to organize. I had originally hoped to make Childers one of the portraits in the book, but was unable to do so when she withdrew from her work as an activist.

I am indebted to Birch Lane editor Hillel Black, for doing what a superb editor does and tactfully teaching me a thing or two about writing, and to everyone else at Birch Lane who worked on the book. Special thanks to my agent Barbara Lowenstein for her support and good work. Finally, I wish to thank my husband Bill Willig for his usual generosity in supporting my work.

Contents

| Author to Reader

W<small>HEN</small> I F<small>INISHED</small> *Roe v. Wade: The Untold Story of the Landmark Supreme Court Case That Legalized Abortion,* it was with a sense of reluctance that I left the subject. I felt there was another story that I had not been able to tell in that book, which ended with the legalization of abortion. This was a story about everything that happened after legalization, the extraordinary changes that the Roe decision brought.

In *Crusaders: Voices from the Abortion Front,* I have taken up that unfinished thread to weave it loosely into the stories of six persons who are currently deeply involved in the abortion debate. Of the people I've chosen to write about, two are unequivocally and clearly pro-life; two are just as firmly pro-choice; and two, although pro-choice, have expressed reservations about the quality of the debate and would like more open dialogue from both sides, which, in turn, holds out the promise of compromise.

My first thought when I began to plan this book was to return to a subject I wasn't about to cover in Roe. I wanted to write about the abortion providers, as the professionals who deliver abortion and abortion-related services call themselves. This female-dominated profession arose overnight after abortion was legalized and did much to change the face of modern medicine, certainly in terms of how women are treated as medical patients. Determined to establish free-standing clinics devoted exclusively to women's reproductive health care, abortion providers pioneered in the delivery of minor surgery on an out-patient basis, a practice unheard of in 1973 that is now considered routine. The providers also set new standards for providing medical treatment in a nurturing, supportive environment.

Their work has gone mostly unrecognized. Few people think to visit an abortion clinic, except under adverse circumstances. The best way to describe the work of the providers, it seemed to me, was to write about an abortion clinic. After considering clinics in New Jersey, Pittsburgh, and Los Angeles, I settled on Reproductive Health Services in St. Louis. That the clinic happened also to have been the plaintiff in the Webster cases was irrelevant. I chose it because the clinic is a model of the kind of supportive atmosphere in which abortion services can and should be provided.

Any portrait of an abortion clinic inevitably must touch upon the daily war that goes on all over the country inside and outside these clinics. In recent years, the providers have worked in what can only be described as a battle zone. All clinics have been picketed and harassed by anti-abortion forces at one time or another. A few clinics have been picketed daily for months and even years. Clinic workers have learned to survive in a daily work environment that includes bomb scares, threatening and obscene telephone calls, written threats to their persons and their families, burglaries and vandalism, and occasional outbursts of a more serious nature, including kidnapping and fire bombings.

My second portrait, the first in the book actually, is of Frank Susman, the pro-choice lawyer who initiated and argued the Webster case in the Supreme Court. In a sense typical of abortion reformers, Susman is also utterly atypical. He is a man in a movement dominated by women, an unaffiliated reformer, an outspoken soul who rankles the pro-choice movement as much as he pleases it. He is nevertheless the quintessential reformer, an expert on the medical and legal aspects of abortion who has worked tirelessly to protect women's right to choose.

An intriguing man in many respects, he is both resented and respected within the pro-choice movement. Susman goes about his work of challenging restrictive abortion laws with little fanfare (except in a case like Webster where extenuating circumstances prevail) and for little monetary gain. Both Susman and Reproductive Health Services, one of his clients, have played an invaluable role in keeping abortion legal in the United States.

Apart from writing about Susman and the clinic, I was also interested in the religious aspects of the abortion issue. This seemed to me to be at the heart of the debate. That led to two portraits, one of Randall Terry, the founder of Operation Rescue, the nation's newest and most vociferous anti-abortion group, and a companion piece about a woman whom we call Moira, a foot solider in his army.

Terry has mined the terrain of fundamentalist Christianity to promote his militant and militaristic anti-abortion, and some say, anti-woman, views. Within a few short months of founding Operation Rescue, he managed to become more of a pro-life mover and shaker than any of his Catholic counterparts did in their decade of existence.

Terry and his followers are part of a movement of conservative Protestants and Catholics determined to roll back the clock to an era when religion played a more pivotal role in our lives than it does at present, a time when the wages of sin functioned as a social deterrent. Terry's proselytizing about abortion is in many ways typical of this fundamentalist fervor, which seeks to punish women for the "sin" of abortion. Their steadfast opposition to abortion is only one item on their much-larger agenda, and it offers, I hope, valuable insights into the fundamentalist revival currently under way in this country.

A companion portrait tells the story of Moira, an uneducated, knockabout, single mother who moved from guru to guru in the Seventies before finally settling on Terry as her prophet. Moira rewrote the script of her already disarrayed life in order to join Terry's army. Both Terry and Operation Rescue had amazing repercussions in her life.

On the pro-choice side, there is also the portrait of Vernice Miller, a young, well-educated African-American who presses the case of minority and poor women. She insists on a more thoughtful discussion about abortion rights, one that will encompass the diverse views of Catholic, Latina, African-American, poor, and young women who have been left out of the debate thus far even though they are the ones who suffer most from misguided abortion politics on the right and the left.

Although she and her constituency are pro-choice, they stand somewhere to the right of center. This has caused the left-leaning pro-choice movement to ignore them. Theirs is an agenda that can include abortion only when it is part of a larger, more general program promoting women's and children's overall health.

Miller, one of the compromise voices in the debate, believes that minority women may hold the key to modulating the debate and preserving the abortion right.

Finally, also on the pro-choice side but with some fascinating reservations, there is Frances Kissling, a self-educated philosopher with some provocative ideas about resolving the abortion issue. As director of a small, iconoclastic but highly influential organization called Catholics for a Free Choice, Kissling challenges the power structure of the Roman Catholic Church.

As is the case with Terry, far more is at stake than women's abortion rights. Kissling seeks nothing less than a complete restructuring of the Catholic Church. She and other dissident Catholics would like to return the Church to its original founding principles. But unlike Terry and other fundamentalists who are seeking to establish a rigid, male hierarchy within their church, Kissling and other Catholic dissidents are striving to dismantle their own male hierarchy. Their goal is to return the Catholic Church to its original founding principles, to reestablish its communal, inclusive structure. Kissling will probably play a pivotal role in the Church's reorganization when it happens..

She supports the abortion right, but like Miller, she calls for more thoughtful dialogue. Where most pro-choice activists insist that abortion is a cut-and-dried civil rights issue, Kissling chooses to see many shades of gray. She is one of the few pro-choice activists who asks and attempts to answer the hard questions about abortion. Hers is a respected voice among pro-choice reformers, and in the wake of the Webster decision, her proposal for compromise has far move relevance than ever.

An underlying theme in this book is my interest in what drives reformers to do what they do. I was curious to know what motivated people to become involved in an issue that is so frustrating and taxing.

I suspect I am typical of most of us in that however much I may be a kindred spirit, I remain an armchair activist at best; at worst, an overwrought critic. In contrast, the persons whom I've chosen to write about are distinguished by the fact they have and continue to act on their convictions. They have organized careers and even lives around their beliefs.

Having observed their activism at close range, I maintain the deepest respect for it, believing as I do that activists are a necessary part of a free and democratic government. It is the so-called "radicals" who carry the banner for social reform and who are the true catalysts for change in our world.

This book is loosely organized around the 1989 Webster decision, in which the Supreme Court found that the states may impose some restrictions on the abortion right. The ruling dramatically affects the future of the abortion right. Even though activists on both sides insist they will not compromise, Webster has reopened the debate among the vast, ambivalent majority that most of us fall into. This time, the debate is not likely to end until some form of compromise is reached.

Abortion, unresolvable and fascinating an issue as it is, is not a subject that can be "writ large." Philosophical discourses on its morality or ethics fall on deaf ears and do little to sway people from one point of view to another. Ultimately such discourse is alienating, so personal is the abortion decision. For that reason, I have chosen to write "small," simply to tell the story of six persons' views, ideas, actions, and feelings about abortion. To the extent that this book helps anyone through the process of deciding how to think and feel about this difficult and painful subject, it is my intention that the real teachers shall be the portraits and not the writer who collected the stories.

In closing, I would like to say a word about the terms I have used to describe the activists on both sides of the debate and also human life, born and unborn. More than any other controversial social issue, abortion requires the careful use of words. Language has become a weapon among activists on both sides of the debate. Although I know pro-choice activists will disapprove, I have used the terms "pro-life" and "right-to-life" to describe those who are opposed to abortion. It is what they call themselves, and what they are called in the popular press. I have also referred to pro-life activists as anti-abortionists because that is what they are.

I have not referred to pro-choice activists as pro-abortion, a term that anti-abortionists use to describe them, because I firmly believe that pro-choice activists are not "for abortion" but rather for the right to choose abortion.

I have broadly used the term *fetus* to describe unborn human life from conception to birth rather than using the more accurate terms blastocyte and embryo to describe various, specific stages of human development. I believe the anti-abortionists' use of the word *baby* to describe potential human life is inaccurate and have avoided its use except in direct quotes.

New York City
April, 1990

CRUSADERS

*Voices from the
Abortion Front*

1 | A Turning Point

ON A SWELTERING MORNING, July 3, 1989, hundreds of people were gathered on the steps of the U.S. Supreme Court. Not since the Nixon tapes case fifteen years earlier had so many congregated at the nation's highest court to await a decision. Americans—indeed, much of the world—had been worked into a frenzy of eager anticipation by an overwrought press that believed it was covering the decision of a decade, possibly even of the century.

In front of the white marble courthouse, the camera crews of several networks pooled resources to set up a spider's web of electrical wires, kleig lights, cameras, and over thirty microphones that they would subsequently use to snare the many VIPs who would be present this morning. In addition, each of the major networks commandeered a small space from which it would be able to broadcast live as soon as there was any word of the decision. Hard at work since 8 a.m., the media had been standing by for this moment for the better part of two weeks and had come from as far away as Japan and Australia. On nearby Maryland Avenue, three vans played nanny to several huge satellite dishes waiting to flash the news 22,000 miles into the heavens to a communications satellite, and then, in an eighth of a second, back down to earth, to cities and towns across America.

Although the Court would not begin its daily business until 10 a.m., the protesters began to gather as early as 8:30. Court guards struggled to confine them to the street sidewalk some one hundred feet from the Court's steps leading to the heavy bronze double doors, but they soon filled and overflowed that space, spilling out onto First Street.

1

In the center of the sidewalk standing side by side were representatives of the two main groups of protesters. Each group was unfurling its own twenty-five-foot-long banner, the kind that is more often seen announcing high school marching bands in parades. But where one would ordinarily have expected to read Central High and Jonesville High were two opposing, political, and to be fair, polemical messages. Eight women unfurled a twenty-foot-long purple banner, sponsored by the National Organization for Women (NOW), whose yellow letters proclaimed, "Keep Abortion and Birth Control Safe and Legal." The competing banner, held by two clean-cut young men who later revealed themselves to be members of American Collegians for Life, a group active on the campuses of Catholic universities, announced: "I am part of society entrusted to protect life."

Hundreds of pro-choice women and a smattering of men milled about carrying round blue and white placards that read: "Keep Abortion Legal." Some hand-lettered signs announced more personal sentiments. A bronzed, youthful-looking mother and her daughter waved signs that said: "Arizona Teen for Choice" and "Arizona Mom Wants Choice." A pregnant woman who said she had traveled from Ohio walked around with a hand-lettered sign that read "No Child Should be Born Unwanted" pinned to her huge belly. One could only wonder at the stories that had prompted these women to travel thousands of miles to offer up their feelings to a group of nine justices, eight of them old men, who would not even deign to look out their windows at the gathering forces.

Abortion foes were out in equal strength and fervor. A banner read: "The child killing must be stopped." Another cluster of men and women representing a group called Americans for Life held up their preprinted placards that alternately asked and announced: "What About the Baby's Body?" and "Abortion is a lie." Dozens of signs reading "Abortion exploits women" bobbed above the sweaty, hot crowd. Beyond the sea of protesters, standing off by themselves, a man and woman wearing faded jeans held up another big banner, which ominously announced: "Operation Rescue will prevail."

The press was a human tidal wave, flowing from one scene of protest to the next. When Molly Yard arrived wearing a beige suit and a grim smile, they descended upon her, listening as she wanly and unbelievably predicted a victory for pro-choice forces.

Next, they flowed over to a pro-life man wearing a brown monk's robe surrounded by a small group carrying large photographs of bloody fetuses. When they knelt to pray, they provided a striking photo opportunity that the press did not fail to seize upon. Then it was on to a stout, blue-suited black man in his thirties who arrived waving a Bible and a handful of small American flags, and emanating the air of a demagogue. Surrounded by a cluster of scrubbed, flag-laden children, he scaled the courthouse steps to position himself for what he wanted to say and soon had launched into a sermon on the evils of Margaret Sanger and what she had done to the black community by introducing birth control.

The press swarmed, for the moment paying rapt attention. But when he pulled two small plastic Kewpie dolls from his front suit pocket and announced, "Here's what a baby in its mother's womb is like at two weeks," a snicker rippled through the crowd, and the press would have moved on had not a young black woman and man shown up at that moment. They were pro-choice delegates obviously sent to deal with their own.

"Killing babies is not the issue here," the young woman insisted. The young man contended: "You forget the woman. You forget the woman." Nothing, however, deterred the self-styled preacher from delivering his message.

The debate grew shrill, and the press moved back in. Maybe, just maybe, this would be high-flown drama that the reporters' editors hungered after for today's headlines. When a cameraman rudely brushed aside an inquisitive tourist to photograph the scene, he seemed to sum up the whole atmosphere when he abruptly told her: "Sorry, ma'am, media event."

The object of all this attention was a lawsuit called *Webster v. Reproductive Health Services*, which the Supreme Court was expected to rule on this very morning. As it had done in another famous case, *Roe v. Wade*, decided in 1973, the Supreme Court was going to make a pronouncement about abortion. The Roe decision had legalized the surgery, even going so far as to make it a basic, specially protected right, like free speech. Now after nearly two decades of legalization, with the Webster decision, the Court was going to make another declaration, one that many people feared would mark the beginning of the end for safe, legalized abortion. For the first time since it was constitutionally established, the right to choose when to procreate was imperiled. And also for the first time in history, the Supreme Court was on the verge of revoking a basic constitutional right.

That the Supreme Court had reached this point was due in large part to the work of activists who had struggled to keep the abortion debate alive since the Roe decision. In recent years, the debate had been dominated by anti-abortion forces, but this had not always been the case.

In 1973 when the Supreme Court had handed down *Roe v. Wade*, there had been only slight opposition to the idea of legalized abortion. Indeed, a solid consensus had existed among a majority of Americans that abortion should be legalized. Although no one could be sure of the numbers, it was estimated that a million women a year obtained illegal operations. These unsafe, septic procedures resulted in the deaths of an estimated 5,000 to 10,000 women annually and maiming and injuries to countless thousands of others. In an era of unprecedented medical advances, Americans had increasingly begun to view this state of affairs as uncivilized. Prior to the mid-nineteenth century, in fact, women had been at liberty to choose whether to bear a child. Most historians believed that the restrictive abortion laws passed in the mid-nineteenth century were intended to protect women from a dangerous surgical procedure rather than to protect the fetus. By the mid-1960s, when abortion was no longer considered dangerous, there seemed little reason not to legalize it.

Opposition to the idea of legalization came mostly from the Catholic Church, and there was remarkably little of that. In Texas, where the *Roe v. Wade* case originated, in the early years of the reform movement, anti-abortion spokespersons frequently and congenially shared the podium with pro-choice spokeswomen as they engaged in remarkably genteel debate about the prospects of legalized abortion. Several prominent Catholics, including a number of clergymen, across the country spoke out in favor of legalization, their reasoning being that if the surgery were legal, the decision to have an abortion would truly be a matter of individual conscience. In any event, none of the abortion opponents thought the threat of legalized abortion was real enough to warrant any kind of organized opposition.

Pro-choice activists would have agreed. Optimistic about their long-term chances of bringing about legalization, they nevertheless believed they would spend much of the next decade in various courtrooms, bringing a series of lawsuits that would only slowly and in a patchwork fashion result in a right to choose when to procreate.

Neither side dreamed that the Supreme Court would legalize abortion in the first decision it ever handed down on the subject. Yet that is exactly what happened on January 23, 1973, when the Supreme Court, overnight, made abortion legal.

The sweep of the decision was breathtaking. The Court placed very few restrictions on the abortion right. Women were at liberty to obtain abortions throughout their pregnancies. In the first trimester, the states could not intervene at all; in the second, they could intervene to protect the mother's health, and in the third and final trimester of pregnancy, they could intervene to protect what the Court called "potential life." The Court declined to rule on when life began, saying only that since the nation's best legal, ethical, religious, and philosophical minds could not agree about this controversial subject, the states would not be permitted to make laws about it, either.

Reassured by such a total victory, the pro-choice activists went home, if not exactly to rest on their laurels, then at least satisfied that the right they had successfully fought to secure was well protected by so expansive a decision as Roe.

As they retired from action, however, the anti-abortion forces belatedly geared up. Finally alerted to the need to organize, they knew they had lost everything with the Roe decision. In reaction, they initiated what at the time looked like a woefully late counteroffensive.

Their efforts yielded little for the next decade. Americans simply were not interested in debating the merits and demerits of legalized abortion. Under any circumstances, abortion is a tough subject with which to capture the public imagination, and this was an issue that for all practical purposes appeared to be settled. Polls taken shortly after the Roe decision showed that a slim majority supported a woman's right to choose; this support would remain largely unchanged during the decade-and-a-half of legalized abortion.

Despite their best efforts to engage the attention of the American public, anti-abortion activists, or pro-lifers as they now insisted on calling themselves, in the immediate post-Roe era were unable to establish themselves as a mainstream force. In fact, most people viewed them as fringe radicals, even though the leadership consisted of respectable and often well-funded groups with ties to the Catholic Church. Occasional outbursts of violence against abortion clinics, which escalated in the late 1970s, did little to enhance their image.

The pro-life groups spent most of the 1980s reshaping themselves into a more middle-of-the-road movement. That accomplished, they set about remolding public opinion on abortion with renewed fervor. The National Right-to-Life Committee, which spearheaded the Catholic Church's anti-abortion activism, responded to criticism that they were male-dominated by hiring two fresh-faced, young women no one had ever heard of as spokespersons. Pro-lifers softened their criticism of feminism. Instead of maintaining their hard-line stance that all abortions were unacceptable, they began to acknowledge that the procedure might be necessary in cases of rape and incest while emphasizing that only 1 to 2 percent of all abortions—a figure the pro-choice forces would consider too low—resulted from those two criminal acts. Within a few years, they had succeeded in turning the discussion around from the rights of the woman to the rights of the fetus, but were never able to stir up much controversy. It was an impossible subject to debate in any event. No one, even the pro-choice activists, would say they were for abortion. At best abortion was viewed as an unpleasant decision that occasionally had to be made.

Not until the late 1980s did something finally happen to once again put the abortion debate center stage in American life. Ironically, this renewed attention to abortion was brought about not by the now mostly mainstream Catholic Right-to-Life groups, but rather, by a ragtag band of born-again Christian fundamentalists. After years of mostly unproductive anti-abortion efforts by highly organized groups, a small, barely organized group succeeded in stoking the flames of the debate as no one else had managed to do.

Although for years women had sporadically been harassed by Right-to-Life protesters as they entered abortion clinics, it took Operation Rescue, with its calculated state of threatened violence and highly organized attempts to physically stop women from obtaining abortions, to move the harassment to new levels. Not only had these new, extremely militant anti-abortion activists succeeded in making the public pay attention to abortion, but they quickly assumed control of the debate. Finally, people began to listen, and they were swayed by what they heard: pro-life's insistence that women acted irresponsibly, destroying a million and half unborn "children" each year. Whoever shapes any debate also decides what questions will be asked and answered, and in the late eighties, this meant that abortion discussion more and more came to be focused on the fetus rather than the woman as the true victim of abortion.

Only when the new pro-life activists' angry faces began to fill people's television screens night after night on the evening news did a new generation of pro-choice activists awaken to the need to respond to this latest threat to abortion. And even then the advocates of free choice were slow to rally their troops, most of whom refused to believe the threat was real. The new activists were tougher, less "ladylike," some said, than the white-gloved reformers of the 1960s. Less given to genteelly discussing the constitutional underpinnings of the abortion right and how it might best be protected in a courtroom, they were angry and action-oriented.

On the West Coast, women broke into pro-life churches at night and painted the walls with pro-choice slogans much as black-power activists had covered buildings with their slogans a few decades earlier. On the East Coast, others disrupted a mass at St. Patrick's Cathedral. Across the country they organized to escort each other into abortion clinics, and when Operation Rescue announced a major attack on the clinics of Southern

California, they organized to physically defend the clinics. Matching Operation Rescue's military tactics with some equally sophisticated maneuvers of their own, the women even managed to infiltrate Operation Rescue at its highest level.

It was just as well if the new pro-choice activists were tough. By the time pro-choice women awakened to the fact that the abortion right was in jeopardy, the right was half gone. The Webster case was already headed into a Supreme Court where two newly appointed, pro-life justices sat, waiting to form a new majority that would presumably undo Roe at the first opportunity. Now, on the eve of Independence Day in 1989, there was little anyone could do but await the decision.

Both sides were poised for battle, and it was difficult to say which was more desperate. If the pro-life forces won and the abortion decision were revoked, outraged women would take to the streets to protest the loss of the right that had the power to change the course of their lives. If the pro-choice forces won, the rage of the unbendingly radical pro-lifers would be equally great, and they would escalate their battle.

Whatever happened, the Webster decision would not be an ending, only a beginning. After years of avoiding the issue, Americans would have no choice but to attend to the abortion debate. In the nearly two decades since abortion had been legalized, it had become the issue that would not die, could not be resolved, where there seemed to be no room for compromise. This was not mere hyperbole. Abortion was the most controversial issue in American life, an intensely painful subject that pitted church against church, men against women, parents against their children, an issue that even reportedly divided the President's family. It was, some said, a test of democracy, of the free world's willingness to tolerate individual freedom.

At the center of the debate were the activists, the new breed of protester, stronger and more agressive than past ones, and determined to fight this holy war to its conclusion. They were the shapers, the propagandists, the apologizers, the explainers, the apex and nadir of the debate. Whatever happened with the Webster decision, one thing was certain: All America would be watching the activists.

2 | The Radical

Frank Susman

F RANK SUSMAN, the lawyer who argued the pro-choice side in the Webster case, is the Lone Ranger of the pro-choice movement. He is a man in a woman's world, a litigator among constitutional lawyers, a freelance reformer in a movement defined by its affiliations. He is also a radical, although he would not use that word to describe himself nor would many people use it to describe him. Yet more than Randall Terry, or for that matter, Molly Yard or Faye Wattleton and many of the other women associated with the pro-choice movement, Susman's work in abortion has been radical, at least in terms of how far it has taken him from the comfortable, decorous world of corporate lawyering that was to have been his destiny.

Reared in comfortable surroundings in Ladue, Missouri, one of St. Louis' richer suburbs, by a full-time mother and a father who founded his own corporate law firm, Susman was slated to follow in his father's footsteps. To a large extent, he did that, building upon the successful corporate practice that Earl Susman had established. But Susman's career also took an unusual, unpredictable turn.

When Susman joined his father's firm after finishing law school, it was taken for granted that he would develop, in addition to his corporate specialties, a pro bono specialty. As a Jew living in the predominantly Roman Catholic city of St. Louis and the Protestant Midwest, Earl Susman had his own ideas about social justice, a term he and his son preferred to civil rights. With Earl Susman at the helm, the firm had played a major role in the 1948 landmark Supreme Court case called *Shelley v. Kraemer*, which broke the back of discriminatory restrictive covenants. Although the covenants could still be written into real estate contracts, the courts could no longer be used to enforce them.

With this legacy to live up to, Frank Susman wasted no time in staking out his own turf. Within months of going to work for his father's firm, he started doing volunteer work. But to everyone's surprise, Susman chose not to work, as everyone expected he would, in the respected and respectable area of civil rights but, rather, in the somewhat subversive world of abortion.

In the late 1960s when Susman became involved with abortion, it was still illegal—and much tainted by its illegality. Except for a few brave physicians who openly performed these procedures in defiance of the law, only shady doctors and illegal practitioners did them. When an abortionist got caught, he had trouble getting a good lawyer to represent him.

Susman, however, had no intention of defending illegal abortionists. Instead he was joining a small cadre of lawyers across the country who were organizing to reform the nation's restrictive abortion laws. Their goal was nothing less than the complete legalization of abortion. Susman and the other lawyers intended to carve out a constitutional right to abortion. They believed that the right to choose an abortion was as basic a civil right as the right to free speech.

Susman became involved with abortion in the late 1960s when the reform movement was just taking shape. In 1967, a group of New York clergymen, headed by the Reverend Howard Moody of the Judson Memorial Church in Greenwich Village, sent a ripple through the abortion reform movement by establishing a telephone service that would counsel women in need and refer them to illegal but safe abortionists.

Howard Moody was a southern Baptist with a liberal New York congregation, so he knew he could do things that other preachers could not get away with so easily. He might never have focused on abortion, though, had a colleague in 1957 not sent him a woman who needed help. To this day, he has not forgotten her or her plight: A middle-aged, widowed mother of two teen-agers, she was pregnant as the result of an affair. Like most women in her predicament at that time, she did not feel she could bear the child.

Knowing little about abortion but determined to help this woman, Moody traveled to New Jersey to the doorstep of an illegal abortionist he had heard about. He intended to set up an appointment for the woman, but as he recalled, "I didn't have the right code word, so I didn't get in." Through other contacts, he found someone safe and reliable who agreed to perform an abortion on the Florida woman.

Moody realized if he could do this for one woman, he could do it for others. Furthermore, his collar would either offer him protection from the law, or if he were arrested, would help to publicize the need for legal abortion.

In the fall of 1966 he began to meet with other clergymen to talk about forming a group to do formally what he was already doing informally, referring women to skilled abortionists. In May 1967, twenty-six ministers and one rabbi began operating the Clergyman Consultation Service (CCS) out of the basement of the Judson Memorial Church. Although the group was ostensibly formed to help women obtain abortions, everyone recognized that this was the most direct challenge to date to the states' mostly unenforced abortion laws.

Moody's group proved to be the perfect forum for testing the abortion laws, and soon branches of CCS were operating across the country, mostly in college towns and cities. In St. Louis, an energetic obstetrics-gynecology nurse named Judith Widdicombe began to make plans to set up an abortion hotline that she would operate out of her home.

At about the same time that Widdicombe was setting up her hotline, one of Frank Susman's corporate contacts, Joseph Sunnen, asked Susman to represent him at a Planned Parenthood meeting in Kansas City. Sunnen, a manufacturer of heavy automotive parts, also owned a small company that manufactured Emko contraceptive foam. Rumor held that he gave away more of the product worldwide than he ever sold, but the company was the source of his unflagging interest in family planning. The Sunnen Foundation gave more money to abortion reform in the 1970s than any other foundation, including the Rockefeller Foundation, which also shared Sunnen's interest in family planning.

That was how Susman found himself sitting around a conference table one day, discussing the need to challenge the abortion laws with three or four Planned Parenthood lawyers. The subject was not a new one for the Planned Parenthood lawyers, but it was to Frank Susman. He was surprised to hear lawyers talking about mounting a broad-based, constitutional attack on the nation's abortion laws. That day, he learned that sixteen or seventeen suits were being prepared for filing in various courts around the country.

When Widdicombe needed legal advice to set up her abortion hotline, someone gave her the name of Frank Susman, a young, local lawyer who had expressed an interest in working on abortion reform. She called him and he quickly agreed to help her. Thus began a partnership that would be influential not only in helping to legalize abortion but also in setting up the most widely emulated model for the delivery of abortion services in the country.

One can easily imagine Frank Susman sitting on the Eighth Circuit Court of Appeals, a federal bench for which he was once a nominee. A tall, somber-faced man, his most striking feature is his prematurely gray hair. Were he older than his forty-eight years, he would be pleased to be described as distinguished. An imposing mustache adds to his aura of authority. A product of his drill sergeant days in the United States Army, it changed his appearance, and he says he will never shave because it gives him extra confidence. Susman dresses like the conservative corporate lawyer that he is most of the time. His only jewelry is a plain watch and a gold wedding band, the gift of his third wife, Nancy.

On first meeting Susman is brusque, not particularly forthcoming. When he wants to give me a copy of his resume, he picks up the telephone and says only one word to his secretary: "Resume." When she appears a few minutes later he takes it without a thank-you. Even his admirers consider him a gruff man. One of his clients, an abortion clinic director, tells me that her staff is scared of him, largely because of his abrupt telephone manner. An impatient man, Susman insists that someone take notes at meetings so he won't have to repeat anything. As we talked, though, his abrupt exterior gave way to a man who was congenial, witty, much at ease with both his strengths and his frailties.

We first met in the law offices of Susman, Schermer, Rimmel & Shifrin, a 26-person law firm. The two-story suite of offices in a high-rise building in Clayton, Missouri, a prosperous suburb of St. Louis, was in the midst of being redecorated, and Susman's office was a sea of calm in the middle of the scaffolding and draped furniture. His office had little to distinguish it from the law office of any other corporate lawyer in a prosperous firm. A large wood desk dominated the room; on it were scattered papers and a scuffed Coach briefcase.

One wall was given over to framed awards. Susman had recently been honored by the National Council of Jewish Women, the American Jewish Congress, and the ACLU. In 1977, he was given the Ethical Humanist of the Year Award for his "courageous fight for the establishment and preservation of women's rights and the separation of church and state." Recently, Susman was awarded the 1989 "Good Guy" Award by the National Women's Political Caucus.

I asked Susman how one got his name first on a law firm's door, and he told me his father had founded the firm fifty years ago, although the name on the door was now his. I asked him to tell me about his family.

The Susmans immigrated from Lithuania and settled in St. Louis. His father, Earl Susman, was the first person in his family to go to college. After graduation, he attended Washington University Law School and then set up his own law practice, possibly because Jews were not welcome at that time at the city's mostly WASP and Catholic law firms.

Susman's mother, Mildred Esther Stone, grew up in California, to which her family always atttributed her great love of the outdoors. Susman believes her family came from Germany, and recalled that his maternal grandfather was known as the Johnny

Appleseed of California, a sobriquet he acquired when he reportedly planted many of the palm trees that line the streets in and around Los Angeles today.

Susman was the middle of three children. As a child, he considered himself a bit of a loner who nevertheless sought out and often won positions of leadership in student organizations. Twenty-five years after the fact, he proudly recalls that he got the largest number of votes for student council during his senior year in college.

Frank Susman's world changed dramatically and forever on December 15, 1956, when his mother died unexpectedly in her sleep of an aneurism. To this day he remembers that it was a Wednesday morning. She was forty-two and he was fifteen, a sophomore in high school. "She went to sleep and didn't wake up. I laid in bed that morning and heard my sister screaming. I was not about to get out of bed and find out what had happened. My father finally came and told me she was dead."

They had enjoyed a remarkably close relationship, not unusual when a parent and child are much alike. Lost in his own reverie, Susman leaned back in his chair and began to describe her. "She never worked. She stayed home and took care of us. But she never cooked, she always had a maid who cooked. She took metalworking classes." He reached behind his desk and picked up a small, well-crafted little brass and copper box she had made and handed it to me.

"She was a great birdwatcher and loved to go on Audubon walks. She would have worn blue jeans every day if she could have. She was very affectionate, as I am. I'm a real handholder.

"I've never come to grips with her death," he continued, and indeed her death has left him with a fatalistic streak. Recently, at a dinner party with friends, Susman posed an unusual question: "If you knew you could stay healthy and live a fulfilling, happy life right up to the end, wouldn't you sign on to check out at age 72 rather than risk dying earlier?" He was genuinely surprised when everyone else present said no.

There are other signs that Susman is a man to hedge his bets. During the summer between his junior and senior year in high school, he and his father took the traditional tour of college campuses. Upon returning home, Susman applied to a number of the schools he had toured, among them Harvard, Yale, Princeton, and Brandeis, a prestigious, predominantly Jewish private school near Boston. When Brandeis offered him early admission, he accepted it even though he wasn't sure it was his first choice and didn't bother to wait to see whether he would get into any of the Ivy League schools. Susman dutifully wrote the other schools to tell them his decision and to withdraw his applications.

At Brandeis he continued a high school interest in student politics and became active in Thespians, which he says he now considers to have been excellent training for his present work. His undergraduate degree was in psychology, in which he graduated with honors, and he would have liked to go on for a doctorate, but turned at the last minute to law, an area, he wryly notes, where he at least knew he could get a job. Earl Susman's firm, founded in the late 1930s, was thriving by the time Frank went to college.

Susman's interest in getting a job may have had something to do with the fact that he had fallen in love with a fellow student, who would become his first wife right after graduation. The newly married couple stayed in Boston, where Susman had been accepted at Boston College Law School. He attended law school full-time while Marilyn finished her senior year at Brandeis. A year later, Susman returned home to St. Louis to complete his last two years of law school at Washington University, his father's alma mater.

Fresh out of law school in 1967, Susman joined his father's law firm, where he was paid a paltry $6000, $1200 less than his wife had earned the previous year teaching grade school. As the only associate in the firm, Susman felt driven to prove himself as quickly as possible. His wife had quit teaching to go back to school for her doctorate, so they needed the money. He was eager to lose his image as the "boss's son." He moved up quickly: "I developed my own practice. I kept one-half of what I brought in plus my salary." Within a few years he was earning more than some of the partners, and had won his partnership.

Frank's tenure at the firm overlapped his father's by more than a decade, and although the two men lunched together two or three times a week, theirs was never a particularly close or warm relationship. His father kept a discreet distance, never interfering with his son's work or life, even when Susman went through two divorces.

Perhaps the only puzzling element in an otherwise tidy life are Susman's three marriages. After seven years of marriage and a son, Andrew, who is now twenty-one, Marilyn and Frank Susman divorced in 1970. A few years later Susman married his secretary. Mary and he had a second son, Adam, now fourteen. After Adam was born, with his wife's agreement, Susman had a vasectomy. That marriage broke up a few years later, and in 1985, he married his present wife Nancy, who is seven years his junior. After years of working for a market research firm, she recently took a job as director of an AIDS foundation.

Susman blames his divorces in part on his inability to communicate with his wives, a problem that dates back, he says, to his childhood. "I never talked to anyone—my wives or my parents—as much as they wanted me to. Nancy wants to know things, and I don't know what to say. I remember my parents and I sitting in the den on more than one occasion. They would say 'Please talk to us.' But I had nothing to say."

Even today, he feels pressure when a law partner presses him for an immediate opinion. Susman frequently demurs, saying he'll give his opinion after he's had some time to think over the problem. "I don't like the process of thinking interrupted. It's not the way I operate," he says. And sometimes, he just wishes everyone would stop asking him to talk.

While Susman insists he is not a workaholic, others who have known him for years say otherwise, and his dedication to his work reportedly played a role in the breakup of two of his marriages. When Susman's second wife Mary gave birth to their son Adam, Susman left just hours later for Washington, D.C., to argue a case in the Supreme Court.

He claims to work very few Saturdays, never comes in on Sunday and leaves the office most nights by 6 p.m. When Nancy gently points out that he has been out of town or at an evening meeting thirteen out of the last fifteen days, he looks genuinely surprised. He is famous for never spending a night away from home if he can help it, though, and colleagues and clients are familiar with Susman's last-minute scrambles to catch the last plane out of wherever he is.

Perhaps because he is away so much, the Susmans tend to keep to themselves when he is home. Most of their socializing revolves around the same three or four couples, none of whom are clients or colleagues. He is close to one of his partners, Tom Blumenthal, a man ten years younger than he who worked with him on Webster and other major cases over the last few years.

Nancy Susman is a skilled horsewoman, and Susman occasionally joins her, but his only regular exercise is a weekly standing game of tennis. He plays at the Westwood Country Club, a mostly Jewish club which, he readily admits when asked, is restrictive in its membership. There are no black members, and women can belong only as auxiliaries of their husbands. Susman says it has bothered him over the years to belong to such a club, and after years of thinking about dropping his membership, he finally did so in September 1989, resigning in protest against the club's restrictive memberhip policies.

Susman parts company with most other lawyers in his need to seek out first-hand experience with whatever problem he is working on. In 1967 when he was appointed to the St. Louis Crime Commission, which was charged with parceling out federal monies to the local police department, he accepted and then promptly signed up to attend the police academy at night. After he was commissioned, Susman worked a beat one night a week in uniform and later as a detective for thirteen years without pay, until, as he puts it, he "got too old to run up and down alleys and get shot at for free." His years on the force, he insists, helped him decide how to allot the money. In 1984, he was appointed by a federal court as a monitor, or watchdog, of the city prison system, a job he takes seriously enough to be a familiar presence in the jails.

Not surprisingly, then, when Judith Widdicombe asked him to help her set up an abortion-referral service, he not only jumped at the chance, but soon was doing more than giving legal advice.

As was the case with all CCS referral groups, Widdicombe's

hotline was essentially a telephone service that women could call for help in dealing with a crisis pregnancy. An abortion was one of several options women were offered. If a woman wanted an abortion, she was told to call back a few days later when an appointment would have been arranged for her. Widdicombe used medical students to pick up women, drive them to the local abortionist, and return them to their homes afterward.

The work was clandestine and dangerous, especially for Susman, whose career would be over were he arrested for so flagrant a violation of the law as the hotline represented. Even today, he recalls how frightening it was to work on the hotline, never knowing if the police might burst into the room and arrest everyone connected with it. "There was always the fear of arrest," he says.

On one occasion, Susman escalated the risk considerably when he and his police partner set up their own unofficial sting operation to catch a person who was using the hotline to guide pregnant women to an abortionist unconnected to CCS. The referral service knew nothing about these abortions, including whether they were safe, and furthermore, the leaks breached a cardinal rule of all referral services, which was to protect a woman's anonymity.

Susman arranged for a woman to set up an appointment to meet the abortion contact at a bar in the Central West End section of St. Louis. When the contact showed up, he turned out to be a law student whose girlfriend was a volunteer at the referral service. She was feeding him the names of potential clients, and he was calling the women to set up abortions with a St. Louis cabdriver who moonlighted as an abortionist. Although charges were pressed, the cab driver eventually got off. But the service was never troubled with misleading referrals again.

Abortion was legalized in New York State in 1970, which in turn legitimized the Judson referral service and brought it above ground as a counseling agency. Missouri activists, however, were in a much tougher position. There was little chance that their conservative southern state would voluntarily ease its restrictive abortion laws, and indeed the St. Louis referral service remained an illegal operation until 1973, when *Roe v. Wade* legalized abortion across the country.

Susman's beliefs about abortion took shape during his early years in the reform movement. Before working on the abortion referral service, he had volunteered on a suicide hotline. Years later, he told a reporter how this experience had made him determined to help women who needed abortions.

"So many of the calls were from women who were faced with the dilemma of an unwanted pregnancy. If that doesn't convince you on the issue, nothing will," he says.

Through his work at the referral service, Susman also saw first hand the tragedy that resulted from illegal abortions. "Women know what they want when they're pregnant," he often tells people who ask him about his views on abortion, "and besides, no one is qualified to sit in judgement—religiously, ethically, or morally—over another person's life."

Susman feels strongly that the right to abortion is a matter of privacy, and that as such it should be constitutionally protected. He does not feel that the regulation of abortion should be left to the states. "No fundamental right is ever left to the majority's whim," he said.

When the Roe ruling legalized abortion, Susman's focus switched from helping women obtain illegal abortions to helping them obtain legal ones. Judith Widdicombe was among those who had seen legalization coming, and she had plans to open what she hoped would be the nation's first abortion clinic. Her clinic, she insisted, would be operated by women. To her shock, Susman was not supportive of her efforts, or at least not of her plans to become the clinic's first director.

"Everyone, including Frank Susman, told me I couldn't do it. People said you can't open a clinic. You're a nurse, you're a woman, you want to open the clinic three blocks from the Cathedral, and you don't have $500,000."

Widdicome did have the promise of $50,000, from Joe Sunnen, who was as interested in supporting the abortion right as he was in promoting birth control. She called a press conference within days after the Roe decision and announced she would open a clinic on March 8, a date she picked out of a hat, because she knew she "had to hook the press." A power struggle ensued when her board and others, including Susman, insisted that the clinic director be a hospital administrator, who would almost certainly be a male as were all hospital administrators in those days. Widdicombe forced the issue with Sunnen, who gave her and not the board the money to open the clinic.

The rift with Susman was deep, even though Widdicombe now admits that Susman's thinking was typical of just about everyone's connected with the clinic in those days. "For two or three years, I didn't use Frank's legal services, but gradually, we began to work together again. After all, he was the best there was. He's the brightest man I know."

He also had another quality that was much needed in those early days of legalization: tenacity. "There's a piece of Frank that's like a terrier. He won't give up. He won't roll over and play dead," Widdicombe says.

Susman's tenaciousness, in fact, is legend. One clinic director and longtime acquaintance of Susman, who has since become a lawyer, recalled sitting in a courtroom with him in Nashville, Tennessee, listening to a judge read a verdict. As it became evident that they had won their case, Susman leaned over to the woman and whispered, "I'll give you a hint about practicing law. Never leave a courtroom without getting an order in writing, especially when it's in your favor."

When Susman asked the judge for a written order, though, the judge declined, saying that his secretary had just left for lunch and there was no one to type it. Susman, who was, as usual, rushing to catch a plane, was not deterred. Did the judge have a typewriter, he asked? The judge did. Could he use it, Susman asked? He could, the judge said, whereupon Susman sat down at the secretary's desk and typed his own order.

After legalization, Susman began to get calls to represent the clinics that were springing up literally overnight to provide abortion services to women. Initially, he spent a great deal of time advising his new clients about practical business matters such as how to set up and operate their new businesses. Beyond that, there were special problems associated with the nature of the work. Clinics were the first facilities routinely to do surgery on an out-patient basis, and this created its own set of problems, such as resistance from local medical and hospital associations that would have liked a hand in regulating the new businesses much as they set standards for other kinds of medical care.

Susman spent hours tackling such unique clinic concerns as liability, standards and quality control, and more routine problems such as how to establish a billing system that would take account of prices based on individuals' ability to pay rather than rigid fees.

"Frank is not only good about giving practical advice," says one clinic director, "but he can tell you how to get around things. Not how to break the law, just how to bend it to make it work for you."

Except for the occasional clinic that kept him on retainer, though, Susman's work with his clinic clients was irregular and never comprised more than ten percent of his practice. The providers, as the new professional deliverers of abortion services called themselves, phoned him when they needed his services. By the mid-1970s when clinics began to be plagued with protesters and episodes of violence, Susman was representing them in court when they pressed criminal charges against offenders. He was using his experience as an ex-cop to advise clinic directors about security.

From the early seventies on, Susman was drawn deeper and deeper into the abortion controversy. He took his first abortion case at the request of the local American Civil Liberties Union several years before the Roe decision. By the time that Roe was moving up through the courts, Susman had developed enough of a reputation as an expert on abortion to have Sarah Weddington, co-counsel in *Roe v. Wade*, call him several times to consult on strategies for Roe.

In 1972, the year before abortion was legalized, Susman took a case called *Rogers v. Danforth* into the Missouri Supreme Court to challenge the restrictive laws the state had passed in 1835. He was back in the same federal court a year later in *Word v. Poelker* challenging restrictions imposed on clinics by the city of St. Louis.

To his dismay he learned in 1976 that he was scheduled to argue *Singleton v. Wulff* in the Supreme Court the same day as another case. When he called the Court to suggest, only-half jokingly, that if they were trying to save him air fare, it wasn't necessary, the clerk apologized but said he was indeed slated to argue two cases on the same day—a rare and not particularly pleasant situation in which to find himself. Later, in court, Justice Rehnquist jokingly asked him if he didn't consider it cruel and unusual punishment to have to argue two cases in one day.

Ostensibly about Medicaid funding, the real issue in *Singleton v. Wulff* was whether physicians had a right to sue in behalf of their women patients, that is, whether an abortion case could be brought without using a woman as a plaintiff. He won the case when the Supreme Court found that physicians did indeed have that right.

Cases like that didn't sit particularly well with pro-choice women, especially those with feminist leanings. Their resentment over the suggestion that physicians had any role to play in the abortion decision dated back to the pre-legalization days when women were excluded from the often condescending decisions that doctors made about their health. In the early stages of legalization, there was much discussion over whether the abortion decision could be made by the woman alone or necessarily had to involve her doctor as well. Pro-choice women, who, for the most part, successfully argued that it was their decision and no one else's, have been guarded about the issue ever since.

Susman believes the issue is more complex than that. While he doesn't think doctors have any role in a woman's decision to terminate a pregnancy, he also doesn't think they can stand outside the litigation process either. As pro-life groups have looked for more inventive ways to restrict the abortion right, they have often sought to restrict the actions of physicians, sometimes making them criminally and civilly liable for actions they undertake in relation to abortion. Under such circumstances, there seems to be no other choice than to assert the interest of the doctors. Historically, too, doctors have been the ones found guilty of abortion, never the women who obtain them.

The issue never seemed more relevant than when Susman, along with co-counsel William Homans, defended a Boston physician, a black man named Kenneth Edelin, who was charged with manslaughter after aborting a woman's third-trimester fetus. It was extremely rare even in the 1970s for anyone to be charged with homicide or manslaughter in connection with abortion, and when the question arose, the only issue was whether an abortionist could be charged if a woman died during an abortion. Never before the Edelin case was a physician charged with murdering a fetus.

Furthermore, when law enforcement agencies cracked down on abortionists, they went after the illegal, unlicensed practitioners, not well-respected persons of the impeccable stature of Kenneth Edelin, a leading obstetrician-gynecologist at Boston City Hospital.

Edelin's case was front-page news, the first big abortion media circus. The courtroom was packed every day of the eight-week trial, and spectators were turned away. All three major networks covered the proceedings as did the two major wire services, United Press International and Associated Press, the local Boston media, and *The New York Times* and the *Washington Post*.

The Commonwealth of Massachusetts charged that Edelin, after two unsuccessful attempts to do a saline abortion, had performed a hysterotomy on a woman. In the course of doing the hysterotomy, the state said that he had taken actions to end the life of the fetus.

The state's star witness, a second-year medical resident named Dr. Enrique Gimenez-Jimeno, vividly described how Edelin had run his finger around the uterine wall to separate the fetus from the placenta and then stood looking at a wall clock for three minutes before removing the fetus from the uterus.

During the trial, Susman and Homans called witnesses who directly refuted Gimenez-Jimeno's testimony, including several who testified that there was no clock in the operating room and that Giminez's view of Edelin was blocked so that he could not have seen what he claimed to see. Edelin denied that he had done the hysterotomy in anything but the most expedient fashion, indicating that any other course of action would have posed unnecessary danger for his patient.

Susman decided not to chance alienating the jury by telling them that officials at Boston City Hospital had attempted on several occasions to discipline and discharge Dr. Gimenez-Jimeno for inefficiency. Nevertheless, he successfully—or so he thought—destroyed Gimenez's testimony, forcing him to retract several broadly inaccurate statements he had made on the witness stand. In a series of reports sent to Robert Sunnen, who was paying Susman's travel expenses on the case, he wrote how the man who had been "an ascending star for the commonwealth became...a descending star under cross-examination."

Susman and Homans also called other witnesses, including several experts who challenged the Commonwealth's contention that the fetus was viable and who attested to Edelin's sound medical practices in performing the surgery. Susman even put Edelin on the stand, where he proved to be a highly credible witness.

Susman's weekly reports to Robert Sunnen, Joe Sunnen's son, were optimistic about Edelin's chances of winning the case, and Susman was as shocked as anyone when the jury found Edelin guilty of manslaughter. The case was lost in part because, over the defense's strenuous objections, the prosecution was able to display a larger-than-life-size photograph of the fetus, which had been preserved as evidence. The composition of the jury, which consisted of eleven Roman Catholics, one Baptist married to a Catholic, only three women, and no African-Americans, couldn't have helped either. Within two hours of the verdict, an alternate juror contacted the defense team to tell them that racial prejudice had played a major factor in the decision. Several jurors used the epithet "that guilty nigger" to refer to Edelin. The case was appealed and Edelin was acquitted in a higher court.

Susman's second Supreme Court abortion case was *Planned Parenthood-Missouri v. Danforth* (428 US 52 (1976), a case that dealt with restrictive statutes including spousal consent, parental consent, and prohibitions against saline abortions, among other restrictions.

In 1977, he took *Poelker v. Doe* into the Supreme Court. The plaintiff, whose real name was never revealed, was a poor woman from St. Louis. A public hospital refused to provide her with an abortion, and although she later got one from Reproductive Health Services, Widdicombe's clinic, Susman used what had happened to her to build a case that would test whether public hospitals had a right to refuse to do the procedure. Susman argued that if women truly had equal protection under the law, then public funds would have to be made available to poor women for abortions. He lost the case when the Court voted 5–4 that public funding of abortions was not required.

The day after the decision, Jane Doe called Susman from Indiana, where she had moved. Severely depressed and threatening suicide, she blamed herself for not having done something more to help win the case. Susman talked to her at length, explaining there was nothing she or perhaps anyone could have done.

Susman's last Supreme Court case prior to Webster was *Planned Parenthood-Kansas City (Missouri) v. Ashcroft*, which he argued in 1983. This time the major issue was a requirement that all second-trimester abortions be performed in hospitals, as well as several other minor restrictions passed by the indefatigable state of Missouri. The Court heard two other abortion cases the same day, *Akron v. Akron Center for Reproductive Health* and *Simopolis v. Virginia*, all dealing with restrictions on late abortions, and then decided the restrictions posed an undue burden on women and struck them down.

Susman has his critics over his handling of abortion cases and his approach to the abortion issue in general; most of them are inside the pro-choice movement. Even among his supporters, he is not considered a feminist, a term he finds chauvinistic and ultimately disparaging, preferring instead to call himself a "humanist." Judith Widdicombe, echoing a view held by many pro-choice women, commented that Susman is "a lot more sensitive to women now than he used to be."

Frances Kissling, another important abortion-rights advocate, says, "Susman can be arrogant. He's very self-assured. He's a trial lawyer, and they're never easy to get along with. Each thinks he's the best at what he does—that's what they're about—and they need that enormous confidence to do what they do."

Perhaps inevitably, there seems to exist a natural rivalry

between him and many of the women who lead the pro-choice movement. They are powerful women, and he is a powerful man. Moreover, many feel and believe that abortion is "the women's case"—and that as such, it is litigation in which men should have little or no role. Just as a man tried to take *Roe v. Wade* away from Sarah Weddington once the case headed into the Supreme Court, in an ironic twist of history, some women would have liked to take Susman's cases away from him so they could be argued by women.

Susman doesn't go out of his way to antagonize the women, but he isn't overly sensitive to them, either. At the Webster oral arguments, Planned Parenthood wanted a woman, their staff lawyer Dara Klassel, to sit at the lawyer's table for appearance's sake. Susman raised no objections, but obviously finds such symbolic gestures empty.

He has also been criticized for his failure to include women as plaintiffs in his cases. He claims it is not always possible or even advisable to include a woman because of the difficulty in protecting her anonymity. Most pro-choice lawyers recognize the truth of what he says. They even admit they often can't find women who are willing to be plaintiffs since lawsuits can drag on for months and sometimes years. Some lawyers, such as Planned Parenthood's director of litigation Roger Evans, however, still try to include a woman as a plaintiff whenever they can while Susman, above all else a practical man, has simply thrown up his hands and decided not to be bothered with the issue.

Many people in the pro-choice movement feel that much of the criticism heaped on Susman has to do with the simple and somewhat snobbish fact that he lives west of the Hudson River and is therefore out of the mainstream of the Washington-New York reproductive rights power axis. There is some truth to this charge, but others who are close to the conflicts that surface fairly regularly between Susman and other pro-choice activists say the issues are also more complicated.

The Planned Parenthood people were appalled, for example, when Susman declined to do any moot courts to prepare for the oral arguments in the Webster case. It would be safe to say that few lawyers who argue in the Supreme Court, even the Solicitor

General according to some reports, do not use moot courts to test their oral arguments. Most moot courts are tougher than Supreme Court oral arguments, for as one lawyer put it: "You agree to expose yourself to a panel of your colleagues and the top experts in the country, who in turn rake you over the coals for several hours—much longer than the oral arguments last."

Another way of looking at the difference: In the oral arguments, the justices look to counsel for information on the issues under discussion, whereas in a moot court, counsel submits himself to a room full of experts who know as much, if not more, about his subject than he does, and who are present for one purpose only: to examine and dissect his thinking far more intensely than will ever happen in the Supreme Court.

Susman's critics feel that his refusal to do moot courts is symptomatic of a deeper problem, namely, his unwillingness to strategize on the intense level that most pro-choice lawyers believe is necessary to bring a big case into the nation's highest court. No one accuses Susman of lacking the intellectual prowess to write the kind of brief that Webster required, but they do suggest that his energies are often split between abortion and the rest of his practice. Roger Evans, for example, as chief litigator for Planned Parenthood, spends all his time working on—and thinking about—abortion. As a result, he believes he wrote a stronger brief than Frank would have "because it's what we do all the time. Frank divides himself between abortion and his trial practice. He sees his function as being that of a trial lawyer. You prepare for the trial, you do the media, and that's all there is to it. He doesn't put the intellecutal probity and strategic thinking into it that we do."

That has upset some people, as has Susman's general unwillingness to spend a lot of time soliciting an array of opinions. "When we were writing the Webster brief, we took all the input we could get from anyone who would talk to us," Evans said. He talked to such constitutional experts as Laurence Tribe at Harvard and Bert Neubourne at New York University.

Collecting opinions simply isn't Susman's style. Susman did travel to Boston with Evans to meet with Tribe, but he was generally uninterested in making a pilgrimage to the other leading constitutional law experts. One feminist who had worked on an important early case called Susman to talk and says he was unreceptive to what she had to say. Susman doesn't even remember the telephone call.

For his part, Susman seems to take a stubborn and sometimes perverse delight in reminding the reproductive rights groups that since they are not his employers, he is under no obligation to go along with their plans. For example, when the major pro-choice groups met after the oral arguments to discuss how to cope with what everyone viewed as their inevitable upcoming loss, Susman escalated the internecine warfare at a particularly painful moment. All agreed that they should not use a legal technicality to make a loss look like a victory, something that would have given them comfort. Instead it was decided to acknowledge whatever losses were incurred and use them to build momentum to preserve the abortion right. Susman attended the meeting, listened to what everyone had to say, and then once again made it clear that while he would probably go along (he did), he was under no obligation to do so, something many at the meeting resented for months afterward. In response to such criticism, Susman observes that as a lawyer, his first loyalty is to his client. For him, the movement comes second.

Despite Susman's disputatious personality, which sometimes serves to exacerbate his woes, Evans says the criticisms heaped on Susman are too broad. "To give him credit," he said, "Frank has been out there fighting this fight for many years. He's fought it simply because it was the right thing to do. And he fought it in Missouri, which is a terrible place to have to do it. He's the guy who carried the banner when no one else was there to do it, and he doesn't always get the respect he's due for doing that. He is often treated to less courtesy and respect than he deserves."

And Susman for his part, often feels that he is fighting a one-man protest against what he considers undue pettiness in the reproductive rights movement. If he tends to let himself be cast in the role of *agent provocateur* a little too often, he is also not a man without antagonists. After the oral arguments in Webster, Planned Parenthood officials called a press conference to which they conveniently forgot to invite their lead lawyer on the case.

On the day of the decision, there was an attempt to deny Susman a copy of the decision, which was in short supply for an hour or so.

Apart from his abortion work, Susman also found time to maintain a thriving law practice (he is his firm's managing partner and second highest biller) and to remain active in community affairs. For many years he taught Sunday School at Temple Israel, where his father was once president, and he was president of the St. Louis chapter of the ACLU from 1980 until 1983. He presently serves on the national board of the ACLU, as well as on the local board. Susman also helped to found the National Abortion Federation, the providers' professional association.

Asked if he has any other specialties besides abortion, his eyes twinkled and he said: "Impeaching mayors." Susman has served as legal counsel to two city councils that subsequently, and with his help, impeached their mayors. Over the years, he has also handled major church-state litigation in Missouri, and he recently brought a successful suit to end police strip searches for minor-offense arrests.

The heart of Missouri is St. Louis, perhaps the most sophisticated city in the Midwest, but one that is dominated by its large, conservative, and politically powerful Roman Catholic population. St. Louis, in turn, is surrounded by some of the poorest rural areas in the nation. That population would prove to be an especially fertile recruiting ground for the largely anti-abortion, born-again Christians throughout the 1970s, and they would join with the big-city Catholics to make Missouri one of the staunchest anti-abortion states in the country. Its part-time legislature could be counted on to churn out piece after piece of restrictive legislation. If Missouri couldn't make abortion illegal, it would do the next best thing, and make it impossible to get.

Since 1973, state legislators had been writing restrictive laws and pro-choice lawyers had been going into state and federal courts to challenge them. Over two dozen cases had gone all the way to the Supreme Court. With the exception of public funding and minors' rights, the advocates of choice had won every case, if that was the way to describe the ongoing process of defining and dissecting Americans' rights that went on in the small white marble chambers of the world's most powerful court. Justice Blackmun, the author of the *Roe v. Wade* opinion, had privately stated (but not so privately that his words had not made the rounds of reproductive rights lawyers) that so long as he and the three justices who had been solidly with him on the majority opinion were still on the bench, there would always be four votes to hear every abortion case. (By 1975, though, Justice William Douglas had retired, but Justice Lewis Powell often cast the deciding vote to hear a case.)

The only two losses had been funding and minors' rights. In 1977, the Court declined to overturn the Hyde Amendment, which denied federal funding for abortions to welfare mothers, ruling that the federal government had no obligation to pay for abortions; by implication the states were not obligated to do so either. Minors' rights had been chipped away in a series of lower court and Supreme Court decisions, producing a patchwork of laws that varied greatly from state to state.

Despite the pro-choice victories, however, the pro-life forces felt they were gaining strength throughout the Eighties. More than anything else, they thought people were beginning to respond to their arguments. Although the polls showed that Americans approved of abortion by a slim majority, they also indicated that they were increasingly ambivalent and conflicted over it. By the mid-eighties, pro-life forces, who had capitalized on that ambivalence, sensed a decided softening in public opinion. The United States had elected two presidents in a row, Jimmy Carter and Ronald Reagan, who had proclaimed themselves to be born-again and pro-life. Anti-abortionists felt the time was right for another Supreme Court challenge, and Missouri was proud to be the state that would produce it.

The law that would become the Webster case was the creation of two longtime right-to-lifers, an activist named Samuel Lee and his attorney Andrew Pudzer. For over a decade Pudzer had been defending Lee on charges stemming from sit-ins and other actions against abortion clinics. In 1983 a St. Louis judge finally sentenced Lee to 314 days in jail for violating injunctions to stay away from the clinics. Lee, who was allowed to leave jail to go to work, instead went to a library every day. There, he set about crafting what he hoped would be an airtight anti-abortion case.

He wrote a law that, among other things, banned any facility that received public funds (or even stood on public ground) from performing abortions, forbade physicians and other public employees from even talking about abortion to patients, and required viability tests on 20-week and older fetuses before doing any abortion. In its most controversial clause, the new law stated that life began at conception—a direct contradiction of the Roe opinion. Pro-life forces pushed the new bill through the Missouri legislature in 1986.

Susman knew he would challenge the law as soon as he heard about it. He walked into the office of his law partner Tom Blumenthal one day with a copy of the new legislation and tossed it on his desk. "What do you think of that?" he asked, and Blumenthal knew he meant, what kind of suit can we bring? Susman and B.J. Isaacson-Jones didn't even need to talk about the new law; they just nodded to one another and got on with the business of building a case. As director of Reproductive Health Services, the clinic that Judith Widdicombe founded, Isaacson-Jones had often lent the clinic's name as plaintiff in lawsuits designed to protect the abortion right. Tom Blumenthal began to draft a complaint, while Susman set about collecting plaintiffs for a case.

Not surprisingly, Susman wasn't the only one interested in challenging the restrictive Missouri law. Across the state, Planned Parenthood of Kansas City was planning to bring its own suit, and Janet Benshoof, director of the national ACLU Reproductive Freedom Project, wanted to file what would have been a third suit.

A small power struggle ensued. Benshoof and Susman were old rivals. After years of arguing abortion cases around the country, Benshoof had yet to argue a case in the Supreme Court, and she thought Missouri might be her chance to do so. Susman, however, felt that Missouri was his turf. Like many members of local ACLU affiliates, he had strong feelings about letting the local chapters handle their own cases. He felt that the national organization, especially the Reproductive Rights Project, was there to provide support, not to take over a case once it was headed into the Supreme Court.

Eventually a deal was struck. Everyone agreed that Susman had the experience in the Missouri courts, as well as in the Supreme Court, and everyone also knew that even if three separate cases were filed, they would be consolidated somewhere along the line. Besides it made no sense for both a local and the national ACLU to file the same suit. National ACLU more or less bowed out (although they would perform an important support function), and Susman and Roger Evans became co-counsel, with Susman representing the ACLU, and Evans, Planned Parenthood. The other plaintiffs in addition to Reproductive Health Services were several physicians, nurses, and social workers who offered abortion-related services.

The resulting case, *Webster v. Reproductive Health Services*, would turn out to be the biggest case of Susman's career. It was, as the cliché goes, a case for the textbooks—and also for the history books.

No lawyer willingly takes a case he knows he will lose, and Susman had no reason to think he would lose Webster when he agreed to organize the lawsuit. In fact he had every reason to think he would win, just as he had won in all three of the four abortion cases he had taken into the Supreme Court.

In his and other abortion cases, the Court had repeatedly declined to limit the abortion right in any substantial way. It had rejected the notion that spouses should be asked to consent to their wives' abortions, that a woman should have to reside in a state for a certain number of days (or weeks or months) in order to obtain an abortion there, that parents always had to consent to a minor's abortion, that women needed a waiting period before they could be given an abortion.

Before the Missouri law could take effect, Susman went to court to get an order to stop the state from enforcing the new law until its constitutionality could be determined. An injunction was issued, and a trial date was set. Susman had deliberately filed suit in the U.S. District Court in Jefferson City, Missouri, the state capital, where he had hoped to get a sympathetic judge. Following a weeklong trial, Scott O. Wright quickly ruled that the new Missouri abortion law was unconstitutional.

The ban on public funds was voided on grounds of "vagueness." The ban on the use of public facilities or employees to counsel on abortion violated a woman's right to privacy. While the state had no obligation to pay for a woman's abortion, Judge Wright said, it also had no right to block her access to a public facility. The viability tests were unconstitutional based on an earlier Supreme Court ruling, *Colautti v. Franklin*, which found that "neither the legislature nor the courts may proclaim one of the elements entering into the ascertainment of viability." Finally, the clause stating that "the life of each human being began at conception" was declared unconstitutional based on the Roe ruling, which specifically said that the states could not adopt one belief about when life began over another.

Missouri appealed the lower court decision, and when the Eighth Circuit Court of Appeals agreed with the trial court, Pudzer and Lee had exactly what they wanted—a test case to take into the Supreme Court. The state appealed to the Supreme Court.

In January 1989, Susman learned that the Supreme Court had agreed to hear oral arguments in *Webster v. Reproductive Health Services*. Webster referred to William Webster, the attorney general of Missouri. His name went on any case that challenged the constitutionality of state laws.

Between January, when he learned that the Supreme Court would hear the oral arguments, and April 26, the day of the arguments, Susman estimated that he spent nearly 80 percent of his time on the case, much of it on such extralegal activities as responding to the massive amount of publicity that surrounded the case. Of the 150 or so cases in which oral arguments are heard by the Supreme Court every year, only a handful attract the attention of the press, and only one every decade attracts the kind of attention Webster did.

What drew the attention of the country—indeed, the world—to the Webster case were several changes of enormous importance that took place in the Supreme Court between the time that Susman filed the case and when he argued it. For years pro-choice people had dreaded, and pro-life people had looked forward to, the day when Ronald Reagan or some other equally conservative president would have an opportunity to reshape the Court to make it more amenable to the idea of restricting abortion. President Nixon, the first president to make abortion an issue in a political campaign, had run in 1978 on the promise that he would do just that, but in the intervening years neither he nor his successors had much opportunity to do anything about the makeup of the Court.

By the mid-1980s, Justices William J. Brennan, Harry A. Blackmun, and Thurgood Marshall, the last of the liberal majority that began under Chief Justice Earl Warren, were old men, all well into their seventies and known to be plagued with a variety of major and minor ailments. Fiercely protective of the legacy of the Warren Court, which had changed the face of civil rights in America, they were reportedly determined to hang on at least until a president was elected who wasn't intent on politicizing the court. So it was not surprising to Court watchers that when a resignation came, it was not one of the old liberal stalwarts but, rather, Chief Justice Warren Burger who stepped aside so a younger—and presumably more conservative—justice could be appointed. The Court's archconservative William H. Rehnquist became the new Chief Justice, and with his replacement, Antonin Scalia, on the bench, the liberal majority was at last near the breaking point.

In *Roe v. Wade*, the vote had been 7-2 for legalization. Now, sixteen years later, crucial abortion votes often came down 5–4, a fragile majority by Supreme Court standards. The final blow came when Justice Lewis F. Powell, the Court's centrist, resigned unexpectedly and without warning at the end of the 1987 Term. He was replaced with Anthony Kennedy.

Kennedy arrived at the Court as the third choice, after a liberal coalition had successfully defeated the nomination of Robert Bork, and a more middle-of-the-road nominee, Douglas Ginsburg, had withdrawn when his use of marijuana in college was revealed.

The backgrounds of the new justices were cause for celebration in pro-life circles. Both men were known conservatives, and although they had never voted in an abortion case, they were practicing Roman Catholics believed to subscribe to the Church's proscription of abortion.

In fact, an earlier appointee, Sandra Day O'Connor, the first woman ever to sit on the Supreme Court, had also been cause for jubilation among pro-life forces. In the 1980s, the acid test for federal judges had seemed to be a jurist's willingness to commit himself, prior to appointment, to an anti-abortion stance. While declining to say how she would vote in any specific case, O'Connor was reported to have assured President Reagan that abortion was "personally repugnant" to her.

With the new lineup of justices, Susman suddenly found himself with a much more problematic case. To the list of concerns that any lawyer must deal with when preparing a case for the Supreme Court, he now had to add to his worries about whether the case could even be won.

The court he would argue before was almost certainly a court inclined to impose some restrictions on the abortion right. Few experts believed the Supreme Court would do anything so drastic as overturning Roe, but pro-choice forces no longer had the luxury of knowing the Supreme Court would hold the line against the states' ongoing attempts to restrict the abortion right.

With Roe every opinion, except that of Justice William O. Douglas, who was known to be in favor of legalization, had been uncertain, but this would not be the case with Webster. Blackmun, Brennan, Stevens, and Marshall were the only clear-cut pro-choice votes remaining. They needed no convincing to remain firmly in that camp. Rehnquist and White had never been in it, having opposed Roe and most other abortion decisions.

The Court was reportedly politicized over the issue. Four of the justices—White, Rehnquist, Scalia, and O'Connor—had criticized Roe. In the fall of 1989, breaking with a longstanding tradition of silence about their work, Justice Blackmun had discussed Roe with a law school class. The abortion right, he predicted, "was about to go down the drain. You can count the votes."

Both Susman and the state's lawyers believed that O'Connor

would be the swing vote. She became, therefore, the person to whom both sides would address their arguments. In the earlier opinion *Akron v. Ohio*, O'Connor had written that Roe was "on a collision course with itself," which most people interpreted as meaning that she felt medical successes in saving fetuses at an earlier age would soon collide with the woman's second-trimester abortion right.

At the time of Roe, fetuses were rarely saved earlier than the twenty-fourth week of pregnancy, and that was undoubtedly a factor in the Court's decision that the state could not intervene to save potential (or fetal) life prior to the twenty-fourth week, or third trimester, of pregnancy. In 1983, when O'Connor wrote the Akron opinion, she believed, incorrectly, that neonatologists were saving fetuses as young as twenty-one and twenty-two weeks. After the Akron opinion the authors of the medical articles upon which she had relied publicly stated her misperception of their studies. More babies were being saved at the twenty-four week stage, but babies were still not being saved earlier than in 1973. The prognosis for such newborns was not good and was unlikely to get any better in the future. By the late 1980s, fetal researchers were acknowledging they would not be able to push back the age of survival any further.

The notion that younger fetuses were being saved undoubtedly contributed to a deepening of the public's ambivalence toward abortion in the mid-1980s. The question of viability—when sentient human life capable of surviving outside the womb began—was the one question the American people most wanted the Supreme Court to answer. Ironically, it was the one they were least likely to resolve, such issues being a matter of individual belief rather than law.

Since writing her *Akron* opinion, O'Connor had dodged the issue, saying only that she did not think that women should be unduly burdened with restrictions on abortion. Chagrined pro-choice activists had taken to joking that O'Connor seemed never to have met a restriction she considered "undue." "O'Connor's opinion on abortion was a little murky," Susman recalled. "She seemed always to want to straddle the fence." Susman hoped he would be able to reach her.

At the trial, Susman and Evans experienced the first of what would be several major clashes over the case. Their differences, which involved both style and content, would continue right up to and during the oral argument. Every day after the court session, the lawyers—Evans and Dara Klassel, the Planned Parenthood staff lawyer who worked closely with him, and Susman and his partner Tom Blumenthal—returned to their hotel where, at the Planned Parenthood lawyers' insistence, they spent most of the evening preparing the witnesses for the next day's testimony.

Evans and Klassel did most of the preparation while Susman and Blumenthal sat by and watched. Blumenthal knew Susman was there only as a matter of courtesy. Susman was in fact appalled at the tedious rehearsing of the witnesses, all of whom had testified for him before in other cases. They were highly qualified expert witnesses whom he wouldn't dream of coaching to such an extent. He began to worry that the witnesses would perform more like puppets than real and likable people once they took the stand. Susman didn't believe in rehearsing witnesses at any great length. After discussing his witnesses' testimony with them, he would put them at ease by telling them to be sure they had their answers right and let him worry about asking the right questions.

"I know this sounds cavalier to those who view us from the outside," Blumenthal told me as we talked at length one day over lunch, "but it's just a matter of style. No one sees the hours we spend—and spent on Webster—sifting through the evidence and going over our strategy."

More serious differences arose over content. Evans didn't want to raise certain issues in court. In contrast Susman, who often litigated cases, believed in using any argument he could to persuade a judge to rule in his favor. Not only that, but the two issues that the Planned Parenthood lawyers didn't want to discuss—free speech and viability—were the very ones that Susman felt he most needed to work with to protect his clients' interests. They were the strongest issues in the case as far as he was concerned. Earlier Supreme Court rulings had established that many restrictions of abortion were illegal because they infringed upon free speech, and the fact that the states could not regulate abortion to protect fetal life prior to viability (considered to be the start of the third trimester) was a principle firmly established in Roe. The Missouri law attempted to protect fetal life from the moment of conception.

The fact that the Missouri law denied public employees the right even to talk to women about abortion was, for Susman, the prime reason that the law should be overturned. The added fact that the state was selectively appealing only one of the sections of the law that dealt with free speech was further confirmation that the state knew it could not win on the free-speech issue.

The Missouri law touched on free speech in three areas: Public employees couldn't talk to women about abortion, nor could those who worked in public hospitals, and finally, wherever public funds were used, women could not be counseled regarding abortion. The trial and appellate courts had found all three regulations unconstitutional, but the state was appealing only the use of public funds. It was a safe ground since earlier Supreme Court rulings had established that denial of public funds for abortions did not impinge on the right to free speech. Obviously worried that they would lose on the issue of free speech, the state's lawyers caved in on the other two.

Furthermore, it was clear from the lower-court trial that the Missouri lawyers were aggressively reshaping their argument to try to show that free speech was not an issue in the Missouri law. They insisted that the state's only purpose was to control the use of public funds, not to chill free speech.

Susman found the state's arguments disingenuous. Worse, he resented the state's attempt to duck the free-speech issue, and had every intention of bringing it up during the oral arguments. He wanted it in the brief.

Evans was equally insistent that they not raise the issue. He argued that it was too risky to take free speech into a Supreme Court that obviously was no longer clearly pro-choice. Furthermore, he said the same issue would come up again a year or so later in the three Title X funding cases that were pending, one of which he would argue in the Supreme Court. If the issue had to come up at all, Evans insisted that it would be more appropriately raised in one of the Title X cases where new government regulations included an outright ban on counseling women about abortion. With the new federal guidelines, the blackout on abortion counseling was so total that a physician or counselor couldn't even take out the Yellow Pages and point to the telephone number of an abortion clinic. The Missouri restrictions, in his view, were less stringent, tied as they were to the control of funding. They cast a chill over free speech but didn't ban it.

Blumenthal thought the real crux of the debate was that the Planned Parenthood people were afraid of how he and Susman would handle the issue of free speech. "That's why they argued it would be better handled in their Title X funding case," he said. Susman felt that Planned Parenthood's lawyers did not want their thunder in the Title X case stolen by Webster. His response to Planned Parenthood's argument that they not bring up the free-speech issue was that, however it was shaded, that was the issue. "Why throw away a chance to raise it?" he asked. The lawyers were still debating the question the night before the oral arguments.

To Susman's dismay, the Planned Parenthood lawyers didn't want to bring up the issue of viability, either. Again, they made the argument that it was too risky to raise with this Court. The viability issue—that is, whether to bring it up in court—had been at the center of countless discussions among pro-choice people going all the way back to *Roe v. Wade*. Pro-choicers' greatest fear was that the Supreme Court would rule on when life began. They had been relieved and thrilled when the Supreme Court had abstained from ruling on this in Roe, and had done what they could to hold the line ever since, mostly by not ever giving the court a chance to rule on it.

Susman took the position that the part of the Missouri law that stated that life began at conception was a direct contradiction of *Roe v. Wade*, which had specifically stated that the states could not make any laws regarding when life began. In the intervening years, the Supreme Court had never deviated from this position. With the force of these precedents behind him, Susman thought they had nothing to lose by bringing up

MADISON COUNTY
Canton Public Library System
Canton, Miss. 39046

viability, and something to win. They might get another ruling reaffirming the Roe position on viability, and that would help the pro-choice cause.

The cloaked issue behind all the discussion about viability was how politicized the Supreme Court had become with Reagan's appointees. Each man's position was ironic: Susman, the tough litigator, was saying he still trusted the Supreme Court to make fair, if not necessarily good, law, while Evans, the abstract theorist, trusted the Court far less and thought there was every chance they would let their politics take precedence over the law.

Their differences over how the case should be handled affected the way Evans and Susman divided the work on the case. After they won in the trial court, the two men sat down to discuss how they would split the rest of the work on the case. It is easy to imagine that this was not an easy conversation. A Supreme Court case is every lawyer's dream, and although a raft of lawyers work behind-the-scenes on such cases, the star— the only person the media wants to talk to—is the person who makes the oral arguments in the Supreme court.

Susman brought his experience—he had argued five other cases in the Supreme Court on abortion—to the discussion. In contrast, Evans hadn't argued a case in the Supreme Court yet and would not do so until several months after the Webster ruling. Perhaps to assuage his ego, he had convinced himself that the oral arguments were mostly for public consumption and actually did little to influence the justices one way or another.

The printed brief was what mattered. It was where one could influence a Supreme Court justice with a startling new idea or concept. Evans decided he could be happy working on the brief, particularly because he believed this would also give him some control over the content of the oral arguments. Lawyers cannot bring up issues during oral arguments that have not been raised in the briefs. Evans believed he had found a way to keep free speech and viability out of the Webster arguments.

Susman's understanding was that while he would devote his time to preparing to argue the case, he would also review and make suggestions and contributions to the brief. Giving up any control on the brief was a major step for him, since unlike many lawyers who let junior partners and law clerks prepare their briefs, he wrote all his own, not only for Supreme Court cases, but for many lesser cases as well. He was dismayed to learn that his input was not appreciated. His conributions to the brief, mostly suggestions to include some discussion on free speech and viability, were largely ignored. The brief contains no detailed discussion of either issue.

Fortunately for Susman, Missouri would raise the issues in its brief and in the oral arguments, thus opening the door for him to discuss both issues in court.

Susman,.who had had misgivings about the division of labor from the start, was surprised when most of his suggestions were ignored. Eventually, he came seriously to regret his decision to let someone else write the brief, but at the time it had looked like the most sensible means of compromise.

They also worked out how the bills, which would mount into hundreds of thousands of dollars, would be paid. It was agreed that Reproductive Health Services would pay only $1 and the rest of the expenses would be shared by Planned Parenthood and the ACLU chapters of Eastern and Western Missouri.

Susman spent much of his time between January and April dealing with the media. He gave hundreds of interviews in the months before the Supreme Court arguments, when interest was building to a fever pitch. At least once a month he traveled to Washington, D.C. or New York to meet with representatives of the major reproductive rights groups about publicity for the case.

He found the meetings frustrating. On one occasion early in 1988, everything came to a head. He had written the heads of the pro-choice groups—NOW, Planned Parenthood, NARAL, NAF—inviting them to a strategy-planning meeting. Susman's letter produced a flurry of telephone calls and escalating rivalries. Half the people were outraged, and wanted to know what right he had to call a meeting. The other half were indignant, and insisted that the next meeting be at their place. Susman insisted that he sponsor the meeting, saying that at least if he called the meeting, everyone would come.

At the first meeting, the directors sent their top assistants instead of appearing themselves. Aware that the aides-de-camp had no real power, Susman insisted on another meeting—one that the directors would attend. The groups finally got together, even going so far as to hire Kathy Bonk, the media expert who had handled the liberals' publicity campaign over Bork's nomination, to coordinate the publicity on Webster. Bonk and Susman formed a close working relationship. Their views on how the case, as well as the issues, should be handled were remarkably similar.

Another disappointment occurred shortly after George Bush's election when the state turned out to have friends in high places. Two days after George Bush was elected president in 1988, in a move many thought was deliberately timed not to alienate pro-choice voters before the election, the Reagan administration filed what many constitutional lawyers viewed as an unusual amicus brief, unusual in that the federal government had no legal interest in the case. The thrust of the Administration's brief was to ask that Roe be overturned. Missouri had also asked the Court to overturn Roe in its brief, at the specific request of Brad Reynolds, the departing head of the Justice Department's Civil Rights division, but Susman did not think the state's request would carry much weight. The state had not asked the courts to overturn Roe in the lower court, so they could not legitimately raise the issue now.

Even more outlandish was a second request, made within days of President Bush's inauguration, that the federal government be permitted to participate in the oral arguments. The Court granted the request, giving the Administration permission to take ten of the thirty minutes allotted to Missouri's lawyers. The Administration's actions seemed puzzling and not, most lawyers agreed, very good law. Since the federal government had no interest in the case, its actions could only be interpreted as a purely political attempt to influence the Supreme Court. The Administration's request to participate in Webster caused a minor rebellion within the Justice Department. Over two hundred Justice Department lawyers signed a petition criticizing the department's intervention and calling it inappropriate. When no one at the Justice Department would agree to press the federal government's case, the Administration had to turn to former Solicitor General Charles Fried, then teaching at Harvard.

"When we heard that Fried was going to argue for the government, we decided we had to get someone of similar stature to counter Fried," Susman recalled. If Fried would represent the Administration, then, he and Evans reasoned, they could ask someone to argue as the representative of Congress. They wrote the Court to request permission to share their argument and then began to consider whom they might ask. After several names were bandied about, Tom Blumenthal suggested Barbara Jordan, the former Congresswoman from Texas who now taught at the Lyndon Baines Johnson School of Government at the University of Texas in Austin. Susman had met and worked with Barbara Jordan in 1972, when the two of them had joined forces with independent Chicago alderman (and former Brandeis classmate of Susman) Bill Singer to successfully challenge the credentials committee of the Democratic Party for its failure to seat enough youth and women. He thought she would be great, but the men still had some doubts. They realized if they got exactly the right person for this job, the results could be spectacular.

Jordan, an African-American, happened to be one of the few politicians of any color in the country who emanated statesmanlike qualities. Retired from politics due to illness, she was still a familiar figure to most Americans. A brilliant orator, people listened when she spoke, and unlike many politicians, she was smart enough to talk only when she had something important to say.

Never particularly active in the area of women's rights, she was nonetheless a supporter and had recently lent her name to the pro-choice cause in Texas. All the men's doubts vanished when they learned that Jordan had recently been on a panel with Justice Sandra Day O'Connor, and that the two had gotten along very well. When they viewed a videotape of the panel discussion, they knew Jordan was their first choice.

The three men arranged a meeting with Jordan at her office in Austin, Texas, so they could formally ask her to share the oral argument. Susman would be flying in from San Francisco, where he had been working on a case, Blumenthal from St. Louis, and Evans from New York.

Evans got there first, only to discover that he was supposed to call his office. When he did, he learned that the Supreme Court had denied the request to share the argument. By the time Susman and Blumenthal arrived, Evans and Jordan were sitting around chatting about what might have been.

The Court's refusal to let them share their argument was a loss, not least for the American people, who were denied the chance to hear what would undoubtedly have been the most eloquent argument that would ever have been presented in behalf of the abortion right.

Although disappointed at the news, Susman realized that if he hurried, he could catch the plane Blumenthal had just arrived on and head back to St. Louis that night. "If you don't mind, I'll kiss you good-by right now and head home," Susman told Jordan, literally walking out the door two minutes after he walked in.

Although he was known for his quick exits and for rushing to get home whenever he could, Susman's need to do so was even more pressing than usual. Since he had started working on the Webster case, the continuous stream of threats he received had escalated.

Nancy Susman had reconciled herself to the hate letters and telephone calls that pervaded their lives, but they never got any easier to take. "My abortion work has caused stress in all my marriages," Frank acknowledges, not because his wives didn't believe in the cause or want him to work on abortion, but because of the harassment that came with the work. Threatening telephone calls and letters were the least of it. There have been times, Susman says, when his wives wouldn't go to the mailbox because they feared what they would encounter there.

On two occasions since he began working on the Webster case, when he and Nancy were out of town, someone placed an advertisement in a St. Louis newspaper announcing that their house was for sale. Another time, a classified ad announced a sale of Harley Davidson motorcycles at their house. For a period of time, Susman had to have his car watched by the police overnight because of threats to plant a bomb in it. He has been subject to repeated death threats, which he downplays, noting that he only gets threats while many of his clients have experienced actual violence. Part of Susman's steeliness about the threats comes from his thirteen years of carrying a badge and a gun. Without elaborating, Susman acknowledges that he takes all necessary security precautions.

The final straw for Nancy, though, came one night when she was home alone. Someone cut the telephone wires outside the house. The Susmans had recently installed a security system, and police believe the intruders thought they were cutting those wires. Nancy Susman was scared enough to ask her husband to get her a gun and show her how to shoot it.

The middle weeks of April were given over to intense preparation for the oral arguments. Susman talked sparingly with Evans about them, but he and Blumenthal, it seemed, never stopped talking about them.

The Planned Parenthood people were still upset at Susman's refusal to do a moot court, and in an attempt to mollify them, he agreed to meet with a group of constitutional law experts they would assemble. The meeting was held in New York on April 17, a week before the arguments. "I listened more than I talked," Susman would say of the meeting afterward. Nothing he heard was particularly new, nor did it change the thrust of his strategy. Since he was scheduled to argue last, his would be a job of reacting to what had been said by the state's lawyers. It would, he felt, be wasted effort to prepare a specific argument.

When he got back to St. Louis, he settled in for a final round of preparation. He and Blumenthal had planned to commandeer one of the firm's conference rooms for several days to go over the possible arguments and the course they might take in court the following week, but that proved impossible with all the interruptions, most from an eager press wanting to gather last-minute details about the case. Even without the Webster-related calls, Susman returns over sixty telephone calls a day.

When Susman realized he couldn't get anything done at his firm, he made arrangements with Lennie Frankel, another local ACLU lawyer, to use his firm's conference room. He and

Blumenthal took all their papers and files there on the Thursday before the arguments. Jackets and shoes off, they settled down for some serious strategizing. Susman drank Classic Coke to keep himself alert. They worked there all day Thursday and Friday and through the weekend, breaking only for meals and sleep.

Through the final weeks of preparation, Susman felt as if an enormous weight rested on his shoulders. Despite the hundreds of interviews he had given in the past few months, the media clamored for more. Friends and colleagues called from around the country to wish him well and offer a few last-minute words of advice and encouragement. It all just added to his burden.

Because of the changes on the Supreme Court, Susman was no longer optimistic about his chances of winning the case, although publicly he continued to deny that he anticipated any kind of loss. Privately, he tried to prepare B.J. Isaacson, the director of Reproductive Health Services, for what he was almost certain would be a loss. Monthly meetings with the reproductive rights groups had turned grim, too, as everyone slowly and in varying degrees confronted the inevitable. The only unknown for pro-choice forces would be the magnitude of the loss. No one could say whether the Court would overturn Roe or simply chip away at it.

A week before the arguments, Susman gave an interview to the St. Louis *Post-Dispatch* in which he hinted for the first time that Webster might not be winnable for abortion-rights advocates. In a statement that reflected hope over reality, he observed that the Supreme Court could uphold every question the state of Missouri brought before it in Webster without overturning Roe. This was an indication of how bleak things had become in recent months for the pro-choice movement and perhaps a vain attempt on Susman's part to send the Court the message that he hoped this was all they would do.

Susman looked so weary that B. J. Isaacson-Jones and other friends and colleagues began to worry about him. He began to talk about how pressured he felt, an enormous admission for him. "It was a very difficult time for me," he recalled several months after the arguments. "Each call just added another one and a half pounds of weight."

On Monday, April 24, Susman and Blumenthal flew to Washington.

They checked into the Hyatt on Capitol Hill where Susman always stayed when he was in Washington. Monday night they attended a press party given by Kathy Bonk.

When he argued in a new courtroom, Susman had his own technique for coping with nerves. He always tried to visit a new court—even a small country one—before he appeared in it. Sometimes he attended a court session, but just as often, he found it valuable to visit a courtroom when nothing was going on. That way, he could become physically comfortable with the surroundings, walking around, listening to his voice to see how loudly he had to speak, standing at the lawyer's podium, checking out where everyone would be sitting.

There is never a time when a lawyer can roam around alone in the Supreme Court, and there was no need for him to do so anyway. Susman was a familiar figure at the Supreme Court. On Tuesday, however, the day before his arguments, he went there anyway since two cases in which he had a special interest were being argued.

One was a union case involving the liability of third party defendant-intervenors for the legal fees of prevailing plaintiffs. Susman was interested because pro-life lawyers often asked to represent fetuses in abortion suits. He had been involved in an Illinois case where a judgment for several hundred thousand dollars had been levied against pro-life physicians who had intervened in an abortion case.

While he was working on Webster, a New York case got a lot of attention when a husband tried to get an abortion for his comatose wife, and two lawyers were able to slow down the process when they petitioned the court to be made the guardians of the fetus. The court eventually ruled in the husband's favor, and the wife underwent an abortion. Susman hoped the arguments he would hear today would result in some guidelines in such cases, preferably ones that would prevent strangers with no personal interest from intervening in others' private lives.

The other case, which challenged the makeup of boards of

freeholders, had originated in Missouri and Susman's interest was personal. "I birthed that case," he said.

Later that afternoon, he returned to the hotel to greet Nancy, who had flown in with B. J. Isaacson. When Isaacson's room in another hotel proved to be unsuitable, Susman spent part of the afternoon arranging for her to move to his hotel. The Susmans dined quietly alone. When he awoke the next morning, Susman found himself looking forward to the arguments. Unlike many lawyers who preferred to work behind the scenes, he enjoyed appearing in a courtroom, and the pressure of a Supreme Court argument simply made his blood flow faster. He prided himself on his ability to stay calm under duress.

Wednesday, April 26, the day of the arguments dawned bright and crisp. As he entered the Court by a side entrance open to those with business at the Court, he caught a glimpse of the protesters, who were squared off against each other. The sound of women chanting "Two, four, six, eight, women must decide their fate" drifted over to him.

Shortly before the arguments began, a group of pro-choice protesters charged the police barricades and ran toward the court. Twenty-five women were arrested. Across the country, pro-choice rallies were held; in New York more than 2,000 people gathered in a small park across from the federal courthouse to protest what many now considered the imminent loss of the abortion right.

Inside the court a hundred or more reporters milled around. The press section was filled to overflowing, and the overflow was accommodated in another room. The oral arguments would be broadcast in the extra room, but someone would have to run in every few minutes to tell the reporters who was speaking.

In the first-floor lawyer's lounge, counsel gathered at 9 a.m., an hour before the arguments, to wish each other well and make some polite conversation before they assumed their adversarial positions in the courtroom.

Assistant Attorney General Mike Boicourt had initially been set to present the case, but at the last minute he had stepped aside so Attorney General William Webster could argue it. In Missouri people were saying that Webster stepped in because he planned to run for governor and thought that arguing the case, which was now winnable, would be a boost to his campaign. Susman wasn't sure that was the whole story, and he cornered Webster to see what he could find out about the last-minute change.

Webster told Susman he hadn't intended to argue the case but that pro-life people had pressured him into it. They pointed out that the former Attorney General John Danforth, now a Republican senator, had argued all the important abortion lawsuits during his tenure. The presence of the state's top law enforcement officer lent stature to a case, they said. In the end he acquiesced even though it wasn't in anyone's best interests. Webster had little time to spend preparing his arguments. Grateful that he had worked so long and hard preparing his arguments, Susman was not displeased that his adversary had not had the same luxury.

A few minutes before the Court was due to convene at 10 A.M., the lawyers entered the courtroom and took their places in front of the imposing raised mahogany bench. While the Court rarely allows more than one lawyer per side to argue a case, it does allow three attorneys to sit at each lawyer's table, and those seats are highly coveted as signs of participation in a Supreme Court case. Susman would of course be seated there, and he wanted his partner Tom Blumenthal beside him, but other than that, he didn't care who was at the table. By all rights, Roger Evans, who was co-counsel, should have sat there, too, but at the last minute Planned Parenthood decided that Dara Klassel, who was Evans' chief assistant on the case, should sit at the lawyer's table, so Evans relinquished his seat to her. Even so, in the weeks following the case, indignant feminists would complain that Susman had not had a woman sitting at the table with him during the arguments.

Most people are surprised to discover how brief oral arguments are, just thirty minutes per side, just as they are surprised to learn that no witnesses are called nor is any testimony permitted. Supreme Court arguments rise and fall entirely on a lawyer's ability to persuade the judge to accept the points of law he or she presents.

Unlike a trial lawyer who makes his opening and closing

arguments without interruption, the normal rules of jurisprudence do not apply to a Supreme Court argument, although the Court does have its own traditions, such as the one that justices do not address each other directly during the oral arguments. But basically, the justices are there to learn whatever they can from lawyers who are presumably (if in fact only rarely) experts on the issues they argue.

Susman would be arguing third, after Webster and Fried, so he assumed—and expected—that his arguments would be peppered with interruptions as the judges questioned him closely, quite possibly on points that had been raised during Webster's and Fried's arguments. Some lawyers would consider going last a major disadvantage; Susman didn't mind.

Only one thing bothered him: He still lacked a strong, dramatic opening line for his argument. He and Blumenthal had batted around several possibilities, but nothing seemed just right. Susman thought he would have to rely on spontaneity when good fortune struck and Charles Fried ironically handed him the perfect opening line. Fried began his argument by noting that the government was asking the Court to overturn Roe. He quickly qualified this by adding: "We are not asking the Court to unravel the fabric of unenumerated and privacy rights.... Rather, we are asking the Court to pull this one thread."

The "unenumerated and privacy" rights to which he referred were a number of expanded liberties that had accrued to the American people over the years even though they were not expressly described in the Constitution. The right to privacy, for example, is mentioned nowhere in the Constitution. The press had speculated that the justices would be concerned with whether they could overturn Roe without also undoing the privacy right, so it was not surprising when Fried opened his arguments this way.

The privacy right had always been the crux of the abortion debate for experts in constitutional law. Although the concept of privacy had roots in common law, the Supreme Court had only begun to shape the right about forty years earlier in a series of cases that dealt with such issues as the right to marry whom one pleased, the right to educate one's children as one saw fit, and in the case of abortion, the right to control one's own body without governmental interference.

Recent polls showed that Americans rated privacy as one of their most cherished rights, on a par with free speech, but not all constitutional law experts were convinced that privacy should provide the extensive protection it did. Some argued that the right of privacy referred only to freedom from government intrusion, not to the assortment of individual rights that had accrued to individuals over the past few decades. The classical argument that even free speech had its limits gave anti-abortionists hope that someday the Court would rule that abortion was not part of the privacy right.

Susman did not believe former Solicitor General Fried when he said he had no intention of unraveling the privacy right. And he knew at last how he would open his own argument.

"I don't now why he did it," Susman would say later, referring, one suspected, both to Fried's opening line and the more general question of why he had agreed to argue a case that his former Justice Department colleagues wanted no part of. "He opened himself to a great deal of damage. I suppose it was a dramatic lead, but it left him exposed.

"Fried handed me my opening line on a silver platter. The moment he said it, I wrote my response in a note and handed it to Tom. He shook his head yes. I wrote a second note that said, 'This will be a laugh.' Then I had some second thoughts. Should I go lighter? Go heavier? Use a pants leg or a sleeve? I never hesitated about saying it though."

The courtroom erupted in laughter when Frank Susman began his argument, saying: "It has always been my personal experience that when I pull a thread, my sleeve falls off." The moment was even more delicious for Susman's wife and a few other people in the courtroom that day who knew that in the Susman family, it was he who did the sewing. After his mother's death, Susman had learned to mend his own clothes, and in all three of his marriages, it was he who sewed on buttons and turned up hems.

Susman wasted no time, however, turning the argument in a more serious direction. He had one fascinating new piece of information he wanted to share with the Court, and he needed

to get it in before the questions started to rain down around
him.

"For better or for worse," he told the Court, "there no longer
exists any bright line between the fundamental right that was
established in Griswold* and the fundamental right of abortion
that was established in Roe. These two rights, because of
advances in medicine and science, now overlap. They coalesce
and merge, and they are not distinct."

When Justice Scalia interrupted to say he didn't see why a
court couldn't separate birth control from abortion "quite
readily," Susman was ready with his answer: "The most common forms of what we generically in common parlance call
contraception today, IUDs, low-dose birth control pills, which
are the safest type of birth control pills available, act as
abortifacients." Susman's implication was that under the Missouri statute, which protected human life from the moment of
conception, all these forms of contraception would be illegal if
abortion were made illegal.

Seventeen years earlier, when Sarah Weddington successfully
persuaded this Court to legalize abortion, she couldn't have
made this argument because the fact that the leading birth
control devices functioned as abortifacients wasn't yet understood. Although the scientific community had known that
some forms of birth control worked this way for several years,
Susman was the first to use this argument in an abortion case.
Many of the lawyers present, including Roger Evans, thought it
was a dazzling new line of argument.

Even if Weddington had known this fact, she probably
wouldn't have seen any reason to use it. In 1972 when she
argued Roe, no one seriously proposed to interfere with a
woman's right to contracept. By 1989, however, it was apparent
that the pro-lifers' agenda included not just abortion but also
birth control. Susman's point was that if the Court in 1989
opened the door to making abortion illegal by ruling on when
life began, it might also be opening the door to making some
forms of birth control illegal as well. Justice Kennedy seemed

---

*An earlier Supreme Court case, *Griswold v. Connecticut,* that established the
right to contracept.

startled by the idea, as did Justice Scalia, who nodded his agreement when Susman explained his point further.

Moving on to his next point, Susman continued, "There can be no ordered liberty for women without control over their education, their employment, their health, their childbearing, and their personal aspirations." Pointing at the long-established custom of leaving women at liberty to obtain abortions, he remarked that this was an even older legal precedent than those forbidding slavery.

This time it was Chief Justice Rehnquist who took exception to Susman's line of argument, interrupting to point out that the states had in fact regulated abortion in the past. While many post-Roe decisions had left the abortion right unrestricted, Rehnquist noted, these had occurred in the post-Roe era. Wasn't Susman ignoring the pre-Roe period in American history when abortion had been strictly regulated by the states? Susman agreed, but countered that even before that, the common law right to abortion had existed for hundreds of years.

Susman and Rehnquist were at odds over the precedent for the abortion right. The Court's conservatives, even more than its liberals, venerated tradition and would want to stand by precedent. *Roe v. Wade* was a precedent-setting case. But if they could prove that the Roe decision was wrong, that it in fact ignored eighty years when abortion had been not only illegal but had been strictly regulated by the states, then the Court would be free to overturn Roe and all the abortion cases that had followed it. They could turn for their precedents to the era of the nineteenth and early twentieth centuries when the states had regulated abortion heavily. Susman wanted to press the point that to do this, the Court would have to ignore hundreds of years of common law history that preceded the regulated era when women were at liberty to get abortions.

As was often the case during oral arguments, the justices who needed no convincing stayed out of the arguments. Blackmun, Brennan, and Marshall said nothing during the oral arguments, while the most active questioners were Scalia and Kennedy, the two Reagan appointees.

Justice Kennedy pressed Susman to say when he thought the

states could intervene to protect the fetus. Susman said he believed the health rights of the woman were supreme throughout pregnancy. Kennedy pressed further, and Susman was forced to concede that he would draw the line at viability or quickening. Viability, the point at which a fetus could survive outside the womb, was the newer medical measure, something that could be based on a doctor's opinion and sonograms. In contrast, quickening, the moment when a woman first felt movement, occurred earlier in the pregnancy, around the beginning of the fifth month, and could only be verified by the woman.

Many feminists would have liked Susman to insist there was no point at which the state could intervene to protect the fetus in order to drive home their widely held view that the fetus should be entirely under the control of the woman throughout the pregnancy. Susman agreed with this completely, but as a lawyer didn't feel he could win this point. Roe had established the right of a state to intervene to protect potential life during the third trimester, and Susman couldn't, as a point of law, deny this well-established principle. Even after he admitted that the states had a right to regulate after viability or quickening, Kennedy said, "But that's line-drawing."

The hearts of pro-choice people sank when they heard this, because Kennedy could be implying that drawing the line anywhere but at conception was an artificial division of pregnancy. Most pro-choice theorists would agree that drawing any line in pregnancy was artificial, but where pro-life people insisted that the line be drawn at conception, pro-choice people wanted to rely on the traditional, older dividing line of birth. To buffer his arguments, Susman quickly pointed out to Kennedy that quickening was a traditional, long-established dividing line in common law and early statute law, however artificial it seemed at the moment.

Kennedy pressed Susman even more about why he would settle on viability and not conception. Susman replied that while viability relied on a body of medical evidence, which suggested a fetus could only survive outside the womb after this point, pinning one's position to conception required an act of faith. Scientists and theologians didn't agree on the point of conception, he noted, since most persons who relied on faith thought conception occurred at the moment of intercourse while scientists believed it occurred a week later, when the united ova and sperm settled on the wall of the uterus.

This led to an exchange between Susman and Justice Scalia that seemed to go the heart of the justice's concerns about abortion. How, Scalia asked, could the right to abortion be considered fundamental if no determination had been made about whether the organism that was destroyed was a human life?

Susman replied that this was a determination that could be made only "by reliance upon faith." Both sides, he said, agreed on the facts of a fetus's physiological development, but disagreed about what those facts represented.

"I agree with you entirely," Scalia said. "But what conclusion does that lead you to? That, therefore, there must be a fundamental right on the part of the woman to destroy this thing that we don't know what it is? Or rather, that whether there is or isn't is a matter that you can vote upon. Since we don't know the answer, people have to make up their minds as best they can." Scalia seemed to be implying that it was begging the question to say that when human life begins is a matter of individual faith. He obviously felt that someone—presumably a Supreme Court justice—had to take the last step and use his personal beliefs to reach a resolution to the question in behalf of all Americans. This view contradicted the position of abortion-right activists, who held that in the absence of any agreement, no one had the right to make this judgment.

When Scalia got to a certain point in this statement, Susman could see the veins pulsating in his head as he struggled for the right word to describe unborn human life. He couldn't bring himself to say "fetus," and he knew "baby" was the wrong word, too. "I could see him struggling with it," Susman recalled, "before he finally resorted to calling a human life 'this thing.'"

Susman and Scalia engaged in another contretemps when Susman cited a historian's brief that expressed the widely held and respected opinion that the restrictive anti-abortion laws passed in the nineteenth-century were intended to protect women from dangerous surgery, not to protect fetal life. When

Scalia suggested that other briefs contradicted that evidence, Susman momentarily lost patience and said he personally had to look at who wrote those briefs—an "organization whose primary purpose is to be opposed to abortion" or "organizations which have been around for one hundred years which are considered to be reputable on a large number of issues."

"I personally cannot put as much stock in a brief filed by the Wyoming Nurses for Life as I can in briefs filed by the American Medical Association and the American College of Obstetricians and Gynecologists, the American Public Health Association, American Public Hospital Association, and other organizations of a similar vein," he asserted.

The quality of the amicus briefs was notoriously uneven. Although advocacy groups could be expected to push their own points of view, certain pro-life groups starting with Roe and continuing through every abortion case since then had misrepresented the medical facts of fetal development as well as the historical precedents for abortion. Not just Susman but many people were appalled that a Supreme Court justice would give any credence to such distorted works. A few well-reasoned antiabortion briefs were filed in every case, but Scalia did not seem to be referring to those, and he remained unconvinced, even after Susman attacked the misleading briefs. "But those briefs cite cases, and they give quotations," Scalia said.

Taking one more stab at convincing Scalia, Susman responded in a tone that was once again entirely respectful, "Justice Scalia, I would not submit that the briefs do not disagree with each other. I do not dispute that. You or I or others might dispute as to whether the facts disagree, but the fact that different parties put different slants or different perspectives or interpretations on those facts, certainly, I could not disagree with."

When Susman changed the topic to free speech, Roger Evans flinched. But Attorney General Webster had brought up the free speech issue in his opening words, and Susman felt he had no choice but to respond. Attorney General Webster had implied that Missouri had no intention of interpreting the law in the strictest sense, but Susman thought the law would impede free speech however it was interpreted. Consider the case, he said, of the woman suffering from a serious heart condition who became pregnant. Without the restrictive Missouri law, her physician would be able to discuss all her medical options, including the fact that it might be necessary to terminate her pregnancy in order to preserve her life. But under the new Missouri law, when the woman asked her physician which course of action he recommended, he would have to say, "I am not permitted to advise you to have an abortion, but I suggest that you consult with someone who can talk to you about this."

At this point, Justice Stevens suggested, somewhat sarcastically some thought, that a doctor could even say he was not permitted to talk to a patient about this "because his freedom to do so had been abridged by this statute."

But Scalia wondered whether such a statement would be any different from that of the physician who declined to perform an abortion because of his religious beliefs. Scalia said that the doctor could tell the woman that she needed an abortion, but that he didn't do them. "This is lawful, isn't it?" he asked.

Susman said he thought a doctor's refusal to perform an abortion on religious grounds was not the same as when a doctor who believed an abortion was in his patient's best interests couldn't tell her she needed one. In the latter case, the state was creating an obstacle to abortion where one had not previously existed.

Although he didn't elaborate because he thought the Court would not be sympathetic, he also felt that the new restrictions were one more burden on indigent women. While any woman, even a poor one, could decide not to go to a physician whose religious beliefs led him to oppose abortion, few poor women could afford a private hospital—or for that matter, a second consultation with a physician who was free to recommend an abortion. Instead, he contented himself with reminding the Court that two lower courts had found this clause in the law so vague as to leave open the very real possibility of restricting free speech.

O'Connor, the justice whom all the lawyers felt they had to persuade, said little during the arguments. Her most intense exchange was with former Solicitor General Fried. Justice Kennedy had asked Fried if the Griswold case, which had established a right to use contraception, in fact stood for the proposition that there was a right to procreate. Fried gave a vague answer, prompting Justice O'Connor to ask him impatiently, "A right to procreate? Do you deny that the Constitution protects that right?"

Fried still hedged the question, and this time O'Connor asked him whether or not he thought the state had a right, at some point in the future, because of a population problem, to require women to have abortions. Fried said he did not, that the two were entirely different issues. Those who thought they had heard O'Connor evincing some support for the abortion right were disappointed when she asked him on what grounds he based that belief, a sign that she was actually concerned that overturning Roe not present new problems for women's liberty.

O'Connor didn't speak again until Susman's argument. When he argued that the Missouri statute was subject to an increasingly narrow interpretation that might lead to the restriction of free speech, O'Connor, an ardent supporter of states' rights, said somewhat reprovingly, "Mr. Susman, I guess the state's courts never had a chance to interpret their own state statute." A slightly chastened Susman replied no.

Susman's arguments, which had now drawn to a close, were far and away the liveliest of the day, perhaps because the justices knew in him they had the one true expert on the legal and medical aspects of abortion among the counsel present that day. In a rare departure from their usual practice of excerpting important oral arguments, *The New York Times* reprinted the Webster oral arguments in full in the next day's paper.

Despite the high quality of arguments, however, little of their content was new. The Court was being asked, yet again, to ponder a question it could not answer. Asking any court to determine when a fetus becomes a person is asking it to answer a question that priests and philosophers as well as ordinary people have been unable to answer in thousands of years of human history. Courts can and have settled certain legal issues regarding fetal personhood. Where fetal life has been granted some rights of personhood, in cases involving, for example, inheritance or damages for injuries sustained in the womb, the rights have always been contingent on live birth. Virtually all societies have declined to grant fetuses legal personhood prior to that point.

From a purely moral-ethical point of view, though, history may offer some precedents, if not outright lessons, for resolving this seemingly irresolvable question. For centuries, many societies have declined to make a commitment to a human life even after it was born. Written and oral history abounds with examples of mothers' often intense ambivalence toward infants whom they did not expect to live. They have refused to suckle them, or name them, or even to hold them. Only in relatively modern times when child mortality rates have dropped, and science has held out the hope of saving young lives, have we as a society begun to commit ourselves to newborn life from the moment of birth.

And yet somehow today we find ourselves on the verge of going even one step further and committing ourselves prior to birth. A segment of our society insists that we make a commitment to fetal life as early as conception, when according to the best medical evidence available, the human life in question is a collection of cells. Others insist that the moment of collective commitment come at some other point in pregnancy when the fetus is incapable of surviving outside the womb.

Throughout history, though, most societies have settled on live birth as the point of communal commitment. It is worth considering that we have no other choice, that, in fact, any other level of commitment to a fetus—either to reject it or to take extraordinary measures to preserve it while it is still in utero—can only be a matter of individual choice. Make abortion illegal and women will still get them when they feel they must. Keep abortion legal and many women will decline to have them even though their own lives may be threatened by a pregnancy.

Susman was buoyant in the minutes immediately after the arguments. As he left the courtroom, he worked his way through a throng of people eager to congratulate him. Like almost everyone else who was present in the courtroom, he felt he had won the oral arguments. His spirits sank, however, when he came down the Supreme Court steps and into the throng of agitated media.

"There were 300 microphones—or what seemed like that

many—waiting for me." He was reminded that his only victory may have been the last thirty minutes in the courtroom. With the new conservative court, nothing—not even his eloquent argument—would be enough to save this case. And one more time, he had to sound as if he believed he had a victory on his hands when he knew he didn't.

Over the next few months, the waiting would become excruciating. Susman tried to fend off questions from the press about what he thought would happen and waited as impatiently as the rest of the country for a decision. It didn't come until the last day of the 1989 Term. Susman had suspected that the judges were still working on the Webster opinion right up to the last minute even though he would not have been surprised to learn that the opinion had been written weeks earlier but held for release until the last day of the term. Who would blame the Court for publishing so controversial an opinion at the last minute and then leaving town as fast as they could? Susman heard rumors, though, that O'Connor was holding up her opinion and had not even let her colleagues read it until ten days before it was due.

The Court doesn't announce in advance when it will issue an opinion, even an eagerly awaited one, so the press had no choice but to camp out in front of the Court starting in mid-June. Susman wanted to be there when the opinion was issued, and so did Evans. He and Susman flew to Washington several Mondays toward the end of the term so they could be in the courtroom if the Court rendered its opinion. In the past, Supreme Court terms had occasionally run as late as the middle of July, but since Rehnquist had become Chief Justice, he had taken pride in ending the term before Independence Day.

Their Monday mornings settled into a small routine. They met to drink hurried cups of coffee together before they headed to the Court to await the decision. One Monday morning they were the only two lawyers sitting in the lawyers' section.

When the decision was not handed down, they left the court together, and were usually set upon by the media. The major networks weren't standing by yet, but the cable news networks were there. Susman and Evans would protest they had nothing to say. The reporters would reply as long as we're here, give us something, so the two men would issue some kind of nonstatement that never made the news. They returned to their respective homes, only to repeat the cycle a few days later.

Washington was abuzz with speculation about whether there would even be a decision before the term ended. Some Court watchers believed the Court would put the decision over until next term, as had happened in Roe. Others said they couldn't, that there were no grounds for reargument, as there had been in Roe when the Court was shy two justices during the arguments.

Susman's pessimism had only grown with the two recent Supreme Court appointments. Neither he nor anyone else in the pro-choice movement had prepared a victory speech. Everyone knew what was going to happen; the decision would just spell out the details of how it would happen.

On Monday, June 27, the Court had announced that it would hand down all the remaining decisions it would deliver next Monday, July 3, a cryptic announcement that most persons took to mean that the Webster decision was at last imminent.

During the week, a telephone call confirmed the worst. Susman had a contact in the Justice Department whom he and Nancy jokingly referred to as their Deep Throat, a reference to the infamous source who kept *Washington Post* reporter Bob Bernstein fueled with leaks during the Watergate scandal. Their Deep Throat had filled them in on the goings-on at the Justice Department when the government had decided to intervene.

Now Deep Throat told Susman the opinion was floating around the Justice Department. The caller had not read it, but had heard enough about it to warn Susman to expect the worst. Prepared as he thought he was for the worst, Susman was stunned. He sat down abruptly on the bed and the color drained from his face when he heard this. It was a shock to have his speculation confirmed. It was even more of a shock to learn that the opinion was circulating in the Justice Department prior to its release.

Decision day for Susman had to be gotten through. He went to Court early that morning so he wouldn't miss anything. Slowly, the pro-choice troops gathered in the small marble courtroom. Officially, Washington had already closed down for the holiday, and it seemed like the abortion activists were the only people in town. This decision ruined a lot of vacations. Evans had stayed at his family's cabin in northern Vermont until after dark the night of July 2 so they could set off their traditional fireworks, then had left at 10:30 P.M., driven until 1:30 A.M., and crashed in a Hartford, Connecticut, hotel for a few hours sleep before getting up to catch a 7 A.M. shuttle to Washington. Of the three or four people on his plane, all were connected to the case. Molly Yard caught the cab ahead of him at Dulles International Airport.

The lawyers' section of the courtroom was relatively empty. None of the members of Congress who had made a point of attending the oral arguments were present. Attendance in the press section was sparse because the reporters knew they could get a copy of the opinion in the press room as soon as the reading of the decision began in the courtroom. That way, they could be outside and at their microphones announcing the decision to the entire world before the justice had finished reading it. Only the spectators' section was jammed full of curious onlookers.

Susman turned to the lawyer sitting next to him as the justices took their seats and predicted: "The Chief Justice will now read the opinion." Not all opinions were read aloud, and even fewer were read by the Chief Justice. Reading an opinion aloud was a justice's prerogative, although it was rarely exercised. But an opinion written and read by a Chief Justice in a case as controversial as Webster would be used to send a signal of unity to the country. After months of negotiations with his fellow justices, for example, Chief Justice Earl Warren had read aloud the unanimous opinion in the school desegregation case *Brown v. the Board of Education* in open court as a symbol of the Court's unity to the entire nation.

True to Susman's prediction, Chief Justice Rehnquist did read the majority opinion. In a 5–4 decision, the Court upheld the constitutionality of the Missouri law. It permitted doctors to test for viability, and reiterated its earlier holdings that public funds and public facilities need not be used for abortions except those performed to save a woman's life. The Court managed to skirt the two most treacherous issues, free speech and whether life began at conception, finding in each instance a reason not to rule on them.

The details of the ruling were not so important, however, as its overall effect. The loss was even more devastating than the pro-choice forces had expected. Without overturning Roe, the Supreme Court had issued an open invitation to the states to pass restrictive laws.

Unlike the school desegregation case, no one mistook Justice Rehnquist's symbolic reading of the Webster opinion as a sign of unity. Four other justices also wrote opinions. Two separate concurring opinions were prepared by Justices O'Connor and Scalia; a partial concurring and dissenting opinion was written by Stevens; and a strong dissenting opinion, joined by Marshall and Brennan, was read aloud by Justice Blackmun.

In a voice that many described as angry and others as sad and eloquent, Justice Blackmun read his opinion in open court, the only time a justice had exercised his prerogative to do so that term. Blackmun insisted that while the opinion had not overturned Roe, it had gutted every principle that it stood for. "I fear for the future. I fear for the liberty and equality of the millions of women who have lived and come of age in the sixteen years since Roe was decided. I fear for the integrity of, and public esteem for, this Court," Blackmun said.

When he finished reading, those present sat in stunned silence. Tears trickled down the cheeks of many of the women sitting in the lawyers' section. Later, everyone would dissect the opinions in minute detail, but for the moment, no one moved or said a word. Everyone sat quietly, trying to absorb the fact that this Court, if given a chance, seemed ready to undo a fundamental freedom that women had enjoyed for most of history. It was worse than anyone could have anticipated in all the months of waiting.

A stunned and momentarily defeated Susman had to pull himself together and face the media outside the court. Then he was expected at a press conference at the ACLU headquarters on nearby Maryland Avenue. He performed admirably, swallowing the bitter blow and talking only about the loss that women had suffered. Only later, when he had time to experience the loss in a more personal sense would he indulge briefly in a moment of rancor, recalling that only one of the women he had worked with on the case came over to him on decision day to tell him what a fine job he had done. "It's tough to lose. It's not an image I want," he would tell me months later.

On an overcast, drizzly day in early October, four months after the fallout from the Webster decision had settled, Frank Susman hopped a plane from St. Louis to Pittsburgh, where he planned to participate in a day-long schedule of events, culminating in a black-tie, fund raising dinner at which he was the main speaker. The dinner would benefit Women's Health Services, one of his oldest clients and also one of the oldest abortion clinics in the country. Women's Health Services was a nonprofit, outpatient facility that provided an array of gynecological and counseling services, including a unique therapy group that met once a week to help its members—all women—get in touch with their sexuality. Sandwiched in between his arrival and the fundraiser would be a brown bag lunch with a group of American Civil Liberties Union colleagues eager to hear the inside scoop on the Webster case; a visit to the clinic, where its employees were eager to meet the man who had argued the most famous—and infamous—abortion case in history; a late afternoon press conference (but not so late that it wouldn't make the evening news); and a radio show at 5 P.M. He had only a few minutes to grab a catnap before dressing for the pre-dinner reception at 6 P.M.

This was not an unusual day as these days went. Paradoxically, losing Webster had made Susman even more of a celebrity. With the abortion right in jeopardy, he was more in demand than ever. His calendar could have been filled with speaking dates had he chosen to accept all the invitations he received. After his speeches, people stood in line waiting to shake his hand and ask him to sign their programs, which he did, always graciously asking the person's name before beginning to write.

Along the way, he had acquired a New York agent to book his speeches. The other new thing was that he had begun to charge a speaking fee, something he had resisted for a long time. For years he had flown around the country speaking for free, but the speaking dates took time away from his practice, and gradually he had become convinced, if not entirely comfortable with the idea, that he should start charging for his speeches. Susman, Schermer, Rimmel & Shifrin had a policy that the partners' outside earnings went into a kitty, so days he took off without pay were a loss to the firm as well as to himself.

Susman was still generous with his time. When he accepted an invitation to give a speech, he typically made himself available not just for the speech but also for whatever else could be arranged in the way of publicity to help the cause. Providers and other pro-choice groups had learned over the years that they could parlay a visit from Susman into a lot of local publicity, and his droll and hard-hitting speeches made him popular on the provider circuit. Susman also had imposed one unbreakable rule on his agent, which was that he always spoke for free at abortion-clinic benefits.

Tonight's main event, a banquet at the local Sheraton Hotel, would ordinarily have been used to raise funds to refurbish the Vivian Campbell Fund, named in honor of a Pittsburgh mother who died of an illegal abortion in 1950. The fund helped poor women get abortions when they needed them. Unfortunately, though, some of tonight's monies would have to be diverted to repair the latest attack on the clinic. It was the second attack on a Pittsburgh clinic within a month, part of the renewed efforts of the pro-life movement in the wake of the Webster decision.

On a Saturday, September 30, six Franciscan University students had broken into a small, locked passageway connected to the clinic. Like most clinics, Women's Health Services has many locked doors, and different keys are required to open each of them. Stuck in the anteroom, the students crouched down to await the arrival of a clinic employee. When the unsuspecting employee, a nurse, arrived, they rushed past her as she opened the door and headed into the clinic. The terrified woman managed to lock herself in a laboratory, where she called the police and then sat trembling as she awaited their arrival.

Meanwhile, the students poured twenty-five gallons of tar along the main hallways of the clinic. It eventually spread throughout the clinic, onto carpeted and tiled floors, on walls and furniture. The damage was extensive: More than $25,000 would be needed just to remove the tar, which was so thick in some places that the entire flooring had to be pulled up and replaced. Adding to the expense of the cleanup was the fact that tar was a hazardous substance; its removal required special precautions. Workers were scheduled to begin removing the tar while everyone was at the banquet, and would work through the weekend.

Actually, the break-in had turned out to be good publicity for the upcoming benefit, and the clinic's director Sue Roselle had spent much of the week prior to the dinner escorting the media through the clinic to view the damage. In addition, the outpouring of support following the Webster decision had made the banquet a more popular cause than in past years.

Mary Litman, the pert blonde publicity director of the clinic told us as she drove us around for the day's events that the turnout was unusually high for this dinner. Not only were nearly 800 people willing to pay $100 a person to attend the dinner, but countless more had sent donations. She and her staff had opened many envelopes in the past few weeks to find checks for $200, $300, even several for $500, from persons sympathetic to the cause who wouldn't—or couldn't—make their views publicly known.

And finally, the fundraiser was also enjoying a little notoriety in some quarters because of the person to whom the clinic had chosen to present its annual special recognition award. In past years the award had gone to a pro-choice activist, usually to reward years of service. Susman, for example, had been honored one year.

This year, it was being given to someone who not only had not yet spent any time working for the pro-choice cause, but who, prior to Webster, might not even have been pro-choice. The recipient was being given the award on the strength of her promise to support pro-choice in the future. The award was going to Elsie Hillman, a well-known Pittsburgh philanthropist and a prominent Republican National Committeewoman. Reportedly close enough to the President and First Lady to spend weekends with them at Camp David, Hillman, like several other

Republican national committeewomen, had recently declared her pro-choice sympathies in the hope that her view would prompt President George Bush to back off from his staunch anti-abortion view.

In the three months since the Webster decision, the mood of the country had become amazingly, profoundly pro-choice. The victory that Randall Terry had grasped in his hand in the days after the Supreme Court ruling seemed to have vanished into thin air as Americans, even those who were still deeply ambivalent about abortion, came down on the side of the right to choose.

Susman was at his most congenial talking at a semiprivate lunch with a group of his fellow ACLU colleagues. "I don't know what a country lawyer from the Ozarks can tell you city people about the Supreme Court," he said as he stood to make a few remarks. Most of the two dozen people in the room were young enough to be flattered by Susman's collegial approach.

"In prior years you had a feeling you could win. There were often surprises, of course. We didn't hold the line on public funding or abortion rights for minors. But for now, the bottom line is that we can't go into the Supreme Court anymore. The votes are no longer there." In fact, Susman thinks the pro-choice movement should stay out of all the courts. "They will not help. We have to change the scene of battle to win. The tactics must be different, the armies larger. You think we lawyers will save you, but we won't always be able to."

Susman has been telling the pro-choice movement for years to stop relying so heavily on lawyers. Mostly because he couldn't get anyone to listen before, he has not always been so outspoken about his belief that the abortion-rights forces must rebuild a grass-roots movement that will protect the abortion right in the polls.

"Webster has the activists playing on a level field for the first time. It remains to be seen who will win," he warns ominously. But there is also a clear note of optimism in his voice.

He believes the majority of Americans are pro-choice, and that the polls present a false picutre when they show only a slim majority of Americans supporting abortion. For example, he points out that the number of people who approve of abortion is always several points higher when a poll is anonymous, then adds: "Anonymous to me means going into the voting booth. That's where people express their real feelings on abortion."

He tells his audience that in the past seven or eight years, pro-lifers have put abortion on the ballot in nonbinding initiatives in several states and have never won. Pro-choice has never put abortion on the ballot, he observes.

Divorced from funding issues, pro-life initiatives have failed in Rhode Island and Massachusetts, both heavily Catholic states, and in Ohio, deep in the heart of the fundamentalist blue-collar constituency. "In those states," Susman says, "pro-lifers chose the language and the voters, and they were defeated. That's what people truly believe about abortion."

Susman is unsure of his feelings regarding his own temporarily diminished role in the abortion movement. He hopes all the action will be in the state legislatures; this is where it has to be if the battle is going to be won. He's working with pro-choice groups in Missouri to develop some pro-choice legislation. And he believes he'll be back in court again before it's all over. Susman once said that abortion appealed to him more than other civil rights issues he might have worked on because it wasn't a single-case issue, and he has no plans to quit now.

There are days when he misses being at the center of all the excitement and attention, the overwhelming passion that surrounded the case. Win or lose, Webster was a case that comes along once in a very few lawyers' careers. But now that it's over, he also finds there a little relief in that, too.

3 | Providers

B.J. Isaacson-Jones and the Women of Reproductive Health Services

GIVEN A CHOICE, most of us would never think of visiting an abortion clinic. This is unfortunate because a morning spent in an abortion clinic, talking to the people who actually do the surgery that has so divided us, watching a frightened teen-ager receive counseling, listening to a woman who desperately wants a baby arrange to terminate a pregnancy because she knows the fetus she is carrying will be so deformed it will not survive, brings home the urgency, the utter need for legalized abortion, and the callousness of those who would make it illegal once again. (If more people had cause to visit a clinic, to see not only the medical service that is provided, but also the supportive and nurturing atmosphere in which it is delivered, more of us might, as one Florida state senator recently did, enter a clinic pro-life and emerge a few hours later in the pro-choice camp)

69

Before it was legalized in 1973, abortion was a clandestine activity, difficult to come by, expensive, and emotionally devastating to the estimated one million women who underwent the procedure each year. A woman who needed to terminate a pregnancy had few choices about how she went about it. She could induce the abortion herself, as many women did, by drinking household bleach or laundry detergent or some other abortifacient. These were, however, systemic poisons that frequently killed her along with the fetus. Or she could seek out her local illegal abortionist, whose tools were often knitting needles and unsterile drug-store catheters. Antiseptic surgery was impossible. Anesthesia was out of the question, as were antibiotics to prevent post-operative complications.

Only a few hundred persistent and lucky women every year managed to obtain a legal abortion, but getting one's physician to perform one required money and connections, and a willingness to lie about the conditions of one's life. To obtain a legal abortion, a woman had to appear before a hospital committee of three male physicians and feign mental illness or threaten suicide.

When it became obvious in the early 1970s that abortion would be legalized in the United States, a few forward-looking persons began thinking about how best to provide women with safe, legal abortions. A St. Louis woman named Judith Widdicombe became interested in the problem when she was a young, newly trained nurse working in obstetrics and gynecology at St. Joseph's Hospital in Kirkwood, a suburb of St. Louis. Over the years, like most medical personnel, she saw women in the hospital emergency room suffering from botched abortions. Most lived, although many were maimed, and occasionally a woman died.

She still remembers her first tragic experience: "I saw my first women die in the emergency room when I was twenty-one. She had a knitting needle abortion, and she hemorrhaged to death. People called the police when they saw she was dying. They all stood around trying to get her to tell them who did it. In the midst of all that, I backed off and thought about what could have made her desperate enough to let someone do this to her."

Widdicombe, a tall, soft-faced blonde woman in her early fifties, and I were talking one December day over lunch in a cozy second-floor restaurant in Washington, D.C., while outside native Washingtonians coped with a rare six inches of snow that had hit their city the night before. The restaurant, the Pan Asian Noodle & Grill House, was a fitting choice for our meeting. While I waited for her, I had read a review that explained that the restaurant was owned and operated by a collective of Asian women from many countries.

Judith Widdicombe, who spent the 1960s juggling marriage, motherhood, and a career, has always considered herself a feminist. Her entire professional life has been spent working in and around women's health. Sensitive from the early stages of her training to what she considered "doctor's insensitivities to women," she has fought not only for legalized abortion but also for a new model of treatment that gives women a measure of control over their health care. For years she watched the conservative medical establishment deny women abortions, a decision she thought belonged to the woman alone.

For the past one and one-half years Widdicombe had been living in Washington, D.C., where she was the spokesperson and fundraiser of Voters for Choice, a PAC group organized around abortion. This had been her idea of a sabbatical, a respite from the twenty-five years she spent on the front lines working as a provider. She came to Washington to learn more about fundraising, and she had been successful, raising more than $250,000 in 1988 alone. Now she was returning to St. Louis to put her skills back to work there in the renewed struggle to save the abortion right.

In the late 1960s, when the movement to legalize abortion had just begun, she organized and operated a telephone referral service to help women obtain safe abortions. It was a branch of the Clergyman's Consultation Service started a few months earlier in New York City. Widdicombe trained about sixty volunteers—some of whom were clergymen. When she could, she sent women to states and countries where abortion was legal. When she had to, she sent them to illegal abortionists whom she had personally checked out beforehand.

After several years of running the telephone hotline, Widdicombe had some specific ideas about how abortion services should be delivered. She believed that abortion should be provided by women, and to this day, most of the people who work in abortion clinics, from directors to laboratory technicians, are female. She wanted abortion delivered on a low-cost basis out of freestanding clinics designed especially to provide abortions and other related women's health services.

Most shocking to the medical establishment, she did not believe that the overnight hospital stay then required for abortions was necessary. Clinics would do them on an out-patient basis, a radical departure in medical treatment that paved the way for many other surgeries to be done the same way. Most important, she thought women should be provided with an objective, nurturing environment in which they could freely decide whether to end a pregnancy.

At the time she founded her clinic, no one, including herself, realized that a brand-new profession, that of abortion-care providers, was being born. The profession of abortion provider sprang up virtually overnight on January 22, 1973, the day that abortion was legalized in the United States. Abortion was quite literally illegal one day and legal the next, a situation that could have led to chaos. Instead it led to something that many women had long sought: more control over their own bodies.

Reproductive Health Services, the clinic Widdicombe founded, was and remains a model of its kind, widely emulated by other abortion providers. Widdicombe's ideas, considered radical at the time of the clinic's inception, are now routine in abortion care, practiced at most clinics across the country. Even though she stepped down as director four years ago, a portrait of her, a photographic icon to her grit and determination, still hangs in a prominent place in the clinic.

Reproductive Health Services is best known for lending its name as the primary plaintiff in the Webster case. It is located in an undistinguished, eleven-story, yellow brick doctors' building in a slightly down-at-the-heels neighborhood of the Central West End section of St. Louis. Most of the gracious old southern-style, brick homes in the surrounding neighborhood have long since been carved into apartments.

Since it opened its doors on May 22, 1973, Reproductive Health Services has been a busy place and has gotten busier each succeeding year of its existence. Reproductive Health Services performed 475 abortions the first year of its existence (but it opened mid-year), and 8,460 in 1988. Eight thousand, six hundred and sixty-three abortions were scheduled, but 203 women did not go through with the procedure. Nearly two-thirds of the abortions in the St. Louis area (city and county combined) and half of those statewide are done at Reproductive Health Services. Two other abortion clinics operate in the St. Louis area, but they only perform first-trimester abortions.

The two large hospitals in the state that used to do them, Truman Medical Center in Kansas City and Barnes Medical Center in St. Louis, have stopped doing the procedure except to save a woman's life.

Each year, women come to Reproductive Health Services from all over the United States and several countries. In 1988, the clinic drew women from twenty-nine states and as far away as England. Over a thousand women drive across the state line from Illinois each year, and they also come from rural states as far away as South Dakota and Nebraska, a telling sign that abortion is not so widespread seventeen years after legalization as it might be. Most of the 2,680 abortion clinics in the country are located in cities and large towns. A survey of abortion services in the United States recently published in Family Planning Journal revealed that only 2 percent—or 32,000 abortions each year—were performed in rural areas. Only one out of ten nonmetropolitan counties has a facility of any kind that performs abortions.

Over 87 percent of all the abortions in the United States are performed at clinics or in private physicians' offices. The number of providers is declining. According to the Alan Guttmacher Institute, between 1982 and 1985, the number of providers dropped from 2,908 to 2,680. The number of hospitals that provided abortion services decreased fifteen percent, from 1,570 to 1,405. In public hospitals, the decline was even more dramatic: Twenty percent stopped providing abortions.

About half of the clinic's patients are black; half are white.

Nationwide, thirty percent of all abortions are performed on black women; seventy percent on white women. Thirty percent of Reproductive Health Services' clients are poor and could not afford an abortion from a private physician or hospital.

Although the clinic services a poor population, even rich women come to Reproductive Health Services. They do so for one simple reason: Reproductive Health Services is the best at what it does. Just as anyone who needs heart surgery tries to find the surgeon with the most experience who will presumably be the most skilled, so, too, do rich women who can afford the best private care come from around the world to get their abortions at Reproductive Health Services.

Reproductive Health Services' budget has grown from $50,000 in 1973 to $2.5 million in 1988. Ninety-three percent of its operating costs come from patient fees and donations; the remaining seven percent is contributed by the Sunnen Foundation, started by Joseph Sunnen to fund family-planning projects.

A routine first trimester abortion at Reproductive Health Services costs $260. The fee escalates by the week to $850 for a late second-trimester abortion. But it is said that if a woman can make her way to Reproductive Health Service's door, she will not be turned away.

The clinic's director, B.J. Isaacson-Jones—the B.J. stands for Bette June—is neither as tough as her initials nor as soft as her name would indicate. A stylishly dressed woman with short blonde hair and luminous skin, she looks as if she would be more at home running a fashion show for the local Junior League than an abortion clinic. In her office, one looks in vain for a tennis racket or a Pierre Deux makeup case and finds neither.

At our first meeting, Isaacson-Jones struck me as demure, even prim. What I mistook for primness, however, was really an intense thoughtfulness. She pauses to think before she answers a visitor's questions, even ones she has heard many times before, and one soon learns that her measured, articulate responses hide a deep well of emotion on the subject of abortion.

Her office contains two bamboo sofas covered in a mauve flowered print material. It looks more like a sun room than the office of a professional woman, but there is a reason for this. Like the people who work here, the office sometimes does double duty and serves as a private recuperation area for prominent or celebrity patients. A large teak-wood desk at one end of the room is balanced by a small blonde table at the other end. Too small for conferences, it is where she eats lunch most days.

Isaacson-Jones is Widdicombe's hand-picked successor, chosen as much for what she didn't bring to the job as what she did. She has no formal training in business management but she is endowed with an instinctive ability to get people to work well together. Widdicombe's self-admitted weakness was her managerial skills, and although she was willing, even eager, to turn over the clinic to someone who would impose more order than she had, she resisted bringing in anyone who might try to insist upon the rigid standards of most business organizations. (Although it is a nonprofit organization, it is not particularly rich, and has no choice but to watch its bottom line carefully.)

Reproductive Health Services had grown over the years, but like most of the female-dominated clinics, it was more organic than most hospitals and medical practices were. If women's health were to continue the advances of the past twenty years, its providers had to remain open to new ideas and directions. Widdicombe needed someone who understood this.

Even better from Widdicombe's point of view, Isaacson-Jones was not political. Although Widdicombe considers herself a feminist, she does not run a feminist clinic. When abortion clinics were first set up, they often divided along feminist-nonfeminist lines, with the feminist clinics tending to be anti-medical and anti-physician. With her nursing background, Widdicombe believed in and wanted a strong, supportive medical environment at her clinic. In the early years of Reproductive Health Services's existence, she successfully fought off an attempted coup among some of her staff, who claimed she wasn't feminist enough. She wanted to be sure the clinic's next director would remain above that fray.

After years of working with Isaacson-Jones as she rose through the ranks, working first as a part-time volunteer counselor, then as a second-trimester coordinator, director of counseling, and finally as associate director, Widdicombe believed Isaacson-Jones understood the special environment in which the clinic operated and had the sensitivity to preserve it.

Although Isaacson-Jones lacks professional management experience, she is not totally uninterested in it, as the bookshelves in her office reveal. Lined up alongside the thick black notebooks where she keeps the details of the clinic's operations are titles such as *The Art of Managing, Passion for Excellence, The Energetic Manager,* and *Influencing Integrity.*

She has imposed a new degree of order on the clinic during her four-year tenure, but she still runs an open shop. During the first hour of our meeting, she pressed several of her huge notebooks on me, one on quality assurance and another on risk management, both big topics at the clinic. The quality-assurance notebook is a record of the clinic's attempts to provide its clients with the highest possible quality of service, and the risk-management notebook is the clinic's log of complications. She gave me free rein in both, asking only that I not mention the names of the few physicians who have had complaints made against them, all of which were settled in the physician's favor.

Isaacson-Jones, who is thirty-nine, became interested in abortion the same way most women her age did, by experiencing it herself or helping a friend through one. In her case, she helped a friend. When a college classmate could not tell her own parents she was pregnant, Isaacson-Jones went to her own father, who gave her the money to help her friend. She took her friend to an abortion clinic in Kansas City, Kansas, where abortion was legal at the time. "The staff at the clinic was wonderful," she recalled. "They made me part of the process." Isaacson-Jones was already coming to the realization that "pregnancy changed women's lives immediately and sometimes forever," and her experience at the clinic reenforced her belief that women had to have access to safe, inexpensive abortions.

After graduating from Stephens College in 1972, she married and soon found herself at home rearing two sons. When her marriage fell apart after eight years, she needed to find a job. That proved to be easy. The hard part was discovering work that was satisfying. The year and a half that she worked in a clothing store was enjoyable enough, but didn't give her the kind of personal fulfillment she was looking for in a career. She went back to graduate school to get a masters degree in education, with an emphasis on counseling.

As part of her degree requirements, she did a practicum at Reproductive Health Services, and she's been there ever since in one capacity or another. Within weeks of coming to work at Reproductive Health Services, Isaacson-Jones knew she had found her calling. Today, as clinic director, she is paid $43,500 a year for what she ruefully describes as a "seven-days-a-week job."

Her four years as director have been among the most harrowing for the clinic and for her personally. She has witnessed the escalation of violence toward clinics, including the fire bombing of her clinic, and she has endured the pain of sitting in her office while television cameras recorded her devastation one sticky summer day in July 1989 when the Supreme Court—in a lawsuit initiated by her clinic—moved to restrict the abortion right for the first time in seventeen years.

Ironically, she says, she and her staff would not mind being put out of business. Last year, she started an adoption service, partly in response to pressure to give women an even wider range of choices when they are faced with a problem pregnancy, and partly because she does not know how much longer she will be in the business of providing women with abortions. It is inevitable that RU 486 or some other new abortifacient that can be taken at home in the early weeks of pregnancy will reduce the number of first-trimester abortions. But she and her staff root for the day when such medications will be licensed for use in the United States. They don't believe a time will arrive when women will not need abortion clinics. "We would still be here for late abortions, for the woman who is too ambivalent to make up her mind in time to use RU 486," she said.

Among the many surprises that await a visitor to an abortion clinic is the fact that most clinics do more than abortions. They typically offer an array of women's health services that young and poor women cannot get anywhere else: routine gynecological checkups, pregnancy and sexually transmitted disease testing, birth control counseling, and in Reproductive Health Services' case, the adoption service. The services offered at this and many other clinics, however, transcend the merely physical, as workers also do their best to support women, to help them emerge from the clinic with their dignity and self-esteem intact.

While the work is exhilarating and rewarding, it must also be wearing, I suggested to two nurses, Carol LaRue and Becky Dye, as we chatted in the staff room. "I should get burnout, but I don't," Dye, a recovery room nurse, said. "We get frustrated and stressed out. I can tell when I'm in that. It lasts a couple of days. But we have periods where there's not so much going on, and we can take extra time."

When I asked her how long she had worked at Reproductive Health Services, LaRue told me she "came with the workbook on how to run the place." An R.N., she does a little of everything, mostly assisting at procedures, but sometimes working in the laboratory and sometimes doing ultrasounds.

She worked with Widdicombe at St. Joseph's. "I knew what Judy was doing out of her house, although I didn't work on the hotline. But when someone called me and told me Judy had opened up a clinic, I called her, and she said come to work tomorrow."

As for the wear and tear on the soul, LaRue manages to keep it all in perspective by comparing what is now and what was: "I don't have any problems with what I do. Maybe it's because I remember the illegal days. I saw a lot of gals have babies that they didn't want. I saw women miscarrying. Twenty years ago, a woman had to lay in bed until she miscarried. Also I see a fair amount of women who are getting an abortion for genetic problems. Even if they had the baby, it wouldn't live. I'm glad we can help them."

A woman's first contact with the clinic is usually by telephone. The hundreds of calls that pour into the clinic each day are answered by the telephone room counselors. The phone room, or "fun room," as it is referred to punningly by the women who work in it, is open whenever the clinic is. Ten part-time workers staff the telephone room. Some work one day a week. Some work four hours twice a week; some work nearly full-time. The only consistent thing seems to be the inconsistency.

The job of Christine Wolf, a laconic woman with long brown

hair, is to juggle not only the phone room workers' schedules but also the schedules of everyone else who works in the clinic. The clinic has learned to cluster activities—counseling, testing appointments, abortion appointments—and Wolf is the woman who makes sure the clustering results in something resembling order.

She trains her own staff, often wooing someone away from counseling when she needs a new worker in the phone room. The counselor's job, Wolf says, is to please the clinic and the client. "We walk a tightrope, and frankly the longer you're here, the better you understand it." One thing the phone room counselors do not do is reduce fees. A woman must come in to talk to someone, often Wolf herself, if she needs a reduced-fee abortion.

The phone room looks like total chaos to the uninitiated. Three or four women, sitting at a large round oak desk are in various stages of consulting with women who have called the clinic for help. One woman is taking a medical history. Another is listening to a woman talk about how depressed she feels taking care of the three children she has and how she can't possibly have another baby right now. The caller is also Catholic and has reservations about abortion. She will be booked for a counseling appointment before she is allowed to have an abortion at Reproductive Health Services.

Another woman who knew exactly what she wanted has just booked an appointment for an abortion and is now being told to bring warm knee socks and a cashier's check or cash when she comes on Saturday. She's also told that she will probably encounter protesters outside the clinic: "If you can't handle it, just go home and call us to reschedule."

Some of the calls are straightforward while others are much more opaque and require considerably more attention on the counselor's part. "You hear a silence or a tone in a woman's voice when you ask her if she's ever considered suicide or suffered from depression. That signals you to ask her to come in for some counseling," says Judy Kirtian in her girlish voice.

Joan Shifter recalls a patient who when asked at first denied she had been the victim of sexual abuse, and then quickly changed her answer to yes. She said she had never told anyone, but an uncle had molested her for five years. She said she didn't want an abortion, but her boyfriend was insisting. She used to protest in front of abortion clinics, she said.

"Why did you stop?" Shifter asked.

"I had a baby and saw how hard it was."

"The important thing to realize is that you must make the decision. And you must learn to forgive yourself for whatever you decide to do. This is a lousy decision, there is no right or wrong."

Since Webster, the callers are more distressed than they have been in the past. Are you still doing abortions? they ask, the anxiety palpable in their voices. Is abortion still legal? they want to know. The phone room counselors, as well as the other counselors, must repeatedly reassure women that abortion is still legal in Missouri. The Supreme Court decision did not affect the day-to-day operation of the clinics. Any clinic that does abortions does not receive federal funds, so counseling is not an issue, and virtually all clinics (certainly all that perform second-trimester abortions) use sonograms to test for viability.

At some point during most phone calls, each woman consults the one master appointment book. Appointments can be made for abortions every day except Sunday and Monday. Sunday the clinic is closed; Monday is a skeleton day when no doctors and nurses are in the clinic. Miniclinics, special counseling sessions designed to educate small groups of women about the abortion procedure, are also booked every day the clinic is open.

Miraculously there never seems to come a time when all three women need to use the appointment book at once. The women, even while carrying on their telephone conversations, seem perfectly attuned to who needs the book next and automatically hand it around the table. Between calls, a serious fashion consultation is ongoing as everyone helps one counselor accessorize her New Year's Eve outfit. She gets two offers of jewelry from her fellow counselors.

I recently spent several days at the clinic. The waiting room, large enough to hold fifty to sixty women, was full at 10 A.M., when I arrived.

Everyone was greeted by a woman who sat behind the in-take

desk. She gave people medical forms to fill out and distributed small plastic cups for the ubiquitous urine samples. To the left of the desk, a rack was filled with literature about a variety of subjects related to women's health.

Most of the women seated in the waiting room were young, in their teens and twenties. Not a single woman, I observed with some surprise, looked pregnant. Later, several of the clinic workers would ask me if I noticed this fact. They told me it's amazing to watch the transformation. The women's stomachs are absolutely flat when they arrive at the clinic, full of fear and anxiety about what they're going to do, many of them not even sure they're pregnant. Once they have been given a pregnancy test, met with a counselor, and at least begun to figure out what they're going to do, only then do they relax. "Then those flat stomachs give way to some pregnant-looking ones," Amelia McCracken, director of community education says.

About half the women brought someone with them, most often another woman. Only two young women were accompanied by young men. One teen-ager brought her two-year-old son and her sister, who will babysit the little boy while his mother keeps her appointment.

Most of the women sit quietly, some keeping up a pretense at conversation, most staring into space, their faces a mask of tension. One apparently blase young woman calmly paints her fingernails fire-engine red as she awaits her appointment.

A closed, locked door separates the big waiting room from the rest of the clinic. Once behind that door, the clinic becomes a maze of narrow hallways, one large and one small laboratory (the latter called the utility room), three procedure rooms, nine primary and clinic counseling rooms and the main counseling room, the adoption agency with its two counseling rooms, several small medical waiting areas, and a dressing room complete with a row of school lockers. The largest is the recovery room, lined on both sides with brown plastic reclining chairs. On the back of each is a neatly folded peach plaid lap blanket.

Every few minutes the reception room door opens, and a clinic counselor calls another name.

"Laura, last initial W., please."

"Julie, last initial S, please."

"Mary Ann, last initial R, please."

One by one the women vanish behind the heavy wood door.

Mary Ann, last initial R, heads for the door, her boyfriend right behind her. Gently and reassuringly the white-coated woman at the door says she wants to see Mary Ann alone. No one but the patient is allowed in for the medical procedure, but if Mary Ann receives any in-depth counseling, her boyfriend will be asked to join her. "Don't worry, I won't forget, I'll come back for you," the woman says closing the door behind Mary Ann and herself.

If Mary Ann's boyfriend is lucky, he'll fall into the grasp of Joan Shifter, who works part-time in the telephone room and also leads what she calls her SO group, SO standing for Significant Other. Shifter rounds up people by going into the waiting room where mothers, grandmothers, aunts, friends, husbands, brothers, and boyfriends all are anxiously waiting for a patient. She usually says she has just made fresh coffee and wouldn't they like to join her for a cup.

"I really have to sell them to get them to join me," Shifter says unabashedly. "I ask, 'Isn't this an awful way to be spending a Wednesday morning?' I promise I'll check on their patients, I tell them I'm a liaison with the clinic, and I say I can help you talk over some of your feelings. Sometimes I get no one and then I go away. When I come back a few minutes later, they've thought it over, and I've got someone—maybe only one person—to go with me.

"I've learned not to judge that a man is the father. Last week, two men came in with a woman. They seemed gay, and I found out they were high school buddies of the girl. Neither was her partner.

"But whoever brings someone here is involved. They have feelings about this, and I try to get them to air those feelings so they can be more supportive of the women later. I say, 'If you think it's over when you walk out of here, you're wrong. You can't tuck this neatly away. Every woman who has an abortion suffers a loss, and so do you. It's best to get those feelings out and move on.'

"Most men haven't dealt with their feelings, their loss. And mothers need to talk about how hard it is to go home with a girl who's really a young woman. I tell them it's not giving their children permission to be sexually active to suggest birth control. Besides, it's too late to give her permission once she's been pregnant. I let the parent off the hook. I say you need to put the burden on your teen-ager. Tell her you think she's too young, but that the decision is all hers. Also tell her if she makes the decision to be sexually active, then she has to assume the burdens and responsibility that go with it."

"Sarah, last initial M." Sarah looks pale and frightened, and Delores McAvoy, a counselor, greets her saying, "My, you've come a long way. Did you have to get up early this morning?" Sarah smiles wanly and relaxes a little as she mumbles an answer.

Delores has Sarah's medical chart in her hand. She checks it and sees that Sarah has booked an appointment for an abortion. She is eight weeks pregnant. She takes Sarah into a small room, where three other women are already seated. Together they will watch a film about what is going to happen to them. Ironically, the nine-minute film is longer than most abortion procedures.

"It's important that you know what's going to happen to you," Delores tells Sarah as she leaves at the door. Afterward, Delores is there to collect her and take her back to the main waiting room. A few minutes later, she is ushered into the clinic again, this time to meet with a primary counselor.

Another of the unusual things about Reproductive Health Services is that every woman who comes through its door receives some form of counseling. Some meet with a counselor in miniclinic, where patients gather in small groups to discuss abortion and other health issues such as birth control. Many meet individually with a counselor, usually for about twenty to thirty minutes but sometimes longer, as long in fact as is necessary for both the client and the counselor to feel comfortable with the woman's decision.

Sarah's counselor, like most of the counselors who meet initially with patients, is a volunteer. She starts by asking her if she has any questions about the film. No, Sarah, says shyly, she doesn't. Did you understand everything? the counselor asks. When Sarah says she did, the counselor begins to talk with her about the kind of support she's getting from her family and friends for this abortion. It's a way of making sure she's getting the approval every woman needs, and also a way of opening the discussion about any ambivalence she might be experiencing.

A woman who expresses an unusual amount of ambivalence during this intake process is encouraged to make an appointment for more in-depth counseling or, if she is unwilling to do this, to go home and reconsider her decision. The miniclinics and individual counseling also give the clinic a chance to educate women about the need to use birth control, after-care, and other issues of women's health.

Since the Webster decision, the counselors have also been using the counseling sessions to talk to women about the fact that legalized abortion is now threatened and what they can do to preserve the right to choose. Women are given post cards they can fill out and mail to their elected officials asking them to support pro-choice. The clinic also prints flyers that educate women about the abortion right.

Much of this and other educational materials that are available at the clinic are run off in the clinic's print shop, which also doubles as the shredding room. The day I visited, I was greeted by a young, smiling black woman named Angela Davis who explained the precautions that are taken to avoid leaving a patient's name around where it might be seen. Extensive records are kept of the clinic's activities, she said, but papers with patients' names on them are routinely shredded. "We don't leave a patient's name lying around on a scrap of paper."

If a woman is prepared to undergo an abortion, as Sarah is, the next step is the laboratory tests. Even though she may already have used a home pregnancy test or been tested by her physician, Sarah's urine will be tested again to make absolutely certain she is pregnant. Blood is drawn to test for diabetes and to type her blood. She will undergo a pelvic exam or an ultrasound.

The clinic has no choice but to charge for these services since it receives no Medicaid reimbursement because it performs abortions. Even if a woman receives treatment and decides not to have an abortion, Medicaid will not reimburse the clinic. At $20 for the pelvic exam and $50 for the ultrasound, the clinic still charges about half what a private physician would, and these fees are often waived.

Along the way, there are administrative details to be attended to: A copy is made of one of Sarah's IDs so she can have it with her during the procedure, consent forms are signed, and the cashier is paid.

Eventually, Sarah is escorted into a small dressing room where she changes into a hospital gown and places her street clothes and purse in one of the lockers. She next goes to a small medical waiting area, which she shares with two or three other women, for what the clinic tries to make the shortest wait of her entire visit.

Within minutes, a nurse comes to get her for the procedure. A counselor will also be present to help Sarah. She is there to hold her hand, offer emotional support, help her with breathing exercises if she needs them to relax, whatever Sarah needs to get through the procedure.

When the doctor arrives, he chats with Sarah for a few more minutes to be sure she is comfortable with her decision. It is rare, but women do occasionally change their minds after they are on the procedure table, and the clinic staff is prepared to support that decision, too.

Sarah's abortion will be done by vacuum aspiration, the most commonly used technique. Over 90 percent of all abortions are done this way. Her cervix is first numbed with a local anesthesia, and then dilators, or rods, are inserted to stretch it. After her cervix is dilated, a small tube called a cannula is inserted into her uterus. The tube is connected to the vacuum aspirator, a machine that suctions out the contents of the uterus. Once the cervix has been dilated, the aspiration takes only five to eight minutes.

Fifteen minutes after the entire surgical procedure is completed, Sarah walks unassisted (as do 98 percent of the women who have abortions), into the recovery room, where she will stay for at least an hour. Two nurses work in the recovery room, monitoring patients' physical and emotional reactions. Sarah is given crackers and soda to rebuild her strength.

Eighty minutes later, she is released, along with four other women, to meet one last time with a counselor, who asks the women how they feel, and talks about how they are likely to feel in the days after having an abortion. She discusses birth control and may offer a month's supply of oral contraceptives to someone who is interested in using them. The clinic does not prescribe or fit diaphragms or IUDs, but under physicians' orders it gives samples of the Pill, which are supplied by drug companies to some women.

She tells the women one more time that the care they are receiving does not end when they walk out of the clinic. Anyone who has an abortion at Reproductive Health Services can call back at any time for additional counseling if she needs to talk to someone about her abortion. Finally, the counselor reminds the women to make an appointment with their own physicians three weeks after their procedure for a follow-up.

Unlike many pro-choice activists, who have sometimes been forced into minimizing the pain associated with the decision to terminate a pregnancy, the women who work at the clinic take a different position. They accept and acknowledge that the abortion decision is a painful one for any woman to make, one that may precipitate a variety of reactions in individual women, and they try to help women cope with their reactions.

"When a woman must undergo a second-trimester abortion, or when she is forced to abort a fetus she might have wanted had the circumstances of her life been different, she often experiences a genuine sense of loss and need to grieve—not least for herself—for having to make so painful a decision," says McCracken, who once worked as a clinic counselor.

One-third of all the women who come to Reproductive Health Services ultimately are referred for more in-depth counseling. All minors must receive counseling, and any woman who is having difficulty deciding what to do about her crisis pregnancy or who is pregnant as the result of rape or incest is steered toward it. If a woman feels she needs counseling for any reason, she can request it.

Women who are aborting an abnormal or genetically impaired fetus receive not only clinic counseling but special treatment the entire time they are in the clinic. These are the most difficult cases any clinic handles because these women badly wanted to have a baby and have now been told or have decided that they should not have the one they are carrying. At Reproductive Health Services the women are accompanied by a counselor the entire time they are in the clinic, and they are given the option to recuperate in a private room if they choose to do so. Some want to be alone; others want to be with other women.

About forty percent of the women who receive primary counseling leave the clinic without an appointment for an abortion. Some call back, but many choose to have the child. For the small percentage of women who need even more in-depth counseling than the clinic is equipped to provide, the counselors are trained to refer patients to clinics and other mental health professionals when necessary.

The staff counseling room is the most electric room in the clinic. Emotions seem always to run high here, and not surprisingly, the main activity after counseling seems to be eating the vast amounts of food that are always around. This is the place where counselors, as many as five or six of them on a busy day, congregate to await their assignments, and it is also where they confer with their supervisors before, after, and even during their counseling sessions.

I hadn't been in the counseling room five minutes when a short, thin, heavily made up woman in her sixties rushed in, wringing her hands, and saying to anyone who would listen, "Whew, it's so painful in there. It's so intense." Immediately she had the attention of Eileen Tamsky, one of the two social workers who were supervising the staff counseling room that day.

The woman explained that she was counseling a woman six and a half months pregnant who will not be able to have an abortion because her pregnancy is too advanced. The woman is not getting along with her husband, who she believes is having an affair with a co-worker. She and her husband fight regularly, she kicks him out, then she takes him back. Even though her pregnancy is very obvious, they have never discussed it. She won't consider adoption and has told the counselor, "If I have the baby, I'll keep it."

The woman's physical needs are first assessed. Thus far, she has received no prenatal care. There is concern about whether the clinic can find a physician to take her on as a patient this late in her pregnancy. Most physicians, fearful of malpractice suits, won't consider treating a woman for the first time at this stage of pregnancy. A slip of paper is pulled from a file; it contains the name of a physician, a sympathetic man, who may be willing to help if the clinic leans on him enough. The supervisor will call him.

Next the discussion turns, as it often does in these sessions, to the woman's support system. Who will help her through this pregnancy? Who will help her care for the child? The woman's own mother is dead, her mother-in-law recently deceased. She has no siblings, no friends, no one she feels she can turn to. She's holding the marriage together because it's all she has, and a baby, the counselors believe, will only aggravate the situation. They must somehow get this woman into more in-depth counseling than the clinic is able to offer her.

Although the woman is middle class, she doesn't work, and her husband controls the money. The woman doesn't even write checks on their checking account. She probably can't get the money for the private counselor they would like to refer her to. Quickly, because the woman has been alone for almost five minutes, a decision is made to send her to a clinic if necessary, and several names are pulled to give to the woman. The counselor heads back to finish her session.

Isaacson-Jones is especially proud of the counseling program at Reproductive Health Services and it is she who has urged me to spend time in this department. Few clinics offer the range of counseling that Reproductive Health Services does, and many offer nothing. Reproductive Health Services' volunteer counseling service is unique, having evolved from Widdicombe's days of operating the telephone referral service.

Says Jody Sova, director of counseling, "I'm not sure every woman who passes through Reproductive Health Services needs the extensive amount of counseling she receives, but we need it. We need to know she's made the best possible decision for her and that she's okay after she makes it."

Unintentionally, the counseling program has also proven to be an excellent form of community outreach. Many women who get abortions are understandably not eager to talk about their experience with an abortion clinic, but volunteer counselors can and do take their experiences back to the community, thus increasing public awareness of the need for legalized abortion.

Arrangements were quickly made for me to sit in on a counseling session. The woman working the in-take desk started asking clients if they would give permission for someone to observe their counseling session. Within thirty minutes she had a list of women who had agreed to have an observer. One was a 26-year-old woman who was 19½ weeks pregnant, too late for a simple first-trimester abortion. Another woman, a mother of four children and pregnant for the fifth time, had already had one abortion and felt she must have another. Another mother of two wanted an abortion because she had recently lost a child to heart disease and felt she couldn't cope with another pregnancy so soon after her loss. Two 15-year-old cousins, both pregnant, wanted abortions but couldn't pay for them; they had spent all their money on one cousin's wedding. And finally there was Tammy, a fifteen-year-old black woman, the mother of a one-year-old child, who is pregnant for the third time and needs a second-trimester abortion.

In 1985, the most recent year for which statistics are available, one million, thirty-one thousand teenagers became pregnant. Of that number 478,000 gave birth; 416,000 underwent abortions; and 137,000 miscarried or had stillbirths. Nearly half of all second-trimester abortions are performed on teen-agers. Experts attribute the high rate to several factors. Many teenagers do not know enough about reproduction to recognize the symptoms of pregnancy. They may not have begun menstruating yet, or may have menstruated only irregularly (many teenagers erroneously believe they cannot get pregnant until they have menstruated regularly for several months). Some, unable to cope with the fact that they are pregnant, simply deny it. The teen-age pregnancy rate is twice as high for nonwhite as for white teens, but both groups choose abortion at about the same rate. Forty-three percent of all teens undergo abortions. In sheer numbers, though, more white than black teens obtain abortions and give birth.

Of women overall who undergo abortions, the Alan Guttmacher Institute reports that the majority are single, poorer on average than other women their age, and young. Eighty percent of women who have abortions are single, that is, never married (63 percent), separated (6 percent), divorced (11 percent), or widowed (1 percent). Only nineteen percent of abortions are performed on married women, although half of all pregnancies are unintentional and half of the women who obtain abortions report using birth control during the month they became pregnant. Sixty-seven percent of all abortions are performed on women whose income is under $25,000. Sixty percent of women who choose abortion are under twenty-five years of age, with the highest ratio (60 abortions per 1000 women) being performed on eighteen and nineteen-year-olds.

Seventy percent of all abortions are performed on white women, but because minority women—blacks and Latinas—are more likely to have an unintended pregnancy, they have more abortions than white women. A black woman is twice as likely to undergo an abortion as a white woman, and although Latina women account for only 13 percent of all abortions, they are more likely than white women to resort to them.

Protestant and Jewish women are least likely to have abortions while a third of all abortions are performed on Catholic women. Women who describe themselves as "born-again" Christians are only half as likely to have an abortion as are all other women.

I decided to sit in on Tammy's counseling session. It took place in a small, gray-walled room, so small that we sat knee to knee on the chairs that were brought in for us. Tiffany, Tammy's year-old daughter, played quietly as we talked. Ronni Handelman, the counselor, is a volunteer but unlike most, she has a masters degree in social work.

Tammy, a black teen-ager, has been pregnant every year since she was thirteen. Her mother Ruth, who accompanied her today, persuaded her to have an abortion when she got pregnant at age thirteen, and Tammy persuaded Ruth to let her have the baby when she got pregnant again at age fourteen. Now Tammy is pregnant again and must decide what to do.

Tammy found out she was pregnant on April 30 (it is now the

end of July) when she went to a local hospital to be treated for rape. A pregnancy test revealed she was one month pregnant. Now into her second-trimester, she has refused to deal with her pregnancy and is here today only at her mother's insistence. In fact, she and her mother are engaged in something of a standoff about what Tammy will do about this pregnancy. Ruth would have liked her to have an abortion right away, but Tammy has refused, claiming she has no money to pay for it. If she decides to have an abortion now, she will have to undergo the much more costly second-trimester abortion.

Ruth, who has two sons, aged eleven and nine, living at home with her in addition to her daughter and granddaughter, doesn't want Tammy to have another child. A practical nurse who plans to go back for an additional degree, she also has some dreams for her daughter, and they include getting an education. The two women are here today because Ruth has finally agreed to pay for her daughter's abortion.

Tammy is pregnant by her nineteen-year-old boyfriend, a high school dropout, who recently was laid off from his assembly line job at a local Chrysler plant. There is, Tammy says, "not much to tell about him." He doesn't know when or whether he'll get his job back, and he says he will support whatever decision she makes. Although they have been together for three and a half years, there is no talk of marriage.

Handelman does not ask whether he is Tiffany's father. Tammy's own father is around and part of her life, but he doesn't live with them, and she sees him only occasionally.

Handelman begins gently with Tammy. She has learned from experience the difficulties of getting through to a teenager. She starts off saying, "First I'd like to tell you how proud I am of you for reporting the rape. It's a very difficult thing to do, but it takes women like you to stop this kind of thing." Asked if she has talked to anyone about the rape, Tammy barely whispers no. She does not look at anyone in the room. "Would you like to?" Handelman asks. Another whispered reply: "Yes."

"You may feel fine now," Handelman continues, "but it might come up again later. It's extremely important for you to get counseling." So important in fact that she interrupts the session to go get the telephone number of a rape counseling center. She presses it on Tammy when she returns.

"Who else knows about this pregnancy?" Handelman asks.

"Everybody," Tammy says, her face brightening. She and her mother both laugh and joke that there are no secrets in their family.

"What are their feelings? Do they know you're here today?"

"Not too many know I'm here," Tammy says. "But they all want me to have an abortion. My auntie, who talked mom into letting me have the baby, she wants me to get an abortion this time. She thinks it will be hard to go to school with two babies."

Asked what grade she is in, Tammy says she is "going for the ninth grade." She doesn't know where she'll go to high school because the family is planning to move out of the inner city, where they now live. Asked how school is going, she stares at the small high window, which is covered with a Venetian blind, for a few seconds before she says, with a slight note of dismay, "Oh, not bad." When Handelman asks her how she is feeling about going to high school next year, she doesn't answer, so Handelman changes the subject. A thunderstorm is raging outside.

"It's good that you have a support system, Tammy," she tells her. "If people approve and support your decision, whatever it is, that helps you. You make the decision, but since you're fifteen, mom has a say in it, too."

Finally she asks: "Do you want an abortion, Tammy?"

"Yes," she whispers.

"Do you have any second thoughts?"

"No."

Handelmann begins to explain what is involved in a second-trimester abortion. She tells Tammy that she will come for two appointments, one to insert a substance that will cause her cervix to dilate and the second, twenty-four hours later, for the surgical procedure. During the first appointment, a laminaria will be inserted into her cervix. She hands Tammy a piece of laminaria. A piece of dried seaweed, it is dull green, less than a half-inch across, and about two inches long. The laminaria will expand as it absorbs the moisture from her cervix, and that will cause the cervix to stretch.

The next day she will return for the surgical procedure, a dilation and evacuation, commonly referred to as a D & E. A vacuum aspirator will be used first, and then the surgeon will use forceps to remove any large pieces of tissue. Finally the physician must use a curette to check the walls of the uterus for any small particles of tissue that may have adhered; they could cause infection later.

When Handelmann finishes explaining the procedure, she tries again to reach Tammy. "Tammy, have you got any hopes or dreams for the future? Do you know what you might like to do?"

"No," Tammy says softly.

Handelmann reassures her, saying, "That's okay, you're very young to have decided."

Tammy stares at the covered window again and Handelmann lets the subject drop. When she speaks again, it is to begin taking Tammy's medical history. Ruth, who has sat by quietly throughout this part of the discussion, answers for her daughter. No, Tammy has no diseases, no venereal disease, she takes no medicine, and she isn't allergic to anything. She has only been hospitalized once, when she had Tiffany.

When Handelman broaches the subject of contraception with Tammy, Ruth gets upset, saying, "She has contraception, she's got the pill, but she won't use it."

Tammy confirms that she won't take the Pill, and Ruth becomes even more agitated, saying, "She'll get them, but she won't use them."

"I hear you, I know what you're saying," Handelmann says to Ruth, "but we need to talk to Tammy about this." Turning back to Tammy, she says, "The Pill could be the wrong contraception for you."

Carefully, meticulously, using a small model of the female genital tract, Handelman explains the various kinds of contraception. Just as she had handed Tammy a piece of laminaria as they talked about her second-trimester abortion, now she hands her a diaphragm as she describes it, and a condom when she talks about it. She tells Tammy that as a sexually active black teen-ager, she is in a high risk group for AIDS, and suggests that using a condom is a good way to protect herself.

Hendelmann asks Tammy how she feels about having another abortion. Tammy sits silently, even after her mother prods her to answer: "She's waiting on you."

Finally Ruth answers for her daughter: "Shocked, that's how she feels."

Shrugging her agreement, Tammy says: "I was shocked. I didn't think about it for a while. My mom finally said it's time to think about it. She made the appointment yesterday."

Handelmann says, "I wish there were an easy way out of a crisis pregnancy, but there isn't. It's not easy to have a baby. It's not easy to adopt out. You must prepare to be a parent because most women who choose adoption don't go through with it. And it's not easy to have an abortion." After waiting a moment, Handelmann gently asks: "Which one do you want to do, Tammy?"

Tammy is silent, and Ruth answers for her again. Handelmann tells the two women that the abortion will cost $400, half the usual fee because Tammy has a Medicaid card.

"Where will you get the money for the abortion, Tammy?" Handelmann asks her. When Tammy says she'll have to get it from her mother because her boyfriend has no money, Ruth chimes in, "She'll give me my money back."

Handelmann goes through the procedure again, this time in greater detail. She says the laminaria may cause some nausea and cramping but assures Tammy that this is normal. On the day of her abortion, she tells Tammy, she will be given a light sedative and an intravenous tube fed with antibiotics. She will also be given a two weeks' supply of antibiotic before she leaves the clinic. Tammy is encouraged to make a follow-up appointment with her own physician.

She is also assured that she will have complete confidentiality. On the day of her surgery, she must give permission even for her immediate family to get information about how she is doing. If anyone calls whom she has not given specific permission to ask about her, the clinic will deny that she is there.

Noticing that Tammy is scared, Handelman reaches out to pat her arm and ask her if she is okay. Tammy doesn't answer, and she starts when a loud thunderclap rattles the window.

Handelman explains that an ultrasound reading will be necessary to determine how many weeks pregnant Tammy is. It is painless, she assures Tammy. The first appointment will take four hours, the actual procedure and recovery, four to six. She suggests that Tammy plan to take off the day from school, and Ruth says she will arrange to take off work, too.

Finally, Handelman tells Tammy that because she is four months pregnant, she may also experience some post-partum depression, which she calls "the blues." They could be hormonal or emotional in origin, but either way, Tammy is assured that she can call the clinic at any time for some counseling if she needs it. An appointment is made for four days later. Turning to Tammy one last time, Handelman asks her: "This is what you want to do?"

Tammy nods yes.

"Are you sure?"

A barely stronger nod from Tammy settles the question. The counseling session is over, one and a half hours after it began.

Back in the counseling room, the counselors gather to analyze the session with Tammy. I express my shock at Tammy's lack of responsiveness to everything—school, the abortion, birth control. The women laugh when I say, only half jokingly, that I would have liked to have Tammy sign a pledge to use some kind of birth control. They tell me most teens are quiet and unresponsive. They come in with their mothers, and their mothers answer for them. Regardless of what they want, they are usually unable to articulate it, and the counselors have learned to read the girls' body language, to explore the relationship between the teen and her mother. If there is real trouble or disagreement between a teen and her mother, it usually erupts sooner or later.

The talk turns to why Tammy has gotten pregnant every year since she was thirteen. Although Ruth is obviously a solid person with the hopes and dreams every mother has for her children, the consensus was that she was overprotecting her daughter.

"Tammy's being rescued," the supervisor said. "She can go on being pregnant because she doesn't suffer the consequences.

She stays in school. Mom takes care of the baby. Mom pays for the abortions."

After we finish talking about Tammy, the conversation turns to another crisis that arose while we were with Tammy. A mother called wanting to know if her daughter was at the clinic. At eighteen, the patient was old enough not to require parental consent, but young enough so her mother might not feel that way. The patient's counselor asked her patient if her mother knew she was getting an abortion today. The girl said absolutely not. A clinic representative returned to the phone to tell the mother that she couldn't reveal whether or not the daughter was there. The counselor told the daughter what the clinic said, and warned her that she'll have to settle the matter with her mother when she gets home.

While the counseling staff moves from one adrenaline-producing crisis to another, Isaacson spends her time on the less emotional day-to-day administration of the clinic. She is a hands-on manager who takes pride in the fact that her door is always open, but with one unusual twist. While she believes her primary responsibility is to support her staff, she says she also must have their support in return.

For her this means that many of the decisions concerning clinic policies, especially those dealing with patient policy, will be jointly made. It means she doesn't pretend to have all the answers. It means she must be able to ask her staff what they think about something and get an honest opinion. The work is too draining, too emotionally treacherous, she maintains, for all the responsibility to rest exclusively on her shoulders.

"I provide what my staff needs in support, but they have to understand that I don't have all the answers. Sometimes I need to go to them and say, 'Help me solve this problem. Let's work out a solution together.'"

Isaacson-Jones is looking for someone to fill a new position she is creating in the medical area. Finding the right kind of person is a major problem, she says, but not for the reason I might suspect, not because people don't want to work around abortion. People tend to self-select themselves for this kind of work, she tells me, adding that she usually starts a job search by asking the volunteers if anyone is interested in moving up. Beyond that, most job leads come to her by word of mouth, and only occasionally does she have to resort to placing a blind ad in the newspaper. While the ad does not mention abortion, it clearly states that this is a "women's clinic."

"But the hardest piece of hiring isn't finding someone pro-choice. It's finding women who fit into the Reproductive Health Services culture. It's threatening to some women because you have real responsibilities here. I make sure everyone partici-pates in most of the decisions. Some women don't like it because we're so inclusive. It isn't a place for a woman who's only interested in her own advancement," she notes, but then quickly adds that Reproductive Health Services has proven to be an excellent launching pad for several volunteers who have gone back to school for counseling degrees and then opened their own practices. "If we've trained someone right, she's ready to do that," she says.

The staff at Reproductive Health Services numbers sixty-eight paid employees plus thirty-five volunteers. Ten people, all of whom report directly to Isaacson-Jones, are considered management: two medical directors, one administrative, one clinical; and directors of nursing, counseling, patient services, adoption services, appointments and scheduling, community education, public affairs, and financial affairs (the comptroller).

Six physicians, including two women, do the abortions on a part-time basis. All have been with the clinic for the ten years that Isaacson-Jones has worked there. That none of the doctors are on staff full-time is a deliberate policy of the clinic, which insists that its physicians have expertise beyond abortion. Like Widdicombe, Isaacson-Jones believes that doing abortions to the exclusion of other medical procedures would be debilitating over time for someone trained to support life, and all their physicians maintain outside gynecological and obstetrical prac-tices. Nurses at the clinic usually do not work exclusively on procedures but are rotated to various functions.

Although she strives for a loosely structured atmosphere, as loosely structured, that is, as is possible in a medical facility, she is very much on the scene every day. "I'm aware of my staff. We have the normal lines of communication. My staff people go first to their supervisors, but they also know it's appropriate to come to me. I walk around. I'm visible. It's the only way I can take a measure of what's going on."

While much of her time is taken up with the routine managerial problems that confront any administrator, some of it is occupied with problems unique to the provider profession or to her clinic. For example, Isaacson-Jones worries about what she pays her staff. Reproductive Health Services' salaries, based on United Way wage scales, are commensurate with pay for the geographic region, but she is aware that some of her top-level staff have taken cuts in pay to work at Reproductive Health Services.

"My director of nursing," she said, "makes less than she would in a similar position in a hospital." She would like to pay them more, but the clinic operates on a tight budget as is, in large part because it is so dedicated to providing reduced-fee abortions to poor women.

She worries about providing her staff the kind of ongoing support they need to do the work they do. That support begins with the hiring process, when prospective applicants are carefully screened to be sure they will be comfortable with the work. New employees are indoctrinated slowly into the day-to-day routine of clinic life. They begin by observing the clinic's work—the counseling and the procedures—through doors and windows, and only when they're comfortable do they move inside the procedures and counseling rooms for closer observation and, eventually, participation.

New staff members go through a special values-clarification exercise that helps them to understand their feelings toward abortion. Regular in-service meetings are scheduled to help the staff deal with such problems as why women choose to undergo second-trimester abortions. The clinic uses a management consultant to help find ways to reduce stress on the staff. Isaacson-Jones considers the work of providing abortions to be among the most stressful in the medical profession, second only to oncology.

"We say that taking care of women is empowering," she said, "but it also causes a lot of tension."

Much of the stress that clinic workers have experienced in the past few years comes not from the daily rigors of working around abortion, but rather, from living day in and day out with the threat of violence, to say nothing of the actual violence that regularly breaks out.

The week before I visited the clinic, two protesters broke into the main waiting room before the clinic opened one morning and chained themselves to two waiting room chairs. The police were called to remove them, and in the process had to saw off the wooden arms of the chairs. The two armless armchairs now stood in the waiting room, symbols of a guerrilla war that never seems to end.

On another occasion, protesters broke into the clinic and chained themselves to huge heavy floor fans. Another time, a protester dived through the heavy plate-glass window in the reception room.

The risk of personal injury became all too real on the night of June 14, 1986. Shortly before midnight, someone entered a second clinic Reproductive Health Services operated in suburban West City and poured six gallons of gasoline in front of the door to an entry atrium. No one was in the clinic at the time, so no lives were lost when the building exploded. Damages were placed at $100,000. What was left of the structure was rebuilt, but because the free-standing clinic was so vulnerable, abortions are no longer done there.

So prevalent has violence become toward abortion clinics that the National Abortion Federation has compiled an information packet detailing the incidents. Since 1977, the first year that violence toward abortion clinics was reported, there have been 712 incidents of serious violence: 32 bombings, 46 arsons, 38 attempted arsons and bombings, 232 invasion of clinics, 226 incidents of vandalism, 48 assaults and batteries, 67 death threats, 3 kidnappings, and 20 burglaries.

Sit-ins are the most common form of harassment that clinics experience. Reproductive Health Services is picketed by a local anti-abortion group almost every Saturday. Although on television sit-ins often look like a peaceful form of protest, in fact, according to a report issued by the National Abortion Federation, "patients are confronted, photographed, or harangued through bullhorns. Large demonstrations may be orchestrated by seasoned activists who travel interstate, boasting arrest records and encouraging local anti-abortion support groups' involvement in harassment."

Furthermore, the potential for an escalation of the violence is present at every sit-in. In 1987 in Chicago a clinic security guard was mowed down by a car driven by anti-abortion demonstrators fleeing a clinic after some mischief. In Washington, D.C. in 1987, terrified patients watched for several hours as police and firefighters worked to unchain ten activists who had broken in during business hours and destroyed furniture before chaining themselves to a heavy piece of equipment.

In 1988 in Southern California, eight clinic defenders were pressed against double plate-glass doors for over forty minutes while a mob of pro-lifers, angry that the women had beaten them to the clinic, surrounded them. Anticipating that the doors would break, the clinic director ordered her staff to call for ambulances and prepared her own clinic to handle the injured. The standoff ended, miraculously without any loss of life or serious harm, only when one of Operation Rescue's leaders arrived with a bullhorn and slowly talked the enraged crowd into backing off.

In St. Louis, the provider community stood by helplessly when Dr. Hector Zevellos, a clinic operator, was kidnapped and held for over a week by a group calling itself the Army of God.

Clinic workers are harassed at home and their children are bothered at school. Jenny Kirby, a former employee at the Northeast Women's Center in Philadelphia received a letter containing a photograph of her child torn into pieces. The message: "We're going to cut your child into little pieces the way you cut up babies." In another state, a clinic physician received a telephone call from someone falsely posing as the local coroner who told him that his child was dead.

The workers at Reproductive Health Services routinely receive threatening telephone calls at home from someone who either screams "Whore" into the telephone or plays the sound of a machine gun firing. All the long-term staff members, including Isaacson-Jones, have been the victims of mail and telephone death threats.

Like most clinics, Reproductive Health Services has taken some special steps to protect its workers. Since security works best when few people know what precautions are being taken. Isaacson-Jones is understandably reluctant to talk about the advice she and her staff have gotten from the Bureau of Alcohol, Tobacco, and Firearms, the government agency that investigates abortion-related violence. The women have been told to vary their routes to and from work and to check anything suspicious about their cars before getting in them. They do not unwrap suspicious packages they receive at home or at the clinic. They have learned to check doorknobs and locks before they open them in the morning when they arrive at work, to survey the clinic for anything out of place when they first arrive. Was there a break-in overnight? Is someone lurking somewhere ready to pounce on the unsuspecting employee?

The stairs leading to the second-floor clinic are always locked, and the floor is sealed at the end of the day. People need keys to visit any of the vulnerable areas such as hallways and restrooms. The building guard checks the clinic and all public restrooms before he leaves work. The guard, I noticed, was armed. When I asked Isaacson-Jones if this was part of their security efforts, she declined to answer, telling me only that some building guards in St. Louis carried guns, and some did not.

Quality assurance is another concern of Isaacson-Jones, who has personally involved herself in making sure that the clinic's patients receive the best possible care. She maintains a risk-management committee modeled after the recommendations of the Joint Committee of Hospital Associations. Both abortions and counseling are monitored on an ongoing basis.

All the practices and procedures that have built up over a number of years at the clinic are geared toward providing patients with the highest quality medical service without sacrificing women's personal needs. Often she must juggle the two, as happened recently, for example, when she tracked feedback forms from 250 clients and discovered what she considered an inordinately high number of complaints—fifteen—about the three and a half hours that were required to do a first-trimester abortion. However, an abortion at Reproductive Health Services takes longer than most places because of the counseling component and an ultraconservative policy regarding the time spent in recovery.

"Our patients spend an hour in recovery, longer than most women stay in the hospital recovery room after giving birth," she says, and it is not a policy that would be lightly revised. "If there's the first sign of trouble, a woman is transferred to Barnes Medical Center, the teaching hospital for Washington University Medical School. We assume full responsibility, and our medical director is in charge of caring for the patient once she enters Barnes."

Nationally, according to the National Abortion Federation, fewer than one-half of one percent experience complications severe enough to warrant hospitalization. In the first quarter of 1989, at Reproductive Health Services, 4 out of 1,789 women were hospitalized.

Isaacson-Jones keeps careful statistics on the clinic's complication rate and compares those statistics with those kept by National Abortion Federation of its member clinics. Abortion is a safe medical procedure, one of the safest in fact. It is seven to nine times safer than childbirth for teen-agers, whose bodies are not mature enough for pregnancy; about as safe as childbirth delivery for all others.

Complications, which include infection, excessive bleeding, and perforation of the uterus, are rare, but they do occur. Of the nearly 208,000 abortions performed in 1988 in the 263 abortion clinics belonging to the National Abortion Federation, no deaths were reported; 321 women were hospitalized, including 62 for perforations, 33 for bleeding problems that were severe enough to require transfusion, and 132 for infections. Of the 8,460 abortions performed at Reproductive Health Services in 1988, 16 women were hospitalized, 1 for perforation, 13 for bleeding, and 2 for infections.

Reproductive Health Services also ensures quality by using the most up-to-date medical techniques. Since legalization, several advances, such as the vacuum aspirator, early pregnancy tests, ultrasound, and new techniques for second-trimester abortions have improved the safety of abortions.

Before the vacuum aspirator came into widespread use, physicians did a dilation and evacuation even for first-trimester pregnancies. Imported from Europe, the vacuum aspiration technique was used in the U.S. by some skilled illegal abortionists in the late 1960s. By the time of legalization, the technique was well enough developed so that many clinics began using vacuum aspiration for first-trimester abortions.

The development of early pregnancy and home pregnancy tests in the late 1970s was another advance in abortion safety. They meant that women could get abortions earlier than ever before, often as early as the fourth to sixth week of pregnancy, when the risk was most minimal. Prior to that physicians did not perform abortions before the seventh or eighth week, which left a woman hanging in a state of crisis for four, five, or even six weeks.

Ultrasound testing, initially used by physicians to monitor pregnant women, is now routinely used in abortion clinic examinations. Before ultrasound physicians had to make educated guesses about the stage of a patient's pregnancy, and a woman who was determined to undergo an abortion might intentionally miscalculate or deny when she got pregnant. With ultrasound, the guesswork is more educated, and there are fewer complications of the kind that used to occur when a physician began an abortion procedure only to discover that the patient who told him she was three months pregnant was actually four and a half months pregnant.

New techniques have also been developed for doing second-trimester abortions. Before 1977, it was widely believed that abortions could not be safely performed between the twelfth and sixteenth week of pregnancy. Second-trimester abortions performed after that time required the use of the saline procedure, an emotionally wrenching process that involved the injecting of a saline solution into a woman's uterus and waiting for her to go through several hours of labor before delivering a dead fetus. Occasionally a fetus was delivered alive. Salines took an enormous toll on patients and staff.

Today, saline abortions are obsolete, and the dilation-and-evacuation procedure is done through the twenty-second week of pregnancy. (Abortions performed after the twenty-second week are rare, comprising only one-half of one percent of all abortions, and they are usually done to preserve the woman's life or health or because the fetus is severely deformed.) At Reproductive Health Services, the only clinic in Missouri that will do a second-trimester abortion, 79.5 percent of all abortions are first trimester, while 19.6 are second trimester.

The clinic has had to struggle with the issue of whether to do second-trimester abortions. The overwhelming majority—75 percent—of physicians and clinics will not perform any abortion after sixteen weeks. The physical risks to the patient are only minimally higher than for first-trimester abortions, and the real problem with late abortions is the toll they take on clinic workers. Reproductive Health Services did not do second-trimester abortions until 1980.

Isaacson-Jones recalled, "Prior to that, people weren't ready. Doctors wouldn't do them. But then Judy Widdicombe did some traveling around the country to various clinics, and she met people who were doing them. She came back with the feeling that we should be doing them, too.

"There is a lot of ambivalence about advanced abortion. Some staff members aren't comfortable doing second-trimester abortions, and those who aren't don't have to do them."

To initiate discussion about second-trimester abortions, Widdicombe began discussing with the staff their feelings about doing them. In-service meetings about second-trimester abortions continue to this day, for while the staff agreed in theory that it would be okay to do some second-trimester abortions, their feelings were not so easily resolved. Some second-trimester abortions are still controversial.

"It's difficult for my staff to understand why some women choose second-trimester abortions," Isaacson-Jones said. "I need to remind them that sometimes we may not like the reasons that a woman has waited to get an abortion or why she chooses to have one, but that's not required of us. I've personally counseled women in cases where I don't agree with the woman's reason, but I don't judge. And we don't do every one we're asked to. The ones we do, we're comfortable with."

There is still occasional insurrection among the staff over specific second-trimester abortions. When this happens, Isaacson-Jones tries to resolve the dilemma. Recently, a problem arose when a woman flew in from Pakistan to get an abortion at Reproductive Health Services. An amniocentesis performed in Pakistan had revealed that she was carrying a female fetus; the sex of the child was the only reason she wanted an abortion. The staff was up in arms and didn't want to do the abortion.

Isaacson-Jones called a staff meeting, where, she said, "I let everyone vent their feelings. We talked about how we did not know what the woman's life would be like were she to have a female child. In male-dominated cultures, women have been beaten or even killed for lesser offenses. Gradually we became reconciled, if not absolutely comfortable, with the fact that the woman should decide for herself whether to terminate the pregnancy."

Like all abortion clinics, Reproductive Health Services has to worry about malpractice. Occasional lawsuits have been filed against the clinic. None has ever been lost. On the advice of Frank Susman and to avoid the nuisance of going to court, however, the clinic has occasionally settled outside court for amounts no larger than $2,500.

To protect itself against malpractice, the clinic follows a strict policy of what it and other clinics call informed consent. This means that any woman who expects to get an abortion at Reproductive Health Services is fully informed of the dangers and complications of abortion, first through the film and also through counseling. "It's important for women to know that risks can and do occur," said Isaacson-Jones. "All our rules are meant to be broken except for risk management, informed consent, and confidentiality."

Among the most commonly broken rules are those involving fees. Every year Isaacson-Jones struggles to set aside money for indigent women's abortions. In 1988, she was extraordinarily successful and squirreled away $400,000 that subsequently enabled the clinic to reduce the fees of 2,538 poor women.

Debate is ongoing among the staff about how much a woman should pay for an abortion. New and inexperienced staff members would often give away abortions, while the more experienced staff members think women should pay something, however little.

"Our object is to help the woman help herself," says Christine Wolf, who as head of scheduling often meets with women who need a reduced-fee abortion. "I try to determine whether this is a woman who really has no resources or who believes she has none. We do abortions for $10, $20. We've found that most women, however, can come up with $150 to $200, if not the full $260."

Isaacson-Jones used to believe in zero-fee abortions, but she no longer does. "I've charged fifty cents, but I charge something. I only did one free, and I regretted it. I listened to my staff after that. I learned from them. We had a very long conversation about the difference between nurturing and caretaking. It is really hard not to give a poor woman everything you can, but it can also be condescending. It's better to charge something, anything." It is a policy the staff is comfortable with, one that preserves a woman's dignity and helps her to feel powerful at a moment when she may feel more powerless than she ever has before.

If its involvement in the Webster case required little of Reproductive Health Services other than to lend its name as plaintiff, the same could not be said for B.J. Isaacson-Jones and the rest of the clinic staff, who were intensely involved in the case, not least because of what it came to represent to the pro-choice movement. It is simply not possible to work on the frontlines the way providers do, witnessing women's painful decisions to terminate pregnancies day in and day out, year after year, and not feel strongly about the need to preserve the abortion right.

And however unsettling the work may become on occasion, it is never without one big reward: the sense of empowerment that comes from women helping women do a task that no one finds pleasant but everyone knows must be done. To find that empowerment threatened is a demoralizing experience.

Like most providers Isaacson-Jones has always found time in addition to her work to be a pro-choice activist. In April 1989 when a half-million women gathered in Washington, D.C., for a pro-choice march, Isaacson-Jones flew to Washington, D.C., where she accepted an award on behalf of the clinic, and then to San Francisco to join in one of the smaller local rallies that were held in key cities around the country.

It was a given then that Reproductive Health Services would challenge the restrictive Missouri laws, as they had on virtually every other occasion when Missouri had attempted to limit the abortion right. When the case began, Isaacson-Jones felt positive about the chances for winning, and her feelings were confirmed with two lower court victories. With very little concerted effort, the pro-choice movement had held the line for sixteen years, and she thought they would do it one more time. She believed from the beginning that the Webster case was headed for the Supreme Court.

Her hopes began to dim, though, as she and others in the pro-choice movement slowly came to the realization that the Webster decision might well be the movement's first big loss. The composition of the Court changed, and even the mood of the country seemed to be shifting from pro-choice to pro-life as anti-abortionists successfully advanced their arguments.

A year before the Webster decision was argued in the Supreme Court, Isaacson-Jones began to prepare for the worst, making preliminary plans to dismantle Reproductive Health Services should it become necessary to do so. "Put $150,000 in an account to give your employees severance pay and pay off your bills, or you'll end up on the front page of the *Post-Dispatch*," her accountant had warned, and she had heeded his advice even though she couldn't bear the thought of closing the clinic. When the clinic's lease came up for renewal, Susman negotiated a clause that would let them out if and when that became necessary. Taking these steps has been painful for her. "We're a family," she says, with tears in her eyes. "And we may not have this much longer."

By the time of the oral arguments in April, Isaacson-Jones was steeled to expect the worst even though she was still hoping for the best. She flew to Washington to be present at the oral arguments. "I can only use the word my children use—awesome—to describe the oral arguments," she said. "Just to realize that these nine people will make the decision for the 10,000 women we see each year in just this clinic brings it all home.

"It was difficult seeing O'Connor," she said, giving voice to a feeling many women across the country had about the oral arguments. "I felt compassion for her. She was the only justice who really looked at everyone in the courtroom. I realize she's not there for women's issues, but in my heart, I wish it were different."

The oral arguments left her feeling buoyant. She felt their side had won, and that perhaps a victory would be theirs after all. But Susman and her accountant and many other people warned her not to expect a good decision.

Despite the warning, Isaacson-Jones was devastated when the ruling finally came down on Monday, July 3, 1989. After weeks of waiting, everyone knew this was the last day in the 1989 term that the Supreme Court would hand down decisions, so most people assumed the Webster decision would be announced then. By coincidence, the clinic was not doing any abortions that day, and everyone who wasn't seeing a client seemed to have gathered in her office. Some people came to the clinic even though it was their day off.

Also, it seemed, the entire local press corps and several national camera crews crowded into her office. Rows of chairs had been set up to accommodate everyone, but even then, the room was so full that people stood lining the walls. Isaacson-Jones sat at her desk and Judy Widdicombe, who had come home to hear the decision, sat to her right.

Although Isaacson-Jones would have liked to go to Washington with Susman on the day of the decision, she had ruled that out for a couple of reasons. First, she felt her staff would need her support—especially if the decision turned out to be as bad as they had come to expect it to be. And second, her presence in St. Louis was a payback to the local media for all the publicity they had given her. As the Webster plaintiff, the clinic had attracted a lot of attention, and it had made a concerted effort to cooperate with the press, even going so far as to accommodate camera crews who wanted to shoot the staff at work, with the hope that this would help to educate people about the need for legalized abortion.

An NBC reporter in her office was connected by a direct line to Washington. Around 9:20 Central Time, they heard that the decision had come down. The camera crews scurried into action. Someone snapped on a television set that had been moved into the office for the occasion. When they saw Carl Stern of NBC News on the air leafing through the decision and saying that Roe had been rolled back, they realized it was over and that the decision had gone against them.

Even though she had told the press they could be present, the deeply emotional Isaacson-Jones had fretted for days about whether she would be able to bear up when she heard the decision. She did not want to fall apart on network television, and she was afraid she might. She did well until the end, when she broke down. She buried her face in her hands. A hushed, respectful press corps and her staff burst into spontaneous applause. She collected herself and finished her statement.

Judith Widdicombe spoke next, "This is a serious, serious setback for women and families in this country. This is an outrage. There's a movement in this country that will not tolerate this. It will become our Viet Nam in the 1990s."

Widdicombe was widely quoted in newspapers and on television, but it was the image of Isaacson-Jones with her face buried in her hands that flashed around the country. In a media geared to soundbites and quick takes, Isaacson-Jones devastation said it all.

Regaining her composure, she requested some time alone with her staff. The television crews collected their equipment and filed out one by one to go prepare their stories.

Although she barely felt up to it, Isaacson-Jones had promised to speak at a local pro-choice rally. Sponsored by the Freedom of Choice Council, it was to be held in Forest Park, a large municipal park, later that day. When she got to the rally, she was amazed at the turnout: Nearly 500 people, almost all women, were there, a large gathering for St. Louis at any time but especially on Independence Day weekend. People stood in small clusters, talking to one another in angry voices. Somehow Isaacson-Jones managed to speak again, this time without breaking down, although she was near tears. She tried to say something reassuring at the same time that she sounded the alarm that the abortion right was now truly and officially endangered.

She had just finished speaking when she saw a familiar figure striding across the stage toward her. It was Frank Susman looking, if possible, even more exhausted than he had the past few months. There was nothing to say; they reached out to embrace one another. She was touched that he would come to the rally after all that he had been through. He could easily have begged off, pleading exhaustion or a plane flight that had arrived too late to attend the rally. Instead, he got off his plane from Washington and rushed there. Here he was, as usual, a steadying presence trying to reassure the crowd that things weren't as bad as they seemed, even though, in his heart, he felt—they all felt—that this was the beginning of the end for the abortion right.

Later that night when she got home, Isaacson-Jones was too exhausted to sleep. Her anger finally spilled out of her. Anger that she had been plugging along in this fight for so long alone. Anger at the thousands of women who came through her clinic every year, the millions who went through clinics like hers, women who should all be standing up for the abortion right— and who, it seemed to her, weren't.

Isaacson-Jones was furious at every celebrity she had ever sheltered—and there had been many over the years—women to whom she had offered the privacy of her office so no one would know they were in the clinic, celebrities who, had they only chosen to speak out, could have influenced millions of people to protect the abortion right. She was angry at the prominent pro-life women, the wives and daughters of pro-life politicians who showed up at her clinic and clinics like hers when they or their daughters needed an abortion. Those women also got VIP treatment from Reproductive Health Services: the privacy of Isaacson-Jones's gaily flowered sofa was offered to them for their recuperation. And for what? she thought. So they could go out after their own abortions and continue to protest other women's choices.

In 1988, Isaacson-Jones had poured out her feelings in a poem she called "An Open Letter to 21 Million women."

Where are you?
For over 16 years we have provided
you with choices
Painful choices
I remember—
I sometimes cried with you.
Choices, nevertheless, when you were desperate.

Remember how we protected your privacy
and treated you with dignity and respect
when you
   were famous
   had been brought to us in shackles
   with an armed guard, or
   were terrified that you would run into
   one of your students?
   I remember each of you.

Our clinic was firebombed.
Do you recall?
Exhausted and terrified we had
been up all night.
We rerouted you to another clinic
because you wanted an abortion that day.
Where are you?

Priding ourselves on providing abortions for
those who cannot pay, we have spent millions
of dollars that we never really
had caring for you. We wanted
to give a choice.
I also gave you cab fare and
money for dinner from my own pocket.
Have you forgotten?

I remember you cried and asked me how
you could carry this pregnancy to term when
you
 were abusing the children you had,
 were having an affair,
 tested positive for AIDS
 could not handle another,
 were raped by your mother's boyfriend,
 pregnant by your father and
 shocked and torn apart when
 your very much wanted and loved
 fetus was found to be
 severely deformed.

Your mother picketed our clinic
regularly. We brought you in after dark.
Have you mustered the courage
to tell her that you are pro-choice?
You are.
Aren't you?

I recall shielding your shaking body, guiding you
and your husband through the picket lines.
They screamed adoption, not abortion!
You wondered how you could explain your
choice to your young children.

You broke our hearts.
You had just celebrated your twelfth birthday
when you came to us. You clutched
your teddy bear, sucked you thumb
and cried out for your mom who asked
you why you had gotten yourself pregnant.
You replied that you just wanted to be grown.
You're twenty today.
Where are you?

I pretend I don't know you in the market,
at social gatherings and on the street.
I told you I would.

After your procedure you told me that you would
fight for reproductive choices (parenthood,
adoption, and abortion) for you mother, daughters, and grandchildren. You will...won't you?

I have no regrets. I care about
each and every one of you and
treasure all that you've taught me.
But I'm angry. I can't do this alone.
I'm not asking you to speak about your abortion, but
You need to speak out and you need to speak
out now. Where are you?

The letter touched the hearts of pro-choice women everywhere and, especially after the Webster decision, it was picked
up and reprinted in countless pro-choice newsletters and other
movement publications. Isaacson Jones received hundreds of
letters from all over the world in response to it.

Over the next few weeks, as she gradually absorbed her loss,
the outgoing Isaacson-Jones became increasingly introspective.
She spent more time alone with her family and with her staff,
her "second family" that she feared might not exist much
longer. She began to think about what she would do if abortion
became illegal.

She says, "We'd flip back to being a volunteer referral service.
We'd still help women get abortions. We'd still be here for
them."

Thus far, her plans to go underground have proven to be
premature. Although most pollsters expected Americans to join
the pro-life bandwagon after the Webster decision, the reverse
happened, and Webster seemed instead to have awakened that
huge sleeping giant, the pro-choice movement. The Webster
decision, in the words of Colorado Representative Pat
Schroeder, sounded "a wakeup call" to the women of America.

Most polls showed that by a two to one margin, Americans
wanted legal abortion. Fifty-three percent disagreed with the
Supreme Court ruling. People were divided over specific issues
such as parental consent (75 percent supported it), federal

funding (61 percent supported the ban on public funds while a seemingly contradictory 57 percent opposed banning public employees from performing abortions), and even whether abortion was murder (in one state poll, 48 percent of those asked thought it was murder even though 67 percent didn't want to see the government interfere with a woman's decision). The bottom line was that poll after poll showed that Americans viewed abortion as a personal decision, one in which the government should have no say.

While the country's attention was riveted on the big picture—preserving the overall abortion right—providers watched several developments that had implications for the future of abortion services. Although most newspapers carried only a brief story on the subject, clinic workers watched intensely to see what would happen in a Pennsylvania case before the Supreme Court in early fall of 1989. They considered it a major victory when the Supreme Court let stand a lower court ruling that permitted the use of a controversial racketeering, or RICO, law against anti-abortionists. The law was a new tool in the clinics' arsenal against the anti-abortionists.

Another case scheduled for argument in the Supreme Court in November 1989 posed far more of a threat to the existence of the clinics than Webster. *Turnock v. Ragsdale* involved a set of regulations passed by the Illinois legislature that basically required clinics to become minihospitals. If enforced, the laws could potentially put 90 percent of the nation's clinics out of business and drive up the cost of abortion prohibitively.

Illinois Attorney General Neil Hartigan, a lukewarm pro-life supporter who nevertheless planned to argue the case himself, had appealed the case to the Supreme Court. In the meantime, Webster was handed down, and Hartigan, who hoped to make a run for governor, found himself on the wrong side of a hot issue. After the Webster decision, everywhere he spoke, he was taunted by angry pro-choice demonstrators. Hartigan was soon eager to ally himself with pro-choice forces, but found this difficult to do while he still had to go into the Supreme Court and argue a case that could potentially do more to destroy the abortion right than Webster. His solution was clever: Hartigan negotiated a rare but not impossible out-of-court settlement before the case was scheduled for Supreme Court argument.

Like providers all over the country, Isaacson-Jones breathed a deep sigh of relief when Ragsdale was settled. The clinics were safe, at least until the next challenge came along.

Like many providers, Isaacson-Jones has vowed to still help women get abortions if they became illegal. The clinics have not, in fact, been standing idly by since the Webster decision. The Federation of Feminist Women's Health Centers has renewed its promotion of menstrual extraction. Popular in the late sixties before abortion became legal, this method of self-abortion, which is practiced by women in self-help groups, is safer than most illegal abortions but not so safe as a clinic abortion. Within two months of the Webster decision, the Federation was distributing a videotape called "No Going Back" that taught women how to practice menstrual extraction.

There was talk of reviving Jane, an underground Chicago network that provided women with illegal abortions from 1969 to 1973. One hundred-fifty Chicago women were trained, mostly by sympathetic physicians, to perform abortions. They ran their clinics, which provided low-cost abortions, out of several Chicago "safe" apartments. Jane was the name women used to contact one another. If abortion became illegal, Jane would undoubtedly revive and become nationwide. Because it would draw on expertise of the thousands of qualified clinic workers, it would be easy to set up.

For the time being, Isaacson-Jones is optimistic that abortion will remain legal. She has been buoyed in recent months by the spirit and intensity of the pro-choice movement. And while she says the current resurgence of interest in protecting the abortion right doesn't surprise her, it also doesn't totally alleviate all her fears. A niggling one is that most women, having never set foot inside an abortion clinic, fail to appreciate what it could mean not to control their own reproduction. She worries that the pro-choice movement will do too little too late. "Sometimes I fear that we may have to lose the right to have it."

4 | Prophet

Randall Terry and Operation Rescue

Aғтеr lisтening to the justices read the Webster opinions (one majority, one dissenting), Randall Terry, a lean, serious-looking young man of thirty, knew he had a victory on his hands. He bounded out of the courtroom and down the steps of the Supreme Court building into the waiting arms of the press. Although he had not been invited to stand by for a live news broadcast by any of the major networks, Terry worked the press with an air of confidence, moving from reporter to reporter to give his soundbite, and leaving Joe Foreman, one of his top aides, behind to offer any follow-up details the reporters might want. Mostly, they didn't want any. They wanted to hear from Randall Terry, who, as the head of Operation Rescue, was the newest ascendent star in the anti-abortion movement.

Operation Rescue had first captured the nation's attention a year earlier by staging protests, which Terry called "rescues," at abortion clinics up and down the East Coast. The group was news because it was more militant than most other pro-life groups. Theologian James Burtchaell of Notre Dame, who had been involved in and a student of anti-abortion groups for several years, promptly dubbed Operation Rescue the intifida of the pro-life movement.

Terry became known not only for the militancy of his views but also for the military precision with which he organized his rescues. He burst into the national spotlight in the summer of 1988 when, in a move much ballyhooed in the media, he went to Atlanta with hundreds of his followers, threatening to disrupt the Democratic Convention.

His threat proved to be greatly exaggerated, not least because the advance publicity had given the Atlanta police ample time to prepare for him. Surrounded by uniformed officers and kept in a roped-off section several yards from the convention center, he failed in his attempt to upset the convention. Even worse from his point of view, he received little national media attention for what happened after the Democratic Convention, four months of ongoing sit-ins at local abortion clinics that Terry liked to refer to as the "second siege of Atlanta."

His bid for media attention, necessary if he were to build a nation-wide organization of thousands of born-again Christians, was rougher going than he had anticipated it would be, and he had experienced many ups and downs in his attempts to deal with the press. But now with a Supreme Court victory in hand, Terry was once again a force to be contended with, and more confident than ever that he could dismantle the abortion right.

"We'll go into state legislatures with equal force to overturn Roe and make child-killing illegal," Terry told reporters as he made the rounds of the news crews. "Blackmun says that Roe is gutted," he said over and over again to anyone who would listen. "The energy is with the pro-life movement. We'll continue to blockade killing centers. This decision will give us the political clout to become a serious political force."

Predicting that he would now have the complete backing of the independent, fundamentalist churches, which had hitherto held back from whole-hearted support of his upstart group, he believed his victory in Webster—and it was his victory, as far as he was concerned—would reinvigorate his movement, giving it new respectability. It would give him entree on a far larger scale than he had previously had to the hundreds of thousands of Americans who called themselves born-again Christians. With the weight of the Webster decision behind him, he expected to have much clout.

Even those reporters who weren't sure who Terry was wrote down every word he said. Terry was patient and self-assured, so self-assured that when reporters leaned in to ask him confidentially what his name was again, he leaned right back into their faces and said emphatically: "Randall Terry. Randall A. Terry." Randall Terry was a man who believed in destiny, particularly his own.

I first met Terry a few weeks after the Webster decision at Operation Rescue's national headquarters in Binghamton, New York. The interview had been scheduled, after much discussion and one week-long postponement while Terry went to jail in Atlanta, six weeks earlier. I was curious, as were most people, about what he was like. Did he hate women, as feminists insisted? Was he truly religious or simply using religion to manipulate his followers? A few months earlier, before a series of scandals culminating with the Jim and Tammy Bakker debacle left the world of televangelists in disarray, that question would not have been asked, but now even his sincerity was up for debate and widely impugned in some circles. I thought all the questions boiled down to one or two issues: Was Terry a real prophet, as he claimed to be, or yet another false prophet come to lead the nation's fundamentalists down the path to nowhere? And false prophet or not, how much political clout was he gathering? He had on several occasions suggested to reporters that he would like to run for public office.

After driving three hours in a steady downpour, I arrived in Binghamton, New York, around noon and headed straight for Operation Rescue headquarters, located in a shabby storefront on Chenango Street, in a rundown neighborhood on the edge of town. No sign announces that this is the national headquarters of Operation Rescue, but a larger-than-life-sized photograph of a bloody fetus in a window was a clue.

The headquarters were a modest five rooms furnished with secondhand metal office furniture that were in the process of being subdivided into smaller cubicles. Sitting in a worn arm-chair was a lanky, white-haired man whom I later learned was Michael Terry, Randall Terry's father. There was no reception-ist, nor did he show any inclination to help me, so I roamed back through the other offices.

A hallway was dominated by a brown folding table on which rested a postal meter and tall stacks of envelopes. A mailing was going out to Vestal, a small town near Binghamton, urging people to join Operation Rescue. I found a meeting area for the staff around the corner and past a cardboard box of bull-horns. I would soon learn that the dozen or so people who worked here (some paid, some volunteer) started their days by gathering in this room for a prayer service and ended them by watching the large black Sony TV to see what media attention Terry had managed to garner during the day.

That morning, for example, Terry had held a press con-ference outside the office of Dr. Salomon N. Epstein, who until recently had been affiliated with the Southern Tier Women's Services. Out of ten thousand abortions he had performed for the clinic, two women had filed malpractice suits against him in 1988. Terry had dug up the complaints and called the press conference to denounce Epstein. He implied that the physician no longer did abortions at the clinic because of his record, but the clinic defended his record, and said Dr. Epstein had left them to devote more time to his private practice. Terry implied that the two women who had filed the malpractice suits had come to him to ask for his support, but neither was present at the press conference, and by the time his staff gathered around to watch their leader on the local evening news that night, one woman had surfaced to say that she was "upset and distraught" over the press conference.

Near the reception area, standing in his shirt sleeves, Terry never took his eyes off me as he asked his press secretary Barbara Magera who I was.

"She's the woman who's going to put you in a book," she answered.

"Oh, no, I'm not talking to her," he said. Magera, a lean, studious-looking young woman, emerged from her office to explain my presence to him again. In a series of paradoxical moves that would define our day together, Terry continued to protest that he would not talk to me even as he slipped into his office to put on his suit jacket and walked down the hall to shake hands with me. His greeting was congenial.

"Really, I won't talk to you. I didn't know about this. I've been stung too many times. But you can talk to her, he said, pointing to Magera. "She'll answer your questions."

Over the next fifteen minutes, Terry roamed in and out of the reception area while I stood around hoping that what seemed to be happening wasn't. I anxiously took Magera aside to ask her what the problem was. She quietly assured me that Terry knew about the interview and would talk to me.

Still protesting, Terry invited me into his office, the only private room in the headquarters. It took us a while to get there, though. Like any good politician, he was adept at creating a flurry of activity around himself and now he took his time, standing in the hallway outside his office talking and joking with everyone about my presence.

As we headed into his office, Terry's secretary, Linda Sclafani, cornered him to say she was having trouble making travel arrangements for Bernard and Adele Nathanson, two heavyweights in the pro-life movement who were coming to Binghamton to lead a seminar for the Operation Rescue staff. (He was a physician who had run one of the largest abortion clinics in the state before becoming a pro-life activist.) The Nathansons insisted on being booked into the first-class hotel, even though Sclafani had explained that Operation Rescue, which was paying their expenses, might not be able to afford that. "So book 'em" was Terry's answer.

Finally, we settled into his office, he behind a large desk and I in a small visitor's chair opposite him. It was no more luxuriously furnished than the rest of the offices.

What did I want, Terry asked? I explained that I was writing a book about abortion activists and felt he would make a good portrait. I wanted to talk with him and accompany him for several days as he worked. In an effort to allay his reservations, I explained that his would be one of several portraits in the book, so my research would be fairly unobtrusive, certainly less than if I were writing a full-blown biography.

At the mention of a biography, his pale face lit up, and he

slammed his fist against the wall next to his desk, a gesture of enthusiasm with which I would soon become familiar. In this case, the enthusiasm was for himself, as he told me: "And there will be biographies written about me. I've no doubt about that."

But then he returned to his previous litany: "Really, I can't give you an interview. I don't need your publicity. I don't need anyone to write anything more about me. If no one ever writes another word about me, I've had all the publicity I need to assure my place in history. Time, Newsweek, they've all been here. I've been in People. Did you see the story about me in People?" Like the thud of his fist against a wall, I would hear his protest several times more throughout the day.

A commotion in the reception area drew his attention, and Terry bounded out of his office, calling over his shoulder to come and meet his family. "My children mean everything to me."

His wife Cindy and three of their four children had unexpectedly stopped by to visit. It wasn't something they did often, a staff member told me later. They were waiting in the reception room, drenched from the rain. Poppy, Terry's 13-year-old black foster son, ran up to him and threw his arms around him. Terry asked his son if he had done his homework, and patted him absent-mindedly when the boy said he had. He brushed past Poppy to walk over to his wife. As they talked, Terry nervously buttoned and unbuttoned his suit jacket.

Their conversation seemed to be about a house they were buying. I would later learn that their house in Windsor, a suburb of Binghamton, was for sale.

"He said it would look bad, but I said I knew it but we might have to do it anyway," Cindy reported.

"So that's the worst of it," Terry said. "We'll lose our—"

"Earnest money," Cindy interjected.

"And that's, what, $500," Terry replied with the air of a man who did not mind letting people know that he could afford to lose this sum of money.

Later Barbara Magera expressed her surprise that the Terrys were buying a new house. It was the first she had heard anything about it. Terry and his wife already owned their house, a "very modest" house, she hastened to assure me.

Terry introduced me to his family only when I asked, and I

was not given an opportunity to talk with Cindy. She and the children roamed around the office for a few minutes, saying hello to various people, while Terry and I returned to his office.

Terry, who is known to take control of interviews, settled down to the serious business of peppering me with questions. What did I want to know about him? Who was my publisher? Did I have a contract to write this book? Did the publisher insist that he be in it? He was pleased when I told him that the publisher was indeed interested in his being one of the portraits in the book.

Just as quickly he changed the subject. Did I know that he spent last week in Houston working on a record album? I said I knew only that he spent at least part of last week in jail in Atlanta. He had gone to Atlanta to address the Christian Booksellers Convention about his new book, titled *Accessory to Murder: An Expose of the Death Movement, Its Profits, and the Failing Church*. The book originally was called *Conspiracy to Murder*, but his publishers, Wolgemuth & Hyatt, worried about libel, had changed the title. While he was addressing the booksellers, he noticed two sheriff's police standing in the back of the room. He wasn't too surprised, he told me, when they arrested him after he finished speaking.

Charged with having missed a court date, Terry claimed he hadn't known about it. He refused to post bond, so he went to jail for a few days, an event that made *The New York Times*. When he was released on his own recognizance, that item did not make *The New York Times*, and many of his followers erroneously believed he was languishing in jail when he wasn't.

But returning to the subject at hand, I told him that I had not known that he had also traveled to Houston to lay down the vocals for a new album of Christian music. I knew he was musical—a singer and songwriter who played saxophone and piano. And I knew, too, that he had cut an earlier album of his anti-abortion songs called "When the Battle Raged." Two of the songs were "I'm Crying for You, Baby" and "If You Believe Abortion Is Murder, Act Like It's Murder."

Terry slammed his fist against the wall again and called out to Linda Sclafani, his secretary: "Has the package arrived yet?"

"What package?"

"They were supposed to Fed Ex the final cut so it would be here today. Have you checked? Are you sure it isn't here?"

She's sure no package has arrived via Federal Express. She isn't sure what was supposed to arrive by Federal Express. Later that day, she will tell me, by way of apology, that Randy, as everyone calls Terry, "has a million things on his mind." His staff reassures themselves several times a day that he doesn't remember what he did yesterday, nor does he know what he will be doing tomorrow, he is *that* busy.

When Terry couldn't play his record for me, he decided to organize lunch. At first, I wasn't sure that I would be included but I soon saw that I, along with Mark Lucas, his punk-haired office manager, and Michael Terry, his father, would be going to lunch together. Although Cindy was standing with us as the plans were made, she was excluded without a word of discussion or explanation.

In the midst of lining up our lunch partners, Terry whirled around to inquire if my publisher paid my expenses. He had asked me this a few minutes earlier in the privacy of his office, and I answered now as I did then, telling him that while I paid my own expenses, I would be happy to take him to lunch. With a magnanimous air, he declared that he couldn't let me pay. Later, over Chinese food he would confide that he wouldn't let me or any other reporter buy him a meal because he will never let himself be indebted to a member of the press.

We drove the three blocks to a Chinese restaurant that was obviously a favorite noontime hangout for Terry and his staff. Terry led the way, greeting the hostess expansively and engaging her in a conversation about the kind of table—round and in the center of the room or rectangular and against a wall—we would need so I could conduct my interview. "We can talk better back there," he announced, settling on the table against the wall.

As soon as we were seated, he said somewhat ominously that he wanted to propose something. I was surprised when the proposal was nothing more riveting than the suggestion that we go Dutch. I wondered if he were so obsessed not to be in my debt that he needed to be triply sure I would not grab the bill, or whether this was his way of showing leadership—or more cynically, if these men usually billed their lunches to Operation Rescue and were now being given a signal that the tab would be divided individually for this one.

Operation Rescue had been under fire in recent weeks for its financial dealings. Despite my (and perhaps everyone's) thoughts about money, the conversation turned instead to the subject of female journalists, who were, as it turned out, a thorn in Terry's side. Despite his claim that he had been attacked by them many times, he still managed to affect a philosophical what-can-a-guy-do-about-it pose. Terry assured me that he understood why the women in the media were so biased and unfair in their treatment of him: "They're trained in liberal journalism schools. They come out hardened. They believe everything they've been taught."

Did female journalists really give him a harder time than male journalists, I asked?

"Oh, yes, they're tougher. They're feminists. They belong to NOW. They don't get married or can't find anyone to marry them," he chortled, wondering aloud who would want to marry a woman with such strident views. By the men's camaraderie and laughter, I could tell that this was an old, familiar luncheon topic. Unable to leave the subject alone, they lapsed into jokes about how ugly the pro-choice and NOW women were.

Terry said he didn't mind if I was not pro-life. (I declined to tell him my views, only that I was interviewing activists on both sides of the debate.) What he cared about was not getting a fair shake from interviewers. He let a local interviewer who was pro-choice talk to him, and considered the articles he wrote to be fair. The articles, by the Binghamton *Press & Sun-Bulletin* reporter Jeff Davis, were good journalism, but they were written in a question-and-answer format that gave Terry ample room to expound his views and Davis little room to editorialize.

Terry's father said he resented the way reporters rode his son's coattails to fame. Understandably, he felt protective toward his son.

I knew that things have not always been this chummy between them. In fact I had been surprised to learn that the man lounging in Operation Rescue's reception area was Randall Terry's father. Now I learned that his mother Doreen Terry was away at a conference, although Terry and his father were close-mouthed about her whereabouts and would not tell me what kind of conference or where she was.

Terry's parents have given few interviews about their son, but I have read enough to know that they are not in agreement over his actions. His mother, who harks from a family of feminist women, was reportedly unhappy with Terry's views on abortion, while after years of strife, his sudden rise to fame had drawn him and his father closer together.

Interrupting his father in mid-sentence, Terry changed the subject. He preferred to talk about feminists and other bad women. Did I know, Terry asked me, that Molly Yard completely supported birth control in China?

"Molly Yard thinks the Chinese birth control program is just wonderful. The one where you can only have one child and can lose your job if you have another one. You can be forced to have an abortion. She thinks that's just great. We did the Oprah Winfrey show together, and I heard her say it. Oprah's the best. She has me on a lot. Phil Donahue has never had me on. I don't know why."

When I suggested that Donahue liked to control his guests to some extent while Oprah was more free rein, he beamed, "That's it. He knows he couldn't control me."

Considerable time was given over to ordering the food. Terry asked me several times if I was sure I could eat the hot, highly seasoned food we were about to consume and ignored his father's repeated suggestion that he would like the lobster and pea pods. Michael Terry shrugged and told me, an unmistakable note of pride in his voice: "You see what happens: The son fathers the father. We've reversed our relationship."

Terry asked me again what I wanted to know about him. I replied that I understood he did not grow up as a born-again-Christian, but was saved at the age of 17. I'd like to know if this caused any problems with this parents, who weren't born-again. I'd like to talk about his childhood, including his reportedly rebellious adolescence. And I'd like to discuss any problems he may be having rearing his own children as fundamentalists. Don't they chafe at the rules fundamentalism imposes, having not undergone the transforming experience of being reborn?

Terry's eyes glazed over. He didn't want to talk about this. Perhaps it was too heavy a subject for a Chinese lunch.

Michael Terry's face took on a wounded look and now he interrupted me to say, "I just want to say that I walk with the Lord."

I explained that I wasn't implying that he wasn't religious, only that Terry was not brought up a fundamentalist Christian.

"I walk with the Lord," Michael Terry repeated. "I've walked with the Lord now for about a year and a half."

When I looked puzzled, Terry explained his father's statement, saying, "My father was born again about a year and a half ago."

"Oh, then you were at the Atlanta rescue." Michael Terry was visibly uncomfortable to have to admit that he wasn't. When I asked him what other rescues he had attended, he sheepishly admitted that he had never participated in a rescue.

"I'll tell you why I can't do it. I would have to miss work, and my department head is—you'll pardon the expression—a bitch." I didn't mind the language but I expected Terry and Lucas, both religious men, to be offended. They weren't.

When I told his father I was surprised to hear such—I struggled for the right word and got it wrong—blasphemous language, Randy burst out laughing and said to his father, "I thought she was going to call you a bastard." The men enjoyed the joke.

Would he, I asked Terry, tell me about the rescues? Gladly. He launched into a description of how he feels when he is arrested during a rescue. According to his resume, he has been arrested more than 33 times. He feigns not to know how many times he has gone to jail. But spending time in jail is, he repeated several times, "exhilarating, a real high." For emphasis he hit his fist against the wall.

Terry hastened to assure me, as he does his followers, that he is also afraid to go to jail. Despite the official disclaimer, he cannot, however, totally hide his enthusiasm for the experience.

Lucas, who had been quiet up to now, told me that some great preaching goes on in jail. Many of the rescuers are ministers or "others gifted with an ability to preach," and impromptu preaching and occasional conversions of prison guards or prisoners are heartwarming highlights of their periods of incarceration.

Later, when Lucas and I talked alone, he talked more about their experiences in jail. "I never understood why war buddies were so tight. My Dad always had his war buddies, and they were his real friends. Now I understand. It's a bond that can't be broken. Usually we're together in a fighting environment," he continued. "We're either out on the street together or in jail together." Now I understand: When these men go to jail, they do not see themselves as commonplace criminals. They are something far nobler: prisoners of war.

As we ate, the men continued to talk nostalgically of battles they had fought together and "retreats" (their word for jail) that were especially inspirational to them. Suddenly, though, Terry's expression changed from fierce to sad, and he began to lament the fact that outsiders only saw the arrests, whereas insiders saw the whole spiritual process. His smooth voice wrapped itself around the words of the sermon he was giving me: "Let's examine this. No, we don't 'want' to get arrested. We only do it to save a child's life.

"I thought abortion was wrong, but what could I do about it? But then I began to see that I could make a difference, that my actions mattered. Abortion was a challenge of my faith."

His voice grew soft. "I'm tired. The first arrest was exhilarating. I loved being in jail. I did some great preaching there, if I say so myself. But now I'm tired."

"Who will you talk to on their side?" Terry asked. Before I could answer, he said, "It doesn't matter who you talk to. They don't have anyone good."

"I'm planning to interview Frank Susman, who argued the pro-choice cause in the Webster case."

"He's not an activist. He doesn't do anything." Nor apparently does Faye Wattleton, director of Planned Parenthood, with whom Terry has shared the air waves several times. Terry recalled how he "laughed out loud" at her one night as she was discussing Planned Parenthood's various activities on "Nightline." "She didn't like that," he added, still obviously quite pleased with himself.

Michael Terry asked me several times what I would want to

talk to him about. Each time, before I could answer, Terry told his father that he would not have to talk to me. Michael Terry was clearly disappointed to hear this.

I told Terry another subject I wanted to discuss with him was destiny.

"Destiny, what about it?"

"Well, I'd like to know if you had any sense that you would be the leader of a movement like this when you were younger? Do you feel that you're destined to do what you do?"

Terry has frequently told reporters that he believes it is his destiny to do what he is doing. With his newfound celebrity, he also has come to the conclusion that it will be his destiny to run for public office at some point. He has made it clear that his agenda is much larger than abortion.

"I do not intend to stop after child killing is made illegal. We plan to restore moral sanity to this country and bring everyone back to the Judeo-Christian ethic. That is going to involve the entertainment world, medicine, the colleges, politics, the judicial system, the prison system, the whole nine yards."

He would indeed be interested in discussing his destiny with me, he said, adding, "I've thought a lot about that."

As the lunch drew to a close, Terry asked his father and Lucas what they thought about granting me an interview. "What do you think? Should we let her talk to me?" he asked, as if I weren't there. Neither man was willing to go out on a limb to answer that question, and Terry seemed pleased at their reluctance to do so.

Back at Operation Rescue headquarters, we settled into his office for a few more minutes of conversation. On his desk were several books, neatly stacked with their titles out facing the guest chair. They were mostly books on born-again Christianity, such as George Grant's *Grand Illusions*, a polemic against Planned Parenthood. Most intriguing was a book called *The Art of War*, written by Chinese scholar-soldier Sun Tzu sometime between 600 and 400 B.C. "I'm reading him to learn how to make war. He was at war, and I'm at war," Terry said.

I asked Terry who his enemies were. He answered, "My enemies are Planned Parenthood, NOW, the ACLU, the pro-aborts, all the people who are killing babies."

Randall Terry may be at war, but not, one suspects, with the groups he named. His enemies aren't Planned Parenthood, the National Organization for Women, or even the killing mills (as he calls abortion clinics), but, rather, women. Women who refuse to stay home and leave all the jobs for men. Women who use birth control to regulate their child-bearing. Women journalists, who ask too many pointed questions. Women who, in short, refuse to acquiesce to the male authority that is at the heart of fundamentalism.

Asked what other books had influenced him, Terry named *The Gold Court* by Amy Carmichael. She was, he told me, a missionary who lived in India, and devoted herself to rescuing "babies from child prostitution in Hindu temples. Her work was very similar to ours," he pronounced.

"And although it makes the liberals angry," Terry added, "because they don't want me to admire King, Coretta King's biography really launched me. I read that book when I was in jail in Atlanta. I was walking vicariously through their experience."

Terry likes to draw a parallel between the anti-abortion movement and the civil rights movement—and implicitly, between himself and Dr. Martin Luther King, Jr. The comparison infuriates liberals and African-Americans, who counter Terry's statement by pointing out that the civil rights movement expanded civil rights to blacks and other minorities, while Terry and Operation Rescue are seeking to deny women their civil rights. Jews are similarly offended with Terry's frequent comparison between the millions of "unborn babies" killed by abortion and the millions of Jews killed during the Holocaust.

Standing to offer me his hand, Terry told me again that he probably would not let me interview him since he didn't need the publicity. And, he added, he recently took one woman reporter to his house for dinner, and she wrote awful things about him, untrue things that no one who knew him would ever believe. Even if he does decide to give me an interview, he warns me, he will never let me visit his home or talk to his wife.

But he assures me I'm free to interview any of his staff, to hang around for a few days if I would like to. He won't be around since he's working at home these days, finishing his book. The book is going to blow the lid off the pro-choice movement, he tells me. "Have you had to do a lot of research to write it?" I asked. "Yeah," he replied, "I've got my staff doing that."

As for his decision to grant me another interview, Terry tells me he'll pray on it—and also consult with his top aides. This studied mention of consultation with his aides is, I'm fairly sure, a reaction to recent accusations that he is something of a loose cannon even among the loosely structured fundamentalist churches.

For a man who claims he doesn't read what is written about him, Terry strikes me as existing in a perpetual state of reaction to the most recent criticism he has received. When someone wrote that he looked stiff in suits, he insisted on changing into a sweater the next time a newspaper photographer came round to take pictures of him.

After lunch as we stood waiting for his father and Lucas to get the car, Terry cracked several jokes and asked me if I didn't think he had a good sense of humor. "*Time* magazine said I don't have any sense of humor," he explained none too subtly.

Now to emphasize the idea that he listens to his advisors, he called out to Linda Sclafani, who sits outside his office and whose primary job seems to be the maintenance of an elaborate set of notebooks that track her employer's busy schedule. "Set up a conference call," he told her.

The surprise obvious in her voice, she asked: "Conference call to who?"

"You know, the loop."

"The loop?"

"The inner loop—" and he rattled off the names of four or five men manning key posts at Operation Rescue field offices around the country.

"And I'll pray on it," he assured me again, standing up to shake my hand.

A few minutes later, as I stood outside his office talking to a staff member, Terry motioned me aside and told me if I really wanted to see him in action, I should come to Los Angeles the first week of August. He was going to stand trial there, and planned to defend himself. Operation Rescue of Southern

California was planning a week of activities around his visit. Not bad, I thought, for someone who wasn't planning to give me an interview.

All families have their mythologies about their famous members, and Terry's is no exception. Terry grew up in the Seventies, too late to join the Weathermen or protest the war that changed America's thinking about itself in the Sixties, too early for the material excesses of the Eighties that might have spurred him into nothing more radical than a job on Wall Street. Randall Terry, who once told a reporter that he was "born out of time," sees himself as a Sixties radical. When he looked around for role models, though, staring back at him from his television set were the televangelists. Along with businessmen like Lee Iacocca, they were the stars of the Seventies, what a young man could aspire to. Given a choice between becoming Lee Iacocca or Pat Robertson, the latter undoubtedly seemed more achievable and closer to his roots.

Terry was born to two middle-class, mainstream Protestant schoolteachers in 1959. He grew up in Henrietta, a bleak, blue-collar suburb of Rochester, a mid-sized city in upstate New York that burned brightly for one brief meteoric moment over a century ago, when it was simultaneously a hotbed of evangelistic activity and the birthplace of the women's movement at nearby Seneca Falls.

Terry's views on abortion were undoubtedly shaped by his mother's family's own experience with it. His mother's three sisters all got pregnant as teen-agers and had abortions before they were legal. Terry's own mother Doreen married his father when she found herself pregnant with him. Terry swears that being conceived out of wedlock has nothing to do with his own militant anti-abortion views, and perhaps he's right. But his aunts' social activism must have had some influence on him, if only to convince him that women had too much power in this world. His three aunts have always worked on behalf of women's issues but have focused most of their energies on reproductive rights. One was a public relations director of Planned Parenthood; another campaigned to legalize abortion in New York

State during the late 1960s; and a third lent her face to a Rochester poster campaign for birth control education.

From his father's family, Terry inherited his musical ability and, most likely, his yearning for stardom. Michael Terry is a failed musician. He won a scholarship for vocal studies to the Eastman School of Music in Rochester, but lasted only a month before dropping out. Terry played the piano and saxophone in high school, and wrote two musicals in college. One retold the story of King David and the other, called *Turn Again*, told the story of the prodigal son.

As a real-life prodigal son, Terry took less time than the Biblical prodigal son to reconcile with his own father. By all accounts, their relationship was rocky during Terry's teen years, and after a fight that reportedly involved physical violence, Terry ran away from home in 1976, four months shy of high school graduation. He had always been a good student, but he also had dreams of being a rock star, so he headed to California to see if he could fulfill his fantasy.

No one in Terry's family agrees about what happened to him during his four months on the road, but everyone agrees that something happened. By all reports, he made it as far as Galveston, Texas, where he worked in a bar during the day and slept on a beach at night. There were rumors of drug use—a small marijuana habit and the use of hallucinogens—but this is not something Terry will talk about today.

His father believes he was held up at gunpoint while sleeping on the beach. His mother says he was robbed in an alley. His Aunt Diane says he was robbed and beaten and left for dead. His Aunt Dawn recalls only that he came home claiming to be Jesus Christ, closed himself in his room for two days, and then came out saying that he had made a mistake. He wasn't Christ; he was the messenger of Christ.

Even his conversion to born-again Christianity is surrounded by mystery. His parents believe he was converted by people he met in Galveston after whatever tragedy happened there, and Terry has confirmed this for several reporters. But then he told another reporter that he was born again several months after he came home. The occasion of that conversion was a nighttime ride around Rochester with a lay minister whom he met while working at the Three Sisters Ice Cream stand in Henrietta. He rode with the minister in his van and listened carefully as the man talked to him about his personal relationship with God.

The high point of the evening for Terry came when the minister let him preach to a woman they picked up on a local road. The taste of preaching imbued Terry with a sense of power he has never been able to shake off, although several years elapsed before he found the subject that became his calling.

According to Terry's official resume, he promptly earned a high school equivalency certificate, and on the recommendation of his pastor, in 1978 was admitted to Elim Bible Institute, a 275-student "transdenominational" school located in Lima, twenty-five miles south of Rochester. In reality, he spent another year in Rochester working at odd jobs and perhaps contemplating his bleak future and how he might best go about shaping it into something grander.

While at Elim, Terry was exposed to the ideas of Francis Schaeffer, a contemporary evangelical writer who was enjoying his heyday. Schaeffer was a disillusioned Presbyterian who turned to fundamentalism, taking up its theme that the modern world was an immoral place and that most people existed in a state of crisis from which they need to saved. Fundamentalists read their Bibles literally and believe in an unchanging moral truth. Mix in the fact that they also believe theirs is the only true religion, and you have the recipe for a great deal of inflexible thinking and a big fall when the rest of the world fails to rush to join the cause.

The fundamentalists formed a splinter group that emerged from the evangelical mainstream tradition in the early part of the twentieth century. They spearheaded two of the more important reform movements in American history: abolition and prohibition. In the 1920s, their despair over the plight of the modern world reached crisis proportions, and they broke with their own tradition of remaining apolitical to make one brief foray into American politics, creating a sensation when they took on the brand-new science of evolution.

The climax to their anti-evolution, anti-modern diatribe was the Scopes "monkey" trial in Dayton, Tennessee. On one side was the fundamentalist, ruralist orator William Jennings Bryan; on the other, the city-slick, modernist Clarence Darrow. Although Bryan won the case, and the teaching of evolution was outlawed for a time, the fundamentalists lost the cause. Even worse, at some point during the course of the trial, they became the laughingstock of the nation.

Their influence over American culture waned overnight. Many people believed they would fade entirely from American life, the last vestige of an Bible-thumping religious order in a world that no longer needed that kind of God, or indeed, as some thought, any kind of God. They did not vanish, though, but instead went underground, becoming what sociologists refer to as a subculture.

The fundamentalists weren't heard from again until the mid-seventies, when the televangelists set about to restore their lost luster and to do war, yet again, with the modern world. By the mid-eighties, the Protestant religious right, which included the Assemblies of God and other pentecostal or charismatic sects, numbered around three and a half million, enough to have considerable political influence. In Francis Schaeffer, eager young religionists like Randall Terry, who sensed that a new day was coming, had found their philosopher-king.

Schaeffer, who lived from 1912 to 1984, brought two new ideas to contemporary fundamentalist theology. The first was an attack on the whole of western culture, which he saw as the seedbed of the moral decay. The second was to raise a call to arms that would send fundamentalists back into the political arena.

From his Swiss study center-retreat called L'Abri, Schaeffer epitomized a reversal of colonial missionizing by moving to Europe with the intention of "rechristianizing" it. There he wrote the books that shaped the thinking of a generation of young fundamentalists. His best-known work is a polemic on the evils of western culture called *How Should We Then Live?* Most of Schaeffer's followers, though, including Terry, saw the videotape rather than read the book.

Schaeffer's 258-page analysis of western culture can be summed up in a few brief sentences: The Renaissance, with its emphasis on man-centeredness, autonomy, and individuality, is bad; the God-centered Reformation, with its emphasis on moral absolutes of right and wrong, is good. Michelangelo's statue *David* is dismissed in one sentence while a minor statue of Swiss reformer Guillaume Farel holding aloft an open Bible is good because it presents "a serious view of the Bible." (It was so minor that its creator goes unnamed even in Schaeffer's book.) Bach and Handel are lauded because their music was God-centered. Renaissance music made "only technical and artistic advances."

As a target for the political action he advocated, Schaeffer found no worthier cause than abortion. In a book about abortion called *Whatever Happened to the Human Race?*, written with C. Everett Koop, Surgeon General under President Ronald Reagan, he wrote:

"Of all the subjects relating to the erosion of the sanctity of human life, abortion is the keystone. It is the first and crucial issue that has been overwhelming in changing attitudes toward the value of life in general."

Schaeffer deserves credit for some of the more outrageous beliefs and claims of the pro-life movement. It was he, for example, who associated abortion with adoption, by claiming (erroneously) that many abortions were done late in pregnancy when the "prospective mother could, with a little more physical trauma, wait to deliver a normal child at full-term and give it up for adoption."

Schaeffer also wrote a small manual, *Christian Manifesto*, that Terry says was his model for the organization of Operation Rescue. In it, Schaeffer described his belief that the founders of America always intended to link the government of the new republic to Christianity, a theme that Terry echoes when he tells his followers that "our Founding Fathers quoted prolifically from the Scriptures and from religious writings because this was a religious society."

With Ronald Reagan's election in 1980, Schaeffer believed that fundamentalists had a rare "open window" for the first time in a half-century through which they could press their religious agenda. But he warned: "In a fallen world, force in some form will always be necessary."

Terry is only following in Schaeffer's footsteps when he insists that civil disobedience is a Christian's duty when the state fails to enforce the laws of God. Schaeffer wrote: "The bottom line is that at a certain point, there is not only the right, but the duty to disobey the state."

Terry claims he doesn't condone or advocate violence, but he teaches his followers that they may have to "physically intervene" to prevent a woman from entering an abortion clinic. "That is the logical response to murder," he says.

Operation Rescue members have been arrested for pouring glue in to the keyholes of a clinic door, for placing fetal remains inside a children's playhouse at a clinic, and for (on several occasions) forming a human wall to prevent women from entering abortion clinics. At an early protest directed by Terry in Binghamton, New York, a pregnant clinic worker was punched in the stomach and injured seriously enough to be taken by ambulance to a hospital. She miscarried a few weeks later.

Frank Susman speaks for many in the pro-choice movement when he says of Terry: "If he doesn't condone violence, he does nothing to speak against it, and by his silence, he encourages it. It is a short step from the lawlessness of Randall Terry and his merry crew to the burning of an abortion clinic."

At Elim, Terry also met Cindy Dean. Cindy grew up in Manchester, a small upstate community in New York. After graduating from high school, she knocked around for several years, working as a bartender and waitress at the local Sheraton hotel. At 23, Cindy was admitted to the Culinary Institute of America in Hyde Park, a prestigious cooking school that trains many of America's finest chefs. In love with cooking, even before she graduated she got a job working in the kitchen of a French restaurant in Rochester and soon was making all their pastries. About that time, she met some born-again Christians and began hanging out with them. A few months later, she had become a born-again Christian; she left school without finishing her course of study.

Cindy's interest in Christianity led her to Elim Bible Institute, where she began taking courses as a commuter student. She met Terry and they were married after he graduated in 1981.

She told one reporter that she was not immediatley attracted to Terry but had been taught to distrust love at first sight in her Elim class on Christian Womanhood. For his part Terry says he was drawn to her because she was "quiet."

That Terry was drawn to his wife because she was quiet is probably no coincidence. Terry is a man who seems uncomfortable in the company of women, or at least strong, independent women. His inner circle is composed entirely of men, who appear to have been chosen at least in part for their willingness to yield to his authority. His humor is misogynist, and women journalists are the bane of his existence. Yet, Terry's attitudes about women are typical of most fundamentalist men and women. Having read their Bibles literally, most relegate women to a position that is inferior to that of men, and believe that they must be subject to male authority.

Given a chance to respond to the charge that he hates women, Terry told *Press & Sun-Bulletin* reporter Jeff Davis: "Oh, dear, me, no. I don't hate women. I do hate the radical feminist agenda, which wants to destroy the traditional family and wants women to have the right to destroy their offspring." Cindy Terry backed her husband, dismissing charges that he hated women as "foolish, inflammatory rhetoric."

He does blame working women for destroying what he calls the "family unit" and has publicly attributed the current high crime rate to the fact that so many women have left the home to work. "We have to thank the feminists for all the crime that young people are involved in. Because of them, these children didn't have a stable home to grow up in," he said, ignoring the two or three weeks out of every month that he spends on the road away from his family.

With the notion that a woman's only role is that of wife and mother comes the corollary that it is the man who provides for his family. For a man with these views, it must have been difficult when the Terrys moved to Binghamton in 1983 and found themselves starting their life together in the midst of the worst recession since World War II. Terry lost two jobs, and Cindy's income kept them solvent. He found himself flipping hamburgers at McDonalds and pumping gas, taking any menial job he could get.

Eventually he landed a job selling cars at Best Pontiac. He held that job until he got his fledgling organization off the ground and put himself on the payroll full-time. His work at Best Pontiac gave rise to the widely held misperception of him as a former used-car salesman, an image his detractors use with relish and his followers find unduly diminishing.

Today, Cindy Terry, dressed in jeans and an expensive-looking green foul-weather coat, is a self-assured, almost Yuppyish young woman whose life undoubtedly has been made easier by her husband's $32,000 a year salary and newfound celebrity. These days Randall Terry travels around the country as the national director of Operation Rescue while Cindy stays home with their children and keeps house. Their quiet suburban life is more likely to be interrupted by a film crew than unemployment. "Everybody does their part," Cindy says, "and this is my part."

But workers at the Southern Tier Women's Services clinic say that Cindy Terry has not always been so sanguine about life. They remember another Cindy Terry, a sad and rather desperate figure who was a lone picketer in front of their clinic during the winter of 1983. One day, she begged a woman entering the clinic for an abortion to have the baby instead and give it to her.

Not until 1986 did she and Terry have Faith, their daughter, now four. Later they added three black foster children to their family, the boy named Poppy, age 10, and two girls, Ebony, 13, and Lila, 3. The foster children are siblings, and Terry claims he "saved" the youngest by talking her mother out of having an abortion.

Cindy was a lone presence at the clinic for several months before Terry joined her, and when he did, there was a kind of desperation in his actions, too. But where Cindy's attempts to pressure women out of abortions were sad, even pathetic, Terry's were undeniably angry. On several occasions, he threw himself against car doors as women tried to get out and clinic workers witnessed him pushing and roughing up women who tried to enter the clinic.

Randall Terry's inspiration to start Operation Rescue came about as a result of an apocalyptic moment in his life. On

January 22, 1984, Terry joined a busload of friends and fellow congregants from his Binghamton church for their annual trek to Washington, D.C., to participate in the March for Life, a pro-life protest held every year since 1974 on the anniversary of the *Roe v. Wade* decision. The march traditionally ended with a prayer vigil on the steps of the Supreme Court.

Despite the stinging cold weather and the pre-dawn hour of their departure, everyone was in high spirits as they boarded the bus for the seven-hour trip to Washington. There was an earnest sense of unity among the group, who worked off their predawn chill singing hymns and chanting anti-abortion chants and "praising the Lord," a favorite—and inevitable—pastime among born-again Christians. Fundamentalists take pride in the fact that whenever they gather, even on social occasions, the talk invariably turns to their personal and intimate experiences with the Lord. On the way down, Terry was as jovial as everyone else, standing several times to lead the singing and once to preach extemporaneously.

Terry had begun to acquire a reputation as one of the stars on the fundamentalist speaking circuit, and indeed, preaching was a time-honored way for a young man to begin his ascent to a position of leadership. He was already viewed as a charismatic figure among the congregation at the Little Church at Pierce Creek, where he worshiped.

In a faith where talking to God is a fairly commonplace activity, Terry was increasingly seen as someone with a special pipeline. Even apart from his obvious ability to stir up a crowd with one of his sermons, people recognized that he had a special gift. One congregant recalled: "Terry is a visionary. He sees what has to be done. He has this understanding, after he prays, after he's alone with the Lord."

When the exhausted group met at the bus for the trip home, it was obvious that Terry's mood had shifted dramatically. He sat apart from the others, alone in the back of the bus. The group was wary and somewhat curious at first, and the word passed that Terry had seen or experienced something during the day that had left him awestruck. No one knew what had happened, but this wasn't the same man who had boarded the bus with them twelve hours earlier.

Terry stayed in the back of the bus, holding his head in his hands as if he were in great pain. Something powerful was taking place, everyone agreed. Part of the time Terry sat quietly; sometimes he could be heard praying; and every once in a while, he cried out, "Oh, Jesus help me." Everyone cast sympathetic looks in his direction, but no one dared go near him. His secretary Linda Sclafani was among those who were with him that day, and she still recalls the moment with awe: "That's when he received the burden. God spoke to him."

Terry's vision was to start Operation Rescue, a new anti-abortion group of national scope that would stage "rescues" at abortion clinics around the country. "Rescue" was a generic name for a type of protest that Catholics and other anti-abortion protesters had been practicing for several years. The protesters gathered at clinics, where they tried to talk women out of having abortions, to "rescue" their babies as it were.

Rescues originated as a form of nonviolent protest. In fact, when anti-abortion violence escalated in the early 1980s, the leading pro-life groups met to discuss the problem and to reenforce their belief in nonviolent protest. The meetings were also an attempt to set some standards and coordinate their activities, which had for the most part been impromptu, disorganized gatherings. Terry showed up at the meetings in 1987 and 1988, but never became active in that pro-life circle, which was mostly Catholic. He found their techniques useful, though, and would adopt several of them for use in his own group.

Most specifically he borrowed from Joseph Scheidler, a Roman Catholic who began his anti-abortion work on the day the Roe decision was handed down and is now director of the Pro-Life Action League. In 1985, Scheidler published *Closed: 99 Ways to Stop Abortion*. Terry used several of Scheidler's ideas, such as the technique of rescuers chaining themselves to cement blocks or other objects, and added some of his own, such as the blitz, when rescuers descend upon the waiting room of a clinic, distributing literature and pleading with women to reconsider their decisions, or the drive-in, when rescuers pull cars in front of the doors and across the driveways of clinics.

Although Terry is now defensive about any suggestion that Scheidler was his mentor, one Binghamton policeman who has followed Operation Rescue's activities from the beginning recalls that in the early days of organizing Operation Rescue, Terry even went so far as to mimic his mentor's dress and his hairstyle.

Terry's contribution to the rescue movement was to organize it with military precision. He instituted "field training," summer training sessions in Binghamton for Operation Rescue followers. He came up with something he called "minutemen raids," small, surprise attacks on clinics. The people who directed rescues were called "field marshals."

If Terry was the Chief of Staff, his followers, according to his training manual, were his warriors, and his instructions to them were clear:

> Warriors take orders and carry them out to the end.
> Warriors know if they don't defeat the enemy
>   the enemy will defeat them. There is
>   no stalemate, no middle ground.
> Warriors don't run into conflict; they run to it.
> Warriors are prepared to die.

Terry instituted rallies the night before a rescue. Officially they were prayer meetings, but their real purpose was to pump up people for the rescue the next day—and for the possibility that they might well be arrested. In fact, according to Terry's plan, if all went well, they would be arrested. The success of a rescue was measured not only in terms of the "babies" saved but also by the number of arrests.

Rescuers met again at a central location in the early morning hours before the rally. They divested themselves of their identification so they could be John Does when arrested. After praying together, they piled into vans so they could be transported to clinics in small groups, a move designed to throw off the police who presumably might be looking for a large caravan of cars.

Unlike the generic rescuers whose goal was to counsel women out of having abortions and to register their disapproval of abortion generally, Terry's goal was to close down clinics, or "killing centers," as he called them. When he closed a clinic, he considered that he had "saved" all the fetuses that would have been aborted that day. Operation Rescue's count of fetuses saved was often erroneous, but the rescuers nevertheless measured their success in terms of the numbers they had "saved." If a woman turned back as a result of their efforts, even if she went home to reschedule her appointment, rescuers talked of how they had saved her "baby."

On January 8, 1986, Terry and seven people broke into the Southern Tier clinic in Binghamton. Before the police got to them, they smashed furniture and ripped out the telephone system. Because he refused to pay his fine, Terry was sentenced to twenty days in the Binghamton jail. Emulating his hero Martin Luther King, Jr., he wrote his first book *Operation Rescue* while encarcerated. He came out of jail, according to Jesse Lee, "with a fire in his heart and bold plans."

Throughout 1986 he tested his strategies in a series of local rescues and continued recruiting people to join Operation Rescue. By fall of 1987, he was ready to stage his first large-scale rally. He had gathered 300 people from around the country for a demonstration against an abortion clinic in Cherry Hill, New Jersey. After that came rescues, each with several hundred people, in larger cities like Indianapolis, Milwaukee, and Boston. In May 1988, he hit New York City for the first time. Two months later, he went to the Democratic convention in Atlanta and stayed for four months to mount daily protests at abortion clinics there. By early 1989 he was preparing to take on Southern California with a week-long series of events and rescues billed as a "Holy Week of Rescues."

Terry was claiming 37,000 arrests across the country, a figure based on reports that are called into national Operation Rescue headquarters each Saturday, the day of most rescues. The figure does not take into account the actual numbers of rescuers, who may be arrested repeatedly.

To make the rescues succeed in a way that would attract the national press, Terry had a constant need for bodies, both generals and foot soldiers. To recruit them, he had begun speaking in the early 1980s on the fundamentalist lecture circuit—at small independent churches, Bible schools like Elim, and always at the pro-life march held in Washington, D.C., on the anniversary of the Roe decision.

Jesse Lee, now co-director of Operation Rescue's Northeast office, met Terry during the 1988 March for Life. "I got to the end of the march—the Supreme Court steps—and there was Terry with a little microphone attached to bullhorns, preaching his heart out."

Terry's theme was well-developed at this point and straight out of Schaeffer. He was advocating civil disobedience. "If God truly never wanted people to disobey civil authority, why did He approve of the Hebrew midwives, Moses' parents, and Rahab the harlot when they defied the commands of kings? Why did he bless the Magi and the apostles for breaking the law?"

"If we say it's murder," he shouted, "why don't we act like it is?"

"God got a hold of me," Lee recalled, as he listened to Terry's speech. "It was like hot oil washing over me. I knew he was right. I had put human life in another category. That quickly, it came to me: This is right."

Mark Lucas, a graphics artist who is now office manager of Terry's Binghamton headquarters, also was recruited when he heard Terry preach in December, 1987, at the Little Church at Pierce Creek. The church's pastor Daniel J. Little fully supported Terry and had even written a booklet, "The Right and Responsibility to Rescue," in support of Operation Rescue. He let Terry use his church to recruit volunteers for a local rescue the next day.

"It was nothing you could put words on," Lucas said, "but I knew I had just been paying lip service to my beliefs. I thought I couldn't do anything else, but Randy showed me how. I began to see I could make a difference. This would be a challenge of my faith. Randy required that we face down the system the whole way. That takes bravery."

Gradually, Terry gathered his entirely male inner circle, the men who would be his generals. They are young men in their twenties and early thirties, with blown-dry hair and suavely cut suits, who carry cellular telephones and leather briefcases. They are often clones of Terry.

Terry offered them what he was trying to buy for himself—a

future they would not otherwise dare to dream about, and lots of excitement. They became war buddies. They strategized together, fought battles together, traveled together, and went to jail together. And these days, they often stand trial together, the inevitable culmination of their many arrests around the country.

If the trials are a draining experience emotionally and financially, they are also high drama. It is a heady experience to walk along the hard marble floors of courthouses all over the country trailed by a press corps that scrambles to cover one's every move. Terry's generals often give up everything to work for him, their jobs, their family lives, their reputations, and their privacy, but so far, they believe it is worthwhile. While the foot soldiers come and go in the organization, rarely lasting more than a year, the generals have been with Terry since he recruited them in 1987 and 1988, and none have dropped out.

Terry understands that civil disobedience is a tough job, and although he enticed his inner circle with the thrill of being on the front line of battle, he has learned to play down the scarier and less rewarding aspects of war in the trenches when he is recruiting foot soldiers. Even though he has repeatedly stated his intention to fill the jails and the courts with rescuers, he softens the message when talking to potential recruits. Then he tells people:

"If you're rescuing with five people, you might spend a few days in jail." There's safety in numbers, though, he insists, saying that most cities could not jail five hundred protesters even if they wanted to. At this point a note of humility enters his voice as he says: "We fancy ourselves like Corrie Ten Boom hiding Jews. But that was a sure way to lose your life. Yet we can save babies from this holocaust with just a little bit of inconvenience or embarrassment." (Corrie Ten Boom was a Dutch woman who hid a Jewish mother and her child during World War II.)

Terry encourages people to refuse to post bond, claiming that most jails will release them after a few hours because they don't have room for them. What he doesn't always say is that Operation Rescue will not post bond for its members, or necessarily provide them with legal support when they go to trial.

It doesn't take long for Terry's foot soldiers to become disenchanted. What sounds noble when Terry is recruiting pales with execution. Terry enlisted an entire Cajun congregation from Louisiana to come to Atlanta, for example, by assuring them they wouldn't be arrested and promising that if they were, they would be out in a few hours. Fully expecting to be released, the rescuers were stunned when they were arrested en masse and jailed. They were even more surprised when Operation Rescue did not spring them.

"We had all these Cajuns in jail," said Atlanta Police Sergeant Carl Pyrdum, Jr., head of the Operation Rescue task force, "and there was no money for their bail. Terry had led all these people to believe he would post bond. But he provided no legal support, and then he got himself sprung from jail after a few days while the rest of them served a month. We almost had a riot when his followers found out he had stranded them."

Sergeant Pyrdum and his task force were ready for Operation Rescue when it came to Atlanta. They had gathered intelligence on Operation Rescue and Terry and had developed a strategy to counter them. Unlike other cities, which had, they believed, been too casual about Operation Rescue, Atlanta's strategy was to be tough.

July 19, 1988, was the day of Terry's first rescue in Atlanta. Three days later, the police had obtained a search warrant to go into Operation Rescue's rooms at Day's Inn to look for identification for the people they had arrested. They believed the identifications were sequestered in one of the "command" rooms Terry had set up. They found a few IDs, but the real surprise was $50,000 in cash stuffed in bags and two fetuses in ice chests. Pyrdum later heard an unconfirmed rumor that Operation Rescue was getting so much mail, most of it containing donations, that it was delivered in duffel bags. Several people reportedly were assigned to the full-time task of opening the mail.

Terry had taken three hundred people to New York and by moving them around to various clinics had managed to get twelve hundred arrests out of the operation. Sergeant Pyrdum decided against using mass arrests. Out of twenty-four rescues over four months in Atlanta, only 1,235 arrests were made. Atlanta police arrested just enough rescuers to throw Operation Rescue into disarray.

"The rest of them could work on their tans for all I cared," Sergeant Pyrdum said. "We were out there to fight him every day of the four months he was in Atlanta. When we arrested people, we made sure they went to jail, too. Every morning, we would go to whatever clinic he was attacking. I saw him personally every day. I watched him position his troops. I would say, 'Ok, Randy, got everyone in position?' He's very predictable and very egotistical, especially as far as his military operation goes. His leaders pushed everyone around, saying you do this, you do that, and you just sit there prayerfully and let us talk to the media. Your pain is nothing compared to the pain of an unborn baby being aborted. But we boondoggled him from Day One.

"One day Randy—I always call him that because he doesn't like anyone but his close friends to call him that—came to me and said, 'This isn't working. We're not doing what we came for.' I told him that was right, we weren't going to let him close down Atlanta clinics."

Pyrdum thinks Terry's frustration over his inability to conquer Atlanta led him into a key strategic error. Terry had originally planned to take Operation Rescue to the Republican Convention held in New Orleans a few weeks after the Democratic Convention. Instead, he got bogged down in his frustrating battle with the Atlanta police, and stayed in that city, thereby missing a golden opportunity to capture some significant publicity.

He should have moved on, as he had planned, to the Republican Convention in New Orleans. There was little to be gained from protesting at the Democratic Convention, where delegates were mostly pro-choice. The Republicans, however, were far more divided over abortion, and Terry could have capitalized on that schism had he gone to New Orleans. Operation Rescue barely made a whimper at the Democratic

Convention, but they would have been the lead story at the Republican Convention.

Terry suffered another disappointment in Southern California, where he expected to recruit thousands of followers from the one hundred or so independent evangelical churches, a dozen with congregations of 5,000 or more, that thrived there. But the much ballyhooed "Holy Week of Rescues" planned for April 1989 was a major disappointment, netting him fewer than 1,000 volunteers.

And in California, for the first time, it wasn't just the police who organized to oppose Operation Rescue but pro-choice women. When Terry announced his California crusade in January, a coalition of the prominent pro-choice groups, including NOW, California Abortion Rights Action League, Planned Parenthood, ACT UP/LA Fired Up for Choice, and Radical Women, began to organize against him. Pro-choice people had been escorting women into abortion clinics for several years, but now the level of activism took a new turn as pro-choice women in Southern California organized to defend the clinics.

The coalition soon raised enough money to support mass mailings that alerted people to Operation Rescue's planned invasion of southern California and recruited them to help with clinic defense. The women borrowed some of Terry's military tactics, appointing their own generals to control their activists during protests and arming themselves with cellular telephones so they could be in constant contact with one another during rescues and when they were en route to the clinics. Several women worked as liaisons with the local police forces. Before the first Operation Rescue action in Southern California, they had persuaded law enforcement authorities not to give Terry what he most wanted—headline-producing mass arrests.

Some of the women proved to be every bit as militant as Terry's rescuers. One group began practicing some civil disobedience of its own, breaking into churches where Operation Rescue rallies were held and painting feminist and pro-choice slogans on the walls. The women also infiltrated Operation Rescue. Some went in as spies to gather information they could give to the pro-choice side while others attended Operation

Rescue rallies as observers looking for any signs of illegal activities, especially those that infringed the civil rights of women.

A few women always attended the pep rallies Operation Rescue held the night before a rescue, or failing that, arose at 4 or 5 A.M. to mingle with the Operation Rescue people at their predawn gathering places. As soon as the pro-choice infiltrators heard which clinics were targeted for the day, they rushed for their cars and cellular telephones to call other clinic defenders who would, in turn, set in action their phone bank. All across Southern California, when they got the call, women roused themselves from their beds in the early morning dawn to throw on jeans and T-shirts (with suitable pro-choice logos) and race to the scene of battle.

At an Operation Rescue rally, the sight of several women rushing for their cars was often the first sign that the rally had been infiltrated, and it usually threw the rescuers into premature action, skewing their own meticulous plans of attack. On several occasions mad chases ensued as defenders and rescuers went head to head on California's freeways, frantically racing one another to be the first to reach a clinic and stake out the most defensible position.

Soon the movement even had a spy working full-time inside Operation Rescue. She was a born-again Christian who belonged to NOW and considered herself a feminist. Her curiosity was piqued when Operation Rescue began to organize in her area, and she began attending meetings. At first she was remarkably casual, stuffing her Operation Rescue brochures in the trunk of her car alongside her NOW flyers.

She began her descent into full-time undercover work by walking into Operation Rescue's main headquarters one day and volunteering her services. Although she would not know it at the time, she would become more and more involved, gaining access to the leadership of Operation Rescue. Her deepening involvement would eventually cost her her job, her apartment, and her car.

The whole undercover operation almost came to a halt before it started, though, in large part because Operation Rescue tends to greet all new volunteers with suspicion. Although Terry claims to recruit from all religions, his nine-page written application asks for such information as the name, address and telephone number of one's church, the name of one's pastor and whether he is aware of the volunteer's pro-life activities. Would-be volunteers are asked to cite three references in the scriptures that support the idea that life begins at conception, along with three other references that reflect scriptural approval of pro-life actions. Denials to the contrary, anyone who hopes to work at Operation Rescue must be a practicing fundamentalist Christian well-versed in his or her religion.

On the day the mole walked into the main headquarters of Operation Rescue-Southern California, she was met with the usual barrage of questions. Before she could answer, though, a woman who had attended Bible college with her spoke up in her behalf, and the questions ended as abruptly as they had begun. She was in, accepted, for the moment.

Before long, she also found herself involved in the most secretive plans of Operation Rescue. It was through her that the clinic defenders learned about the pre-rescue rallies, as well as the post-rally debriefing sessions that Terry held in local churches. Soon she was alerting pro-choice forces to times and places of minutemen raids.

Terry slowly realized that he had an infiltrator in his Southern California operation. When the pre-rescue rallies were infiltrated by pro-choice women, he suspected he had a spy in his midst, but when even the minutemen attacks weren't kept secret, he no longer had any doubts.

Gradually, what had started as a lark became intensely, at times frighteningly, serious. The woman's actions of necessity became more and more clandestine. She lived an increasingly isolated life, unable to contact her old friends, unwilling to get too close to her new ones. Worst of all from her point of view, she had no one with whom she could share the crisis of faith that Operation Rescue provoked in her. And always, she lived with the fear of being discovered.

On the one hand, too many people in the pro-choice movement knew about her presence to guarantee her the secrecy she needed to operate in complete safety. At Operation Rescue protests, she often came face to face with women she knew from the pro-choice movement who were startled to find one of their members helping to direct a rescue. On the other hand, no one in the pro-choice movement was willing to acknowledge her presence to the police, since some officers' loyalties were considered suspect. "She was," in the words of one activist, "hung out to dry." Some pro-choicers even believed she was a double-agent.

The national leaders of Operation Rescue, including Terry, converged on the Southern California offices in spring 1989 to try to find out who was leaking information. Unwilling to let anyone but his top four or five staff members know there was a spy in their midst, Terry only added to his difficulties in finding her. When he couldn't resolve the problem, he finally resorted to hiring a private investigator.

Suddenly the stakes were even higher for the spy. Feeling that her days were numbered and that there was at least some risk of violence when she was discovered, she spent several months trying to extricate herself from Operation Rescue. In a final act of frustration because she could find no other way out, she dropped her cover in the simplest and most efficient way, by calling Sue Finn, who ran the Operation Rescue office and telling her she was the spy. To her immense relief and that of Operation Rescue, it was over at last.

Two other Southern California clinic defense people, a gay man and lesbian woman who were active in the radical group called ACT UP, had more fun and assumed less risk when they infiltrated Operation Rescue. Posing as a married couple, they joined a local congregation, St. Norbert's, that had many Operation Rescue members. Soon they were participating in rescues, and eventually they climbed through the ranks to become highly placed field marshals at rescues.

When they wanted out, they simply showed up at a rescue dressed in their Operation Rescue T-shirts and field marshal's armbands. At one point during the rescue, they stripped off the Operation Rescue T-shirts to reveal their ACT UP T-shirts and used the armbands to tie their hair into pony tails. The Operation Rescue people were understandably distraught; the clinic defenders amused and delighted. Terry, reportedly, was infuriated.

The downside of civil disobedience is that Terry and his followers would soon be faced with a multitude of civil and criminal lawsuits around the country. Just two years after its founding, Operation Rescue is burdened with lawsuits and legal actions in several states, among them Georgia, New York, Pennsylvania, Massachusetts, and California. More than a dozen major legal actions were pending against Operation Rescue in the summer of 1989 alone, actions that could potentially result in hundreds of thousands of dollars in fines and lawyers' fees. Some of the suits were the result of criminal charges after the mass arrests, but others grew out of charges filed by the ACLU and other civil rights groups, who charged that women's civil rights were being infringed by Operation Rescue.

Oblivious to the threat that the escalating fines and court costs would pose to his organization, Terry was elated to enter this next phase of action: the trials. Through them he believed he would at last be able to get what he coveted most, a national platform from which to present his anti-abortion case to the American people.

That opportunity presented itself the first week of August, when I next saw Terry. The setting was the Los Angeles Municipal Court; the occasion, a trial—his first—before a jury of his peers. Terry did his best to turn his trial into a media event. A week of pro-life activities, designed to culminate in a round of ten clinic rescues, had been planned to kick off what was referred to as "Terry's trial," even though there were four other defendants.

An expensive-looking brochure, trumpeting the theme "Let Them Live LA," announced the week's events: a kickoff rally for Terry Monday night, a memorial service for dead fetuses on Tuesday, an evening prayer and repentance service for women who had been exploited by abortion on Wednesday, a survivors' prayer march on Thursday, the rescue rally on Friday, and the rescues on Saturday. There were also plans to pack the courtroom during the trial.

Monday morning, August 7, found Randall Terry and his co-defendants gathering under the hot morning sun outside the Los Angeles Municipal Courthouse. Only a small crowd, fewer than two dozen and hardly the number needed to pack the courtroom, had gathered to support Terry.

Even the press wasn't out in full force. A few cable stations and Channel 9 were setting up their gear and getting ready to cover the trial.

I walked up to Terry, who didn't recognize me despite having spent a day with me only two weeks earlier. He apologized, saying he had flown in late last night and was exhausted.

He told me he was sorry I had come all the way across the country to Los Angeles because he meant to have someone from his office call me to tell me not to come. He had decided he didn't want to be in my book after all.

When I said I'd like to follow him around for a few days as long as I was there, he laughed and told me to go ahead. "It's a free country," he said, shrugging his shoulders.

I told him that I would probably write about him anyway. He looked surprised and asked: "You will? I thought you wouldn't write about me if I told you not to."

Russ Neil, one of the leaders of Operation Rescue–Southern California, joined us, and Terry introduced us, getting my name wrong. I told Neil I was writing a book about abortion activists.

Terry added, "Yeah, don't talk to her."

We both looked at him for confirmation, unable to detect from his tone whether he was joking or serious. When Neil asked him, Terry didn't answer but stood, lips pursed and arms wrapped tightly across his chest. Almost imperceptibly, he nodded his head no. Neil moved away from me quickly. Terry, however, continued to make small talk with me.

We were interrupted when a man and woman and their child of about eleven walked up to him. The man said, "I just want to tell you how much we admire you. We fully support what you're doing. Bless you."

"God bless you," Terry responded, all smiles again. Beyond that, though, he didn't ask the people where they were from or make any attempt at small talk.

A Channel 9 reporter, trailing heavy black electrical cords and shadowed by his videocamera, came over to interview Terry.

"Isn't it true that your strength has been waning in California?" he asked in a pleasant, nonconfrontational voice.

"I don't see how you get that," Terry responded. "Eight

hundred people were arrested here in March." He was referring to the rescue operation for which he was now standing trial on charges of trespassing and conspiring to obstruct a business.

"But only a few dozen people have shown up here today."

Terry said, "I'm grateful that anyone showed up."

Upstairs near the fourth floor courtroom, about a hundred people were gathered. The crowd consisted of some more media people, about 90 Operation Rescue followers, and some pro-choice advocates who were sitting in as court watchers.

Betty Ann Downing, an ACLU field representative who tracked the activities of Operation Rescue, had come as a court watcher. She was there to gather information about Operation Rescue that could be used in the various lawsuits that the California Civil Liberties Union brought against Operation Rescue when they violated women's civil rights.

After what seemed like an endless wait in stuffy, airless halls, the bailiffs opened the courtroom, and we all hustled for seats. Only 45 of us would get them, and the rest, including many of Terry's followers, would patiently line the hall outside the courtroom, reading their Bibles and praying, distributing their literature to passers-by. In the coming days, their presence would be an ongoing bone of contention with the prosecution, who feared that their literature would taint the prospective jurors as they were brought in.

As we waited for the judge to appear, Terry and the other defendants roamed in and out of the courtroom, talking among themselves and ignoring the spectators. On trial along with Terry were Mike McMonagle, a Catholic lay reformer from Philadelphia and West Point graduate; Jeff White, the son of a policeman and a mover and shaker in Southern California's OR office who recently was released from a 45-day jail stint on Operation Rescue's behalf; Don Bennette; and Andrew Epping. Terry, McMonagle, and White had petitioned the court to be allowed to defend themselves.

Twice, Russ Neil came in to lead the spectators in prayer. Heads were bowed and hands were clasped while they asked for the strength to survive this ordeal they were going through. They prayed that the trial would serve as a means to an end— the end being to stop the "baby killing."

When Gloria Allred, a feminist attorney, entered the courtroom, a titter rippled through the pro-life spectators. They had all seen her on television touting her causes. Most recently, she had called a press conference to demand that Saks Fifth Avenue and other stores give women the same free alterations on the clothes that they had been giving men for years. After the Webster decision, she appeared at a press conference alongside Norma McCorvey, the Roe in *Roe v. Wade*. Although she wasn't especially active in any of the feminist or reproductive rights organizations in Southern California, she had been tapped as an enemy of the rescuers, who mostly based their enemies list on what they saw and heard on television.

"Roe's a puppet, and then Allred grabbed her. She controls her now," a freckle-faced, red-haired boy sitting behind me announced to the crowd generally. Hearing his own bitter words, though, he added, "I shouldn't speak against Allred. The Lord can turn something around. Maybe she's here today because she's meant to hear something Terry will say."

Finally, the trial got underway. Terry and the defendants entered the courtroom first, trailed by an unusually large group of lawyers for men who were defending themselves. The lead lawyer Cyrus Zal was technically defending only Bennette and Epping, but he often stood to protest something in Terry's behalf as well, and the judge seemed inclined to be lenient about this. Also present was a high-powered criminal lawyer, wearing black cowboy boots in need of a shine and a disheveled blue shirt with a missing cuff button. I was told he was the only hired gun, the only lawyer with no emotional ax to grind.

I was surprised to see four women among the pro-life counselors. Only one, Mary Murphy Quintero, actually sat at the defense table, while the others lined a wall behind the defense table, more a presence than anything else. Downing, with whom I'd been chatting, explained to me that they were just that, a response to recent criticisms that Operation Rescue was male-dominated. The women, she said, would not have been present a few weeks earlier.

Several pre-trial motions needed to be settled before jury selection could begin. Judge Richard Paez's first order of business this morning was to ascertain whether Terry,

McMonagle and White were competent to defend themselves. After a brief interview with each, he decided they were.

In these preliminary stages of the trial (later he would clash repeatedly with the judge), Terry revealed himself to be surprisingly acquiescent in the face of authority, a trait he shares with many fundamentalists but which nevertheless strikes a false note in a man who preaches civil disobedience. This boded badly, I suspected, for those of us who relished trials that challenged, or at least stretched, the system. I realized with a slight twinge of disappointment that whatever disruptions occurred in this courtroom would be relatively minor. These defendants were no Chicago Seven.

The most pressing pre-trial issue—it would determine the course of the proceedings—was whether the defendants would be permitted to use the necessity defense. Terry hoped that the trial would provide him with a public forum from which to promulgate his views about abortion, but to do this, he had to be able to use the necessity defense. He had made much of his intention to use it in the press and among his followers.

The necessity defense comes out of common law and is based on the principle that it is sometimes necessary to break the law to do some good, most typically, to save the life of another human being. As it is taught in law school, the classic illustration of its use is the example of the "drowning child." A person may willfully and legally disobey a "No Trespass" sign in order to cross a field and save a child from drowning in a pond.

In recent years, the defense has been successfully used by anti-nuclear protestors, and Terry's followers felt their cause was far more important than anti-nuclear protests. A young woman in the spectator section was wearing a T-shirt that reflected her views on this:

> Be a hero, save a whale.
> Save a baby, go to jail.

The city prosecutors had filed a pretrial motion to prevent Terry and the other defendants from using the necessity defense on grounds that it was inappropriate in a simple trespass case. They would argue that the only appropriate focus of this trial was the trespass charge and the other misdemeanors the defendants were charged with. A fetus, they would tell the court, was not a person and could not be defended in California.

Judge Paez said he would give each defendant an opportunity to address this issue. Now each was permitted to speak in turn, with Terry, in a pattern that would become familiar to those in the courtroom, speaking last.

Terry began with an obsequious apology to Judge Paez for turning his courtroom into a media circus. When Paez stared blankly at this overt attempt at ingratiation, Terry quickly got down to the matter at hand. The other defendants had addressed points of law; in another pattern that would soon reveal itself, Terry turned his attention to emotional matters.

"We are saving lives, we are saving viable children. The prosecution's insistence that if we can close down an abortion clinic one week, we can also decide they don't like organ transplants the next and close down hospitals, or close down the entire city the week after that is nothing but a red herring."

"Your honor, we support justice, and the preserving of life is the highest goal of justice." Imbued with the spirit of the message he was conveying, he misjudged his audience. Judge Paez impatiently interrupted to tell Terry point-blank that he was naive about the law.

Terry tried again: "Today is one of the most exciting days of my life because it's the beginning of a trial by my peers. I want to tell you why as family men we want to sit in front of the door of an abortuary." He didn't sit in front of abortion clinics, or "killing rooms," as he called them, because he wanted to, but because he was morally obliged to.

"Lastly," Terry said, his voice soft, his slender, almost feminine hands emphasizing his points, "this trial is about justice. Abortion is not a settled issue. That's a cold hard reality. Abortion is not a settled part of our history. This era will be remembered as a brief, dark window in American history."

Much was at stake here. If Judge Paez ruled that the necessity defense could be used, the men of Operation Rescue would do their best to put abortion on trial, using not the evidence required by law, but magnified and bloody photographs of fetuses and their inflammatory and often misleading literature. They would cite out-of-context passages of the Bible as evidence of why they should be permitted to trespass on abortion clinics and interfere with women's lives. Terry would attempt, as he had on other occasions, to preach in the courtroom.

In contrast, the city's lawyers, prepared to argue only the misdemeanor charges brought against these plaintiffs, would not have prepared any rebuttal to this kind of defense, nor was it within their charge to do so.

Around noon, after listening to everyone's arguments, Judge Paez announced a recess until the next morning, at which time he would rule on the necessity defense.

Terry was fairly buoyant about the morning's session. The judge's views on abortion were not known, and Terry hoped that Paez, a Mormon by birth, might be on their side. With his rigid ideas about right and wrong, Terry could not conceive of a judge who personally found abortion repugnant but would still enforce the law of the state of California, which permitted abortion. You were either on his side and right, or you were not on his side, and were wrong.

Partly this was his fundamentalist vision of the world, and partly it was Terry's own flawed thinking. Terry had no heart for compromise, and he saw no reason to have laws he disapproved of or found morally wrong. After months of observing Terry at close range, Sergeant Pyrdum had observed of him: "He fits the Messiah complex, as far as I'm concerned. He's transcended from this plane of logic. He won't listen to people."

Terry was thrilled with the events of the first day. His followers had packed the courtroom, and it was their appearence that counted on television, not the fact that fewer than one hundred out of Southern California's thousands of fundamentalists had shown up. The media coverage, if not spectacular, was adequate. His entry into the courthouse had been impressive. He had given several interviews before the trial began and had held a press conference after the morning session ended. Of course, the major networks weren't covering the trial as he had hoped, but he was still confident they would show up when the trial got hot. He thought he could promise some theatrics somewhere along the line. And tonight he would be the featured speaker at a kickoff rally, expected to draw a thousand or more people.

To hear Terry speak is to understand the source of his power to recruit people to his cause. I heard him at the Central Baptist Church in suburban Pomona. The white stucco building normally seated 800. This night it held at least another one hundred people.

The altarpiece was a huge videoscreen. The sound system could have held its own at a Rolling Stones concert, but tonight it served a Latino electric guitar band.

They were playing to a white, predominantly blue-collar audience. Only a handful of Latinos were sprinkled throughout the crowd, and there were even fewer African-American faces. In front of the altar, five uniformly blonde and overweight middle-aged women swayed to the music and held aloft huge sequined banners that read "Lamb of God" and "Jesus Reigns." For over an hour people stood, arms raised, singing hosannahs as the pews slowly filled. Their children played quietly in the pews.

Two women, obviously there to warm up the crowd, spoke first. They looked like soap opera stars with their carefully coifed hair and heavy-duty makeup. The crowd loved it when the first woman railed against the evils of sex, telling the people that if nothing else, making abortion illegal would stop the fornication that runs rampant in our society. They roared when she described "liberal-style sex education—the kind that teaches your children to have sex, that using birth control is okay."

The second woman struck a more somber note with a story of having visited an abortion "survivor," a tiny premature baby being treated in a hospital's neonatal intensive care unit.

Terry was obviously the eagerly awaited star of the evening, though, and the excitement was palpable as the moment of his speech drew closer. During the women's speeches, he sat with several of his men in a pew off to one side in the back of the church. Shortly before he was due to speak, they moved out of the pews and vanished into a large reception area at the back of the church.

When he was introduced, everyone waited for him to emerge from behind the altar as the other speakers had, but nothing happened. The audience was on its feet and thundering its applause. After what seemed like an interminable wait but was only a highly charged few minutes, Terry came bounding down the eighty-foot aisle of the church and leapt onto the stage. Apologizing for his lateness, he spoke a line of Spanish and told the crowd that he had been giving an interview to Spanish radio.

A natural speaker, he had a sense of timing that many accomplished actors would envy, and an amazing ability to build rapport with his audience. After a few jokes about Molly Yard and feminist women, Terry launched into his main message:

"The Webster ruling is simply a dawning. We aren't even in the heat of the day yet. But we have a crisis in the evangelical movement. We burn bright and we're gone."

The audience was on its feet, as it would be many more times during this speech, thundering its approval.

"Our day of distress only began with Webster," Terry continued. "Our adversaries are in deadly earnest. Our enemies have been launching a counterattack."

Terry's plea was more urgent than it would have been even a few weeks earlier. Although the Webster decision had initially been seen as a victory for pro-life forces, the outpouring of support for the abortion right had surprised everyone and had weakened Terry's support. As the euphoria of the Webster decision had faded, so, too, had Operation Rescue's promise to move on the state legislatures. The need to win converts to Operation Rescue's cause was more pressing then ever before. Terry needed and would ask for money tonight, but more than that, he needed bodies, people who would unquestioningly follow him into battle in his Holy War, people who would do so quickly while there was still a cause to fight for. The sympathy he and other pro-life groups had built over the past few years seemed to be fading—inexplicably—before their eyes since the Webster decision.

"Folks, we have got to impact on the political process," Terry said. "Are you hearing me?"

The crowd roared its agreement.

Pointing his finger at the audience, Terry cajoled: "Most churches won't get involved, not because what we're doing is illegal, but because it's controversial."

Terry recounted the Biblical story of David's disappointment when he was told he could not fight the Philistines, that he must return instead to base camp to join his wife and children. On his return, he discovered that the camp had been raided the day before. "Talk about a bad day," said Terry, who, like all good teachers, knew how to make the story personal to his listeners.

Unsure what to do, David talked to his preacher, who told him: "Pursue, for you shall surely overtake and shall surely rescue."

"They were goin' on a rescue mission," Terry announced triumphantly, lapsing as he occasionally does into his version of a Jewish accent and gestures.

"And why did David fight?" Terry asked. "He wanted to save the wives and children. He did not want to surrender his children to the enemy."

The audience was totally caught up with his speech, even though they had heard it before. It is Terry's standard speech, and there are audio and videotapes of it in the homes of most of the people present. The listeners never tire of hearing the next part.

"What keeps you in the movement? We are doing it for our children and our children's children. Some of you have lost children, and you know what I'm talking about. Sometimes I think what would happen if I lost my baby. I can't even think about it. Jesus help us, folks," he moaned.

The threat of losing children is real and terrifying to evangelicals, who look upon others more worldly than they as having already lost theirs. In a religion with more than its share of naysaying rules, there is much to rebel against, and evangelicals live in constant fear that they will lose their children either through a lack of vigilance over their moral values or from too much vigilance. Pro-choicers are a good example of what has gone wrong, as Terry reminded the audience: "They have already sacrificed their children on the altar of idolatry."

He slammed his fist against the podium as he drove home his

message: "We—must—stop—the—child—killing. Those of you who try to protect your world and keep it just so, if you don't defeat child-killing, you won't have your little world. This is our last chance. If we don't save babies, our children will curse our memories.

"I want to take the weak, foolish, wormy types—you and me—and use us to change the course of history in a way that affects the next one hundred years."

The standing ovation was long and deafening. A sense of unity pervaded the sanctuary. After Terry left the altar, someone else would come up to make a plea for money and a collection would be taken. The church's baskets would be stuffed full of donations for Operation Rescue before the evening was over.

Money isn't a subject Terry likes to discuss, perhaps because he feels so vulnerable in this area. Operation Rescue alone among the leading pro-choice and pro-life groups does not evoke a nonprofit tax status. It operates under Terry's name, and all monies, many of which are received in cash, go to him personally. Terry insists his for-profit status keeps his enemies from seizing his assets, even though there is nothing inherent in this organizational structure that would protect him in that way.

While Terry expects his followers to pay their own fines and has no fund set up to help indigent rescuers pay fines, he has personally refused to pay his fines.

Not surprisingly, since Terry and Operation Rescue have been fined in several courts and states at this point, guessing how much money Operation Rescue has and where it is (at one point, no one could locate any bank accounts for Operation Rescue or Terry) has become a favorite pro-choice pastime.

Legal watchdog groups and lawyers who have brought suits against Operation Rescue speculate that it is a rich organization. In a deposition Terry gave in New York in 1989, he claimed he took in $300,000 in 1988, but most experts believe that figure is too low. Sergeant Pyrdum thinks $2 to $10 million would not be too high an estimate of Operation Rescue's annual income.

Pyrdum said, "Every time he went on Falwell's, or Bakker's, or

Swaggart's shows, he appealed for money. Just rattling the can from one of those viewer bases can let him walk away with a million."

In the course of talking with Terry's followers, I met several young women who said they sent $25 a month to Operation Rescue. Assuming that Terry has a fairly modest base of only 2000 supporters who send him $25 a month, then he collects $600,000 a year from them alone. Operation Rescue also gets injections of money every time Terry speaks before a big crowd like the one at Central Baptist Church, and he has often said that the money pours in after a successful, well-publicized rescue operation. Donations soar every time Randall Terry spends a night in jail.

This doesn't even count the big donors, such as the $10,000 in seed money that Jerry Falwell provided to help the group get started or the regular infusions, some reportedly as large as $60,000, that come from Tom Monaghan, president of Domino's Pizza and an ardent anti-abortion supporter.

Sensitive to the suggestion that he is becoming a rich man at the expense of his loyal followers, Terry has restricted talk about money by those who work for Operation Rescue. His staff will no longer discuss their earnings. Magera and Lucas, whom one would expect to be among his better-paid staff members, went out of their way to assure me of their poverty. Barbara Magera joked with me one day that she, too, would like to write a book. She would call it *I Could Be Making Money, But I've Decided to Make History Instead.* According to a deposition Terry gave in New York, Lucas earned $22,000 a year, but Lucas told me that he earned less than he had as a waiter in the Binghamton area.

Day Two of the trial was even more low key than Day One. Gone were the crowds of ardent supporters, and the media had dwindled to one or two lone reporters. Twenty minutes before the session began, there were no picketers outside the courthouse and only fifteen people waiting to be admitted to the courtroom. No photographers or videocams tailed Terry and his men as they walked to the courtroom on this day.

Among his hard core followers who were present, the big topic of conversation was how inspirational Terry's speech had been the previous night. The talk, as it often does among Operation Rescue followers, revolved around Terry. His emotional state, his views, what he had said recently, what he wanted or needed done, all are analyzed in minute detail. This morning, the women were worried about whether Terry was upset over the course of the trial. Yesterday, they said, he took time during his lunch break to explain to them that the court might not let him defend himself the way he needed to in order to be able to present the pro-life case.

The talk turned to the ten rescues planned for the weekend. Officially, Terry insists he has no national organization, that each group operates independently and the headquarters in Binghamton is merely a clearinghouse and information center that binds the various independent groups together. He has attempted to use this strategy in court to prove that he cannot be held responsible for the actions of other groups that just happen to call themselves Operation Rescue. But this was not the impression one gets from listening to his followers, who frequently reminisce about rescues they have participated in.

One follower who worked for Operation Rescue-Southern California proudly told me: "We don't make a move without him. During a rescue last month, people were on the telephone to him constantly, saying this has happened, that has happened, what do you want us to do now?"

A few minutes before the trial began, a handsome, Latino man wearing a court marshal's uniform slipped into the courtroom and took a seat in the back. He began talking to the man next to him. He said he wanted to be here today to let everyone know that he was sympathetic to their cause. "I'm all for abortion," he said, "but at age 30. Let people live until they're 30, and if they're bad, then flush them."

A young mother, who had driven forty miles with her two-year-old child, twisted in her chair toward the marshal and giggled, "I know what you mean. I'm a pro-lifer, and I'm for capital punishment. I know some people don't understand that, but it's how I feel." Then, obviously feeling she had spoken out of turn, she apologized for eavesdropping. The men barely acknowledged her presence before returning to their conversation.

The marshal continued: "I hear women will go underground if abortion is illegal, and that's okay. There's two things about that, as I see it. The first is the stigma will return to unwed women who get pregnant. A child is a precious thing to me. God put that seed there for a reason.

"The second thing is, let's say we lose a thousand women a year from underground abortions. We'd still be saving two hundred thousand—maybe even three hundred thousand—babies. I mean, the lives would still be there."

A solemn-faced Terry finally entered the courtroom. He nodded and smiled at me.

Judge Paez took his seat and the session started. He told the defendants he had done some research overnight and presumed they might have as well. For that reason, he would invite additional comment if anyone wished to speak. The fireworks began immediately.

When Terry raised his hand to speak, though, the judge admonished him to keep it short. Terry coyly asked, "Sir, I didn't take too long yesterday, did I?" When this met with the same blank response as his earlier attempts to ingratiate himself, he plowed ahead: "Judge, the issue is viability. We need to show that the clinic we picketed was doing abortions up to 24 weeks. We know they were because that's what their ad in the phone book says."

Terry's voice suddenly took on a humble tone. "Your honor, I had the privilege of being in Washington, D.C., for the Webster decision. I heard Blackmun say that Webster gutted Roe. And Rehnquist said the states' interest begins before viability."

A look of confusion momentarily crossed Judge Paez's face when Terry invoked Blackmun's name for the pro-life cause. Terry had said the same thing outside the Supreme Court on the day of the Webster decision, but no one knew enough then about the Webster decision to question him.

Now Paez informed Terry that Blackmun had not in fact said that Roe was overturned; that wasn't what the justice had meant when he said Roe was gutted. Terry was genuinely unable to let go of this idea, however, and kept insisting that the justice who had written the Roe opinion supported his belief that Roe was overturned.

Frustrated that Judge Paez didn't see things his way, Terry's voice took on an angry, then a condescending tone: "Judge, please try and grasp this. It's not the case that we're protesters. Your Honor can take a few hours and look at our videotape footage and our training manuals. We never mention the word protest or demonstration. We're not about protest. A rescue takes people from a place of danger to a place of safety. If you rule against us, not only have you denied us our defense, you've failed to see the purpose of our rescues."

It was his usual defense, to deny that he was a protester or even that he had practiced civil disobedience, but it is still shocking to hear if you've heard him say the exact opposite at a rally the night before.

Tensions heightened as Judge Paez obviously prepared to rule on the necessity defense. This single ruling would shape the course of the entire trial to come. Either Terry would be allowed to use the necessity defense to put the morality of abortion on trial or he would stand trial of the much more ignoble misdemeanor of trespass.

But in reality, much more was at stake, for Terry personally and for fundamentalism. Given a forum from which he could put abortion on trial, much as evolution had been put on trial some fifty years earlier in a Tennessee courtroom, Terry not only stood to become a hero to hundreds of thousands of fundamentalists across the country, but his defense of abortion could become their long-awaited vindication for their sixty-five years of suffering since the Scopes trial.

Terry, determined to have the last word, asked: "Your Honor, if Roe were overturned, could we be prosecuted like this?"

"I suspect you could."

Disgust and disagreement was written all over his face as he sat down.

Now it was Judge Paez's turn. "I know that the word abortion brings on high emotions. I respect that. But I'm a judge of law. Because of that, I have ruled out the necessity defense." Paez went on to cite a string of California cases that established that the necessity defense could not be used for political protest.

The judge was still speaking, but Terry had stopped listening. Red-faced, he shook his head in disbelief, and whirled in his chair to face the spectators, giving them a full view of his anger. For the first time that morning, he looked directly at his followers as they sat watching him in shocked silence.

Paez was still speaking: "A woman still has a right to an abortion in California up to 24 weeks. Webster did not change that."

Terry's anger spilled over outside the courtroom, where reporters and videocameras pressed close to him. Claiming that his defense has been destroyed, he asked:

"Can pro-lifers get a fair trial anywhere in this country? This legal arm of our government has become the lapdog of the death industry. This is just going to be a slam-bam, thank-you-ma'am trial."

He took the defeat hard. I saw him a few minutes after the press conference, slumped on a wooden bench outside the courtroom and looking like a high school basketball team's star player on an off night. His aides and lawyers clustered around him, trying to buoy his spirits and rally him to finish the fight. They talked eagerly of what could be salvaged of their original defense. He and the other defendants could still take the stand to explain their actions, that much the judge had promised. And Judge Paez had refused the city attorneys' request to prohibit them from praying at "strategic moments" during their arguments or from prominently displaying the Bible in the courtroom. That was a good sign. In the coming days of the trial, they could use their Bibles, they could use their Christianity, just as they had always planned to do.

Virtually overnight, the men reshaped their defense. They would argue that they had not resisted arrest, as charged, but rather, that they were defending themselves against police brutality. As a defense tactic, it would prove every bit as effective as the necessity defense. Effecting a martyred pose that served him well, in the coming days of the trial, Terry would manage to convince the jury that he was the abused rather than the abuser.

On Thursday, August 10, two days after Judge Paez ruled that the defendants could not use the necessity defense, Operation Rescue filed a lawsuit against the Los Angeles Police Department charging them with singling out Operation Rescue participants for unnecessary force, specifically the use of what police call pain-compliance techniques, which involved the application of increasingly painful increments of force when people failed to respond to officers' requests to move. The technique had been in use for several years by various police departments, who claimed there was less risk of injury with it than when people were dragged away bodily for arrest. The lawsuit had been in the works for several weeks, but it was nonetheless well-timed.

Operation Rescue also claimed it wanted to stop the use of nunchakus, wooden sticks about fifteen-inches long that were placed firmly along a person's arm and used to lift him out of a crowd and into a police van. The group went into federal court to request a restraining order that would stop the police from using these martial arts devices. The order was denied, but in papers filed in response to the order, Los Angeles Police Captain Patrick McKinley observed that "the demonstrators have an unusual capacity to withstand pain."

For their first defense witness, Terry and the other defendants called Captain McKinley, who was led to repeat his statement about their ability to withstand pain out of context on the witness stand. The jurors also watched Operation Rescue videotapes of the arrests, and were asked to observe that only pro-life activists were arrested. It was true: Representatives of the pro-choice forces had worked with the police for months to persuade them that they did not want to be arrested and in fact would help the police deter the pro-choice crowds from any kind of physical confrontation that might lead to arrest. Operation Rescue on the other hand invited arrest; it was their policy.

The videotapes plainly showed the use of the pain-compliance techniques. The jurors watched pictures of the police sticking a knuckle in a rescuer's ear, a finger in a nose, and putting nunchakus along a rescuer's arm to facilitate getting him into a police van. The defendants talked about their injuries—sore wrists from the nunchakus, one man's bloody nose, another's reported broken arm. The abuses, according to the defendants' testimony, were directed at those who were most ill-equipped to tolerate them—the women and the elderly.

Lost in the passion of the moment was the fact that despite a thorough police investigation, no one was ever shown to have suffered a fractured limb. There was no one in the courtroom to dispute the charge that the elderly and women were the special targets of the police; had there been, the jury would have learned that virtually no rescuers were elderly and that it was the men and not the women who occupied the trenches at a rescue.

The climax of the trial occurred August 31, when after nearly a month of other testimony, Terry took the stand. The courtroom was packed for the first time since the opening day of the trial. Terry was the last of the five defendants to testify.

Fewer than ten minutes into his testimony, Terry was in trouble with Judge Paez, as he had been throughout the trial, for using inflammatory language within hearing of the jury. This time, he had called a medical clinic an "aboratorium." On other occasions, he had insisted on calling abortion clinics "abortuariums" and "killing centers." Against the judge's warning, he had insisted on comparing legalized abortion to the Holocaust.

Terry tried to explain why he felt morally justified in blockading medical clinics during the Holy Week rescues even though a U.S. District Judge had issued a statewide injunction just days before the scheduled rescues forbidding Operation Rescue to do that.

At first he pled ignorance, claiming he had not known about the injunction. Besides, he told the jury, looking straight at them, he had been named in twenty other injunctions across the country forbidding him from rescue operations.

"The bottom line is that these injunctions are meaningless, and I give them no more attention than a stray piece of paper laying in the street." No federal judge, he said, can "tell us not to save babies."

In emotional tones, Terry described a Good Friday service held at the Heavenly Hall Church auditorium during the April Holy Week of Rescues. The service, which he called a "funeral," was like countless others held across the country for his followers and potential recruits. It was for Baby Choice, one of the two fetuses he traveled with. Terry's voice cracked as he described the service. "That night there were 2,000 of us filing past the dead baby in the coffin, and it took two hours for the crowd to file past," he said, his body gripped with sobs. Terry didn't tell the jury how he had sat on the altar under a spotlight at the piano playing hymns for the entire time, as people filed past him, too.

Judge Paez asked him if he would like a break.

"No," Terry sobbed, "I'll be okay."

The judge ordered a break. Throughout it, Terry remained on the witness stand, his back to a courtroom packed once again for his testimony with his followers. Blowing his nose with a handkerchief and rubbing his eyes with his fists, he sobbed, his body heaving, for the entire thirty-minute break. Several times, he could be heard singing to himself and praying.

The trial ended shortly after Terry's outburst, and then began the wait for the jury's verdict.

Despite Terry's presence as the centerpiece of the much-publicized "Let Them Live L.A." week, most of the planned events could only be described as flops. A major hitch occurred at the last minute when the archdiocese lawyers got nervous about letting Operation Rescue use its facilities, and several of the events had to be rescheduled from Catholic churches to fundamentalist churches.

Over 900 people showed up at Central Baptist in Pomona to hear Terry preach on the first night of the trial, but after that, the numbers steadily dwindled. Fewer than 125 people showed up for the evening prayer and repentance service on Wednesday and the survivors' march on Thursday, and no more than a dozen people came to the cemetery for the memorial service for 17,000 dead fetuses on Tuesday.

The numbers were up again—2,000 to 3,000—on Friday night at the pre-rescue rally, but that was because Archbishop Roger Mahoney was a guest speaker, along with Terry. The archbishop was speaking out publicly for the first time in support of Operation Rescue.

On Saturday, Operation Rescue struck nine rather than the ten clinics it had announced, but this was still more than it had ever hit in one day—and more than their numbers could support, as it turned out. The effectiveness of the protests was further diminished by several odd mistakes of the kind that Operation Rescue did not usually make.

The Sherman Oaks Clinic was among those blockaded, for example, even though it was not doing any abortions that day. Operation Rescue, which had to strike clinics that were actually doing abortions in order to be able to claim they had saved any lives, usually went to great lengths to make sure any clinic they struck had at least one abortion scheduled on the day of a protest. In fact, often a rescuer made an appointment for an abortion at a clinic that Operation Rescue planned to blockade to be sure that at least one abortion was planned for the day of a rescue.

Operation Rescue also struck a clinic that was closed. While the clinic defenders waited for the rescuers at an open clinic a block away, the pro-life group belligerently stood its ground at the closed clinic. The field marshals yelled at their followers through bullhorns: "The pro-aborts are at the wrong clinic."

Observers, including Betty Ann Downing, noted that Operation Rescue was moving the same people around from clinic to clinic, a sign that their numbers were too low to cover all the clinics at once. Their numbers also seemed to be down from past demonstrations.

Through all nine rescues, Terry was chauffeured from site to site like an honored guest. He didn't personally direct any of the rescues. In fact, he rarely directs rescues these days. He spent the last two hours of the downtown Los Angeles rescue sitting with his co-defendant Jeff White in a McDonald's across the street from a clinic.

After four days of deliberation, in a verdict that shocked many people, especially the pro-choice activists, Terry and his co-defendants were acquitted of the charges of trespass and resisting arrest. The jury deadlocked 8–4 on the conspiracy charges against Terry, White, and McMonagle, causing the judge to declare a mistrial. In effect, the jury had bought the defendants' arguments that they were the victims of police brutality.

Terry's victory was short-lived, though. Two weeks later, he stood trial again, in Atlanta, his old nemesis, on similar charges. This time, without any charges of police brutality to wave in front of the jury, Terry was unable to muster the sympathy he had in Los Angeles. He was found guilty.

On October 5, 1989, after pleading with the judge to grant him leniency, Terry was sentenced to a year in jail on each charge, the sentences to run concurrently, and two $500 fines. The judge offered to suspend the sentence if Terry would agree to stay out of the Atlanta metropolitan area for two years.

When Terry declared he couldn't pay the fine as a matter of conscience, he was taken to Fulton County Jail. Although his previous pattern had been to spend a few days in jail and then quietly get himself sprung, this time he planned to serve his entire sentence, in part because it was the only way to avoid being banned from Atlanta for two years. Besides, sentences like his were usually automatically reduced by two-thirds, so Terry had reason to believe he would be a free man in four months.

While incarcerated in Fulton County Jail, Terry seemed, not for the first time in his brief career as a protester, to let himself become mired in petty grievances. In a series of letters written "in the name of Jesus from the Fulton County jail," he attempted to stir up sympathy not for the pro-life cause, but for himself, maltreated by prison officials who denied him the use of a fax machine and wouldn't let him give interviews to reporters.

Terry's antipathy toward the Atlanta police grew even stronger, and he became more determined than ever to "take Atlanta." Operation Rescue hotlines around the country buzzed in early January of 1990 with a plea asking "single" volunteers to move to Atlanta for a year. What the hotlines didn't say was that Randall Terry had unfinished, personal business there.

Terry also seemed to be edging Operation Rescue toward an even more fanatic position. In December, 1989, the Atlanta hotline message bristled against a government that "has aligned itself with the children of Satan" and Operation Rescue followers were urged to "join us...as we stand against those who worship the goddess and continue to practice their vile sacrifices."

From Fulton County jail, he wrote his followers: "I am deeply troubled by what I see happening to the Rescue movement nationwide. In city after city (with a couple of exceptions), the numbers of rescuers are shrinking, and the average number of rescue missions per week is dropping."

On January 31, 1990, Terry let an anonymous supporter pay his fine so he could leave jail. He went directly to Washington, D.C., where he held a press conference to announce the closing of Operation Rescue's Binghamton office. Terry claimed the headquarters were $70,000 in debt. He insisted the rescue movement would not affect the efforts of his 125 local affiliates.

Terry's scorned mentor, Joseph Scheidler, said of the closing: "Rescues are now a phenomenon happening all over the country. You don't need to get directions from Binghamton."

The pro-choice groups were even more cynical, insisting that this was another attempt on Terry's part to manipulate the press and his followers. "Anything to get in the news," Molly Yard, president of NOW commented. "We know churches take up collections for him. He's not going to be without money."

Lawyers who had successfully brought suit against Operation Rescue in 1988 (and had been frustrated when none of the fines were collected) pointed out that the U.S. attorney's office in Manhattan had recently gone after Operation Rescue's assets to settle one $50,000 fine. While Terry was in jail, seven thousand dollars was seized in an Operation Rescue bank account. "They're trying to escape responsibility for their actions. This is a clever strategy to avoid all the court actions we have against them," said Mary Gundrum, an attorney for the Center for Constitutional Rights who was involved in a suit against Operation Rescue.

It remains to be seen whether Terry has outsmarted his enemies or whether, as he said during his speech in Pomona, he has simply burned bright and is gone.

5 | Foot Soldier

Moira

MOIRA BENTSON,* a sweet-voiced, fallen-away Catholic, is a foot soldier in Randall Terry's army. She is part of a battalion possibly numbering in the thousands but more likely in the hundreds of fair-faced, naive young men and women, moderate sinners even by their own descriptions, who nevertheless lived their lives a little too fast and easy for a little too long. Lost in the Seventies, they sought repentence in the Eighties. And Randall Terry was there to give it to them. He was their Prophet, some said their Messiah.

Moira first met Terry in 1987 during the annual Right-to-Life March. She was ripe for the meeting and for his message. Opposed to abortion since she was sixteen, at age twenty-nine, she had written more than her share of letters to the President and other high government officials pleading with them to do something. Even though she was beginning to feel that nothing would ever change, she had recently signed yet another petition, this one for a fundamentalist group called Last Days that operated out of Tyler, Texas.

When a contingent from Last Days had decided to travel to Washington for the 1987 Right-to-Life March, Moira knew she wanted to go with them and somehow managed to scrape together enough money for the trip. She had enough to pay for

*Some names and identifying details have been changed.

173

her room if she shared it with someone and to buy skimpy meals, which was all she was used to; but best of all, someone had offered her a free ride. Almost free, that is; she had to buy a tank of gas.

The group hoped to present its petition personally to President Ronald Reagan. Pro-lifers had waited a long time to see someone in the White House who truly supported their cause, and Ronald Reagan was their man. Jubilant over his election, they had escalated their activities, with every expectation he would do what he could—through Supreme Court appointees, through legislative action, maybe even by signing a bill—to bring about their goal of making abortion illegal once again. There was even speculation that it might happen all at once instead of step-by-step, if they could come up with a bill that Reagan would push through Congress. After all, hadn't seven humanist, liberal judges managed to make abortion legal overnight? All anti-abortionists agreed that had been a dark moment in our nation's history, but with Reagan's election they believed that victory was at hand.

A rumor circulated, as it had every year since he was elected, that the president would make a surprise appearance before the marchers. That was part of the reason Moira wanted to go. She didn't want to miss an opportunity to hear him. The rumor proved to be unfounded, but the president did send the group a personally taped message, which was almost as good. It was played during the official program held on the green in front of the Capitol. It was the first time that a president of the United States had ever spoken to the thousands of marchers since they had begun their long, uphill struggle in 1973 to make abortion illegal again.

Moira found herself marching alongside a group she had never heard of before, called Operation Rescue. Their leader Randall Terry was going to preach on the steps of the Supreme Court later in the day and they urged her to hear him. She would, they promised, be absolutely dumbfounded by his talk. Terry wasn't like the other speakers, the ones who were part of the official program. One reformer solemnly told her his message was completely different, a true and radical call to arms.

At the end of the rally, more out of curiosity than anything else, Moira hung around the steps of the Supreme Court, hoping to hear this Randall Terry speak. When he did, she was not disappointed. His speech, his manner, were completely different from anyone else she had ever heard talk about abortion. Tears ran down his cheeks as he described the millions of fetuses that died every year because women aborted them. He raged at them, the people who had gathered to hear him speak. He begged them to do something concrete and real to stop the killing of innocent "babies." He told them they weren't good Christians if they didn't act. "If we say it's murder," he asked the crowd, "then why don't we act like it is?"

Moira thought, "This man is talking action, not just talking." This was real Christianity, the very thing she had been longing for.

Moira had been feeling this way for years, and she had been doing her part, but until she met Terry she had not seen anyone else as worked up over this issue as she was. She agreed with everything he said. Real Christians didn't just stand around and let their fellow human beings die. They did something to stop it. But all the Christians Moira knew, the "rich Christians" that she especially hated, just sat in their churches and did not help poor people at all. She, on the other hand, who had little money and always seemed to be scraping just to feed herself and her little girl, still managed to eke a few dollars here and there to give to groups that were fighting abortion. And now Terry was suggesting not only that she give her money but that she give of herself as well.

After he spoke, Randy—everyone told her to call him that— talked to the small, admiring crowd that gathered around him. He told them about his plans for a new group he was organizing. It was called Operation Rescue. He gave it that name because the group was going to stage rescues all over the country, huge demonstrations that would close down the nation's abortion clinics, or "aborttuaries," as he called them. If the government could not or would not stop the killing, they as Christian soldiers would form an army that would.

Terry admitted there would be some danger in becoming one of his followers. He was asking people to commit civil disobedience, to risk arrest. If hundreds of people gathered outside "killing centers" around the country, the police would be there to meet them and would probably even arrest them. That was what he wanted, to fill up the nation's jails with anti-abortion protesters. To make the police let drug dealers and murderers go if they had to put the pro-life protesters in jail. Then, he told them, the American people would sit up and take note.

He had been jailed once for twenty days in Binghamton, New York, where he lived and where Operation Rescue's national headquarters were located. He'd even written a book while he was in jail, just like the Reverend Martin Luther King, Jr.

After the speech, Moira was thrilled when Randy talked to her personally. He asked if she were married, and when she told him no, not at the moment, but she had a little girl from a previous marriage who meant everything to her, he seemed especially pleased. He asked her little girl's name and how old she was. Then he asked if she would come to New York in November 1988 for a big rescue he was planning. He had been running some "field tests," he told her, in Binghamton, but this would be his first major test in a big city. Her presence in New York would be important, something worthwhile she could do if she were truly serious about working to end the killing industry.

If they made a good showing in New York, the media would have to pay attention, and it would send a message to America. The message would be that if they could close down the killing industry in New York, then they could go into any city and close down its abortuaries. And that's exactly what he planned to do.

But to do all this, Terry told her, he needed bodies, enough people to impress the media, who would then pick up their story and give Operation Rescue credibility. What the group lacked most now was credibility. They were still small, just starting out, and no one even knew they existed. That's why he was going around the country personally recruiting members, talking to people like herself and even whole congregations, persuading them to join him and really do something. He hoped Moira would talk up what he was doing at her church.

He'd been curious about that too, asking her how long she had walked with God and what church she belonged to. He had seemed really impressed when she told him she went to Mt.

Paran, a big church with over 10,000 members in Atlanta, where she lived. When he told her good-by, he had patted her arm and looked her right in the eye and said, "God bless."

Moira understood what Randy was saying. When he walked away from her a few minutes later to talk to some other people, she believed he had offered her nothing less than a chance to change the course of American history. She promised Terry she would do her best to come to New York for him.

Moira Bentson, grew up in Newport Beach, California, an affluent community in southern California. She was the product of a broken home, twice broken, actually, once by her parents' divorce when she was eight, and repeatedly by her parents' ambivalence toward their children.

After her parents' divorce, Moira and her brother went to live with her mother's parents for a while. Her father, who was a short-order cook, wasn't around much. When her mother pulled her life together three years later, she collected Moira and her brother and took them home to a small, shabby apartment she had rented. It was only a few miles from her grandparents', so she continued to see a lot of them.

They lived on what her mother could earn working as a secretary, and on alimony and child support. They couldn't count on the latter; more often than not her father didn't bother to send it, and after a while, her mother had no idea where to find him to collect it. It was tough making ends meet, unless her mother had a boyfriend. Then there was more money, and her mother was happier.

Moira, who was a timid child, found her mother difficult to live with. She felt overpowered by her and resented her mother for constantly belittling her. Moira grew up feeling she wasn't quite good enough for whatever she tried or whomever she wanted to love.

Her mother had an opinion on everything. "My mom thinks any woman with four or five kids is retarded. She thinks you should only have two children. I was supposed to be aborted," Moira told me. "My Mom was real young when she got pregnant with me. She wasn't married, and she wasn't ready to deal with kids. She wanted to get an abortion, but my dad wanted to marry her. He talked her into going through with the marriage."

She always resented him for doing that and mostly took it out on her children. She never raised a hand to hurt them physically but never stopped battering them emotionally. Never did she miss an opportunity to remind Moira how much she had ruined her life.

Moira preferred living with her grandparents, even though her grandmother was stern and perhaps too rigid to be rearing two young children. She was always passing judgment on someone, whether it was Moira's mother, one of her favorite subjects for disdain, or her neighbors, whose comings and goings she obsessively tracked. Her grandfather was less stern, but paid Moira and her brother little attention. He didn't seem to know what to say to them.

While living with her grandparents, Moira had occasionally been taken to the Roman Catholic Church they belonged to. When her grandparents didn't go to Church, her Aunt Rose sometimes stopped by on Sunday morning to take her niece and nephew with her to services. Moira liked going to church. She was baptized, something her mother had neglected to do when she was born, and she took First Communion while she was living with her grandparents.

By the time she went to live with her mother again, Moira had absorbed enough religion to know that she disapproved of her mother's liberated life. She was shocked when her mother took up with a group of nudists, attending their camps and other activities and touting their philosophy to her children. Moira resented that her mother never took her to Church. "My mother was worldly, and it was me, me, me first," she said.

Even though she disapproved of her mother more intensely every day, Moira herself grew wilder as she entered her teens— "the way California kids are," she recalled. She was hardly alone among her peers when she started having sex with her boyfriend when she was sixteen. It was easy enough to bring her boyfriend home with her after school when her mother was still at work, and she sometimes sneaked him into her bedroom at night when her mother was out, which was often.

Her mother never checked on her when she got home.

Besides, Moira made no secret about what she and her boy-friend were doing and even asked her mother to help her get the Pill so she wouldn't get pregnant. She was surprised when her mother got angry because she was having sex and refused to let her take the Pill.

"I should have used something else, but I didn't. I was stupid, and I got pregnant right away," she said.

Her boyfriend Jimmy was a young Marine four years older than she who was stationed at Camp Pendleton. His parents weren't divorced, but they fought all the time, and he had enlisted right out of high school so he wouldn't have to live at home anymore.

Moira had met him through the high school ROTC program she had joined. She was a "junior jarhead" she proudly told me, and he was a full-fledged "jarhead," the name Southern Californians use for Marines.

When she told Jimmy she was pregnant, he was happy right away. He said he wanted to marry her, and that they would have a really good life in the Marines. Moira dropped out of high school, and she and Jimmy began making plans to get married.

Her mother had other ideas, though. Determined that Moira not ruin her life with an early marriage like she had, she told her daughter she would have an abortion. She insisted, in fact, and stormed around the house for days raging that she was too young to be a grandmother. When Moira told her mother about her plans to get married, she just got angrier, demanding that Moira give her the telephone number of Jimmy's parents. She called and tried to get them to help her pay for an abortion. When they said they didn't care what happened, she exploded again and insisted she would pay for the abortion herself.

Without consulting Moira, she made an appointment for her at a local women's clinic. Moira was confused and did not know whether she would—or could—keep the appointment. She could see how she and her brother had ruined her mother's life, and she wasn't sure that she didn't want an abortion. At first, she had felt very grown up at the thought of getting married and being a wife and mother, but then she looked at how her mother's life had turned out, and she wasn't so sure. But every time she and her mother talked, they got into a fight, and Moira couldn't tell her how she was really feeling. There was no one, in fact, with whom she could discuss her doubts.

Even after she went to live with her mother, her aunt had still come by sometimes to take Moira and her brother to church. Her brother refused to go, but Moira went. She liked the people who paid attention to her after the service, and she liked the service too. It was pretty.

Now with her pregnancy hanging over her head, Moira began to think about how her local priest had railed against abortion a few months ago when it was suddenly legalized. He had said that only an irresponsible woman would not find room in her life to love one small child. And children, he said, repaid all the time and attention they took. The rewards of being a parent were among the greatest any human being could know. As Moira thought back over the priest's sermon, she came to the conclusion that she agreed with everything he had said. She, too, thought abortion was wrong. She couldn't give up her baby; she wanted it. It would be someone of her own to love and care for.

Moira worried that her mother could force her to have an abortion, especially since she was a minor. She didn't know where to turn. Two days before she was scheduled to have the operation, out of desperation, she walked into a Right-to-Life meeting sponsored by a group of local Catholics. She had read about the group in a church flyer. At the meeting, everyone listened while she talked about her problem. When she told them she was three months pregnant, they showed her pictures of a three-month-old fetus so she could see what her baby looked like. Moira broke down and cried.

She told the sympathetic people who surrounded her and were patting and hugging her that she was afraid her mother would force her to go through with an abortion. Could she do that? The people assured her that her mother could not, that it was her decision entirely. Moira walked out of the meeting with a new strength. She realized she would never go through with the abortion, no matter what her mother wanted.

A few days later, Moira and her boyfriend drove to Mexico, where they were married by a local justice of the peace. When she returned, she did not go home but lived instead with Jimmy, who had already rented an apartment for them off the base.

Three weeks after she got married, Moira enrolled in a special high school for pregnant teens. She had no idea that her mother had reported her as a missing child, and that the police regularly checked the records of teens attending the high school for runaways. They picked her up two days after she started school, and since she was still a minor, took her home to live with her mother. Because she had married without a parent's permission, her mother managed to have her marriage annulled.

Moira lived with her mother for three months, until she was six months pregnant. "I made her life so miserable that she finally gave up and told me I could get married again. At first Moira went to her priest and asked him to marry her, but he refused to do so when he saw that she was six months pregnant. Then she and Jimmy went to Las Vegas and got married again.

This time they lived in Camp Pendleton base housing, a nice two-bedroom apartment that Moira spent most of her time fixing up for the baby. Jessica was born in the spring of 1977. And the nice thing was the Marines paid for everything.

Although Moira hated to admit it, marriage was harder than she had ever imagined it would be. They moved every two years, and Jimmy was gone a lot. She didn't get along very well by herself, especially after she had Jessica. Tough as she found marriage, though, she liked being a mother. She never took out her depressions or bad moods on Jessica the way her mother had on her. And she was a much more relaxed and casual parent than her mother had been.

In 1978, when Jessica was a year old, Jimmy got out of the Marines, and they all moved to Atlanta so he could take a job with a computer company there. Even though things should have been better, because now they wouldn't be moving every couple years, the move proved to be more than the marriage could handle. Actually, their marriage had been coming apart for some time, and it finally collapsed shortly after the move.

When she and Jimmy divorced in December 1979, she was twenty-two and the mother of a two-year-old daughter, whom she would now have to rear alone the way her mother had reared her.

Marriage had stolen Moira's teen years, and after her divorce she became determined to make up for lost time. "I don't know if you've ever been divorced so you know what it's like," she told me as we chatted one June afternoon, "but I went through a wild period. Everyone does. I cut my hair, got long nails, and partied for about five years. I lived with different men."

And for a while, she enjoyed it. "I seemingly had a good life, at least that's how I acted when I was out." But eventually, Moira discovered that the euphoria she felt when she was out partying didn't last when she was faced with the day-to-day responsibility of running her life and taking care of her child. "When I was home, it was different. I was miserable."

Bit by bit, Moira's party-girl facade crumpled. She was consumed, once again, by the feelings of insecurity she had experienced throughout childhood. An old familiar feeling that something was missing in her life settled over her and this time, it refused to budge. Since she had been a little girl living with her mother, Moira had struggled with feelings that she wasn't as good as everyone else—or as good as she could be. That's why she had taken so much comfort in the Catholic Church. The Church had shown her how to be good, and had made her feel like she was someone.

But when the local priest had refused to marry her because she was pregnant, she had "condemned" the Church and vowed she would never return. The Right-to-Life group had been there for her when she needed them, but Moira couldn't be a reformer when she felt her own life was in such disarray. How could she help others when she was too paralyzed to help herself, when she couldn't even pull her own life together? She was looking for someone or something to reform her, not the other way around.

However low she felt, though, she never stopped looking for the answer. Her search was the one organizing force in her untidy, disheveled life. Like many people who came of age in the 1970s, Moira turned to the Eastern religions, which she now believes were cults. For the next three years, her life was taken over by a series of gurus whose names she no longer recalls.

Moira recalls somewhat sheepishly that she talked to spirits. "Yes, I spoke to spirits. There were four spirits I spoke to, and then two spirits." Actually, there were lots of different spirits with whom she communed, but now that she is a born-again Christian, she says it is a part of her life she would prefer to forget.

The mysticism didn't provide her with the self-discipline she was so desperately seeking. "I rolled from one cult to another trying to find God. I was always looking for God. I felt there had to be a God. But I still went to bed at night saying I'm not good enough. I wasn't disciplined. I couldn't get up early enough to meditate. I didn't do my mantras like I was supposed to." She did go to many weekend retreats; they soon replaced the wild parties in her life.

Through it all, Moira was never unhappy with her decision to have her daughter. Jessie was the one thing in the morning to get up for. After her marriage broke up, they often lived hand to mouth. There were times when over an entire week, they ate only potato chips, or when she and Jessie had only a bag of oranges to last for several days. It nearly killed her when Jessie needed shoes she could not afford to buy, but through it all, she had no regrets about her decision to be a mother. When she was her wildest and when she was at her most mystic, she still managed to take care of Jessie. Jessie was a pretty child, just as Moira had been, pretty enough so that Moira had turned down several offers to buy her over the years.

Moira worked at a series of odd jobs, often as a carpenter and sometimes as a car mechanic, skills she says she acquired from living alone after her marriage dissolved. Moira dreamed of a better, more stable job, had difficulty finding anything without a high school diploma. She thought about going back to school, but she never seemed to get her life organized enough to do that. Some day, she kept promising herself, she would go back to school.

One day Moira was befriended by a woman she often saw at the local health food store. The friendship started slowly, with nods when they passed in the aisles, and brief conversations in the check-out line as they waited to pay for their groceries. At first they shared snatches of their lives with one another, but soon they were visiting each other at their homes. It was one of those friendships where they replayed their entire lives for each other over the course of several long evenings. Dee was a good listener, and although Moira sometimes thought she was kind of boring, she liked having someone to talk to. Dee would brew a pot of cinnamon and apple tea, and the two women would sit and talk for hours.

Eventually, Dee, who at forty-six was twice-divorced and had no children of her own, even began to offer to babysit Jessie when Moira went on weekend retreats. "I thought she was stupid to watch my daughter for no pay, but if she wanted to, I let her," Moira said. Jessie was always happy and well-cared for when she returned, and gradually this softened her attitude toward this woman who went out of her way to make Moira's life easier.

When they did talk about Dee's life, it was about her religion. Dee was a born-again Christian who never hid the fact that she was trying to convert Moira. But Dee was smart enough to keep her efforts at converting her friend low key. "When I came home from my weekend retreats, she would read to me from the Bible, and I would let her for awhile. She never pressured me. When I said, 'Okay, that's enough,' she quit. She kept loving me, though. I know that now."

Dee also introduced Moira to a man whom she describes as "an old hippy." Like her, Ben was divorced and rearing a child alone. They began to trade babysitting and gradually became friends. "He took me to Christian concerts. I was real surprised to learn that they had some good music, and that this old hippy liked it."

Even though they lived in different worlds, he never reproached her for her beliefs. Like Dee, he took care of her daughter while she went to weekend retreats. "He saw my picture of the Ascended Master, but he never criticized it."

One year when Ben asked her what she would like for Christmas, she teased him, saying, "Whatever you do, don't give me a cross. I'll give it back." He gave her a cross, and true to her word, she gave it back.

Meanwhile, Dee was still in her life, gently trying to pull her into the Christian fold. At first, she asked Moira to pick her up at church. Happy to oblige, Moira always sat outside in her car waiting for her friend. Then Dee asked her to come inside for a few minutes at the end of the service, and Moira thought why not. If nothing else, she would show Dee that this tactic wouldn't work. She came in and sat in the back of the church.

Dee began introducing her to people she knew in the congregation. They always took great interest in Moira, and in Jessie, too, for that matter. Bit by bit, Moira was warming to what she saw and experienced at the fundamentalist church. It was so different, so nonjudgmental, compared to what she remembered of the Catholicism she grew up with.

For one thing, there was no criticism, only understanding and sympathy. She thought people would look down at her for how she lived, for being a single mother and a divorced woman, but they didn't. There was a real sense of community, and she seemed welcome to join it or not, as she chose. For the first time in her life, she felt approval from people for her struggle to make sense of her life. The people she met seemed to be struggling with theirs, too.

For a long time, though, Moira would not let herself trust what was happening. She was sure that at any moment one of these kind, sympathetic women would turn into her mother, demanding and critical. Unable to believe these people were as sincere as they seemed, she challenged the friendships she was offered. Each time she moved one step closer, she pushed herself two steps away. "Dee kept asking me to pick her up at church. After a while, I didn't like that because I could see what she was doing. I wanted to resist. I'd stall before going to pick her up. Then I'd drink a few beers. That gave me the courage to tell myself I could get up and leave at any time. But God has a sense of humor. Did you know that? And one night when I went to pick up Dee, God picked me up instead and took me into that church and sat me down right in the middle of the aisle. I'd been taught you couldn't leave a church service, so I just sat there."

That was the beginning of a new life for Moira. Within weeks, she was asking her old hippy if she could have her cross back, this time so she could wear it proudly. "I was finally saved during a big service with lots of important people. There was a local radio talk show host, who was saved that night, too. When the preacher asked who wanted to be saved, I stood up and walked down the aisle and stood beside the talk show host and said yes."

Since Moira was saved three years ago, she says her life has turned around. "It was like someone put rose-colored glasses on me. I used to hate rich people, especially rich Christians, but I didn't anymore. Friends had to be there for me or I would dump them like that. I didn't have anything to do with them if they weren't always there for me. After I got saved, I called up everyone I was on the outs with and made up with them. Those rose-colored glasses were everything."

Like most born-again Christians, Moira immersed herself in the culture, going to Christian bookstores and buying books like Mary Pride's *The Way Home: Beyond Feminism and Back to Reality*, which began: "Today's women are the victims of the second biggest con game in history. (The first was when the serpent persuaded Eve she needed to upgrade her lifestyle and 'become like God.')"

The book went on to disparage "uncommitted sex," "contract marriages" in which each partner has "a sharp eye out for his or her rights," and birth control, which Pride considered "the mother of abortion." Even seeking to space one's family came in for criticism when Pride pronounced it an attempt "to usurp God's sovereignty by self-crafting one's family." Moira also took several classes in parenting at her church, which showed her, she says, how to be a better mother.

When she returned to Atlanta after meeting Terry, she was less sure whether she could become involved in Operation Rescue in the way he wanted. Her problem, as always, was money. She couldn't afford to travel to New York in November, or to risk spending much time in jail. There was no one but her to support her daughter.

Moira spent the next few months wavering back and forth about whether she would go, but then just a few days before the November rescues, fate stepped in to tell her that going to New York was the right thing to do. "I didn't want to drive, but a friend said she would. I was still undecided, but then the day before the New York rescue, I met a guy from Florida who wanted to go. I knew I was meant to go, and we drove to New York together."

New York was Moira's first rescue. She attended the rally the night before, and then got up at 4 a.m. to go to the rescue. At the rescue, she and the other women formed a prayer column, standing off to one side while the men locked arms and blocked the entrance to the clinic. For hours she stood there with her arms raised singing Hosannah and "Jesus Loves the Little Children."

At the rally, she walked up to Randy to remind him who she was. He said he remembered her and thanked her for coming so far to help. He asked how Jessie was and told her to remember she was doing this for her and for Jessie's children. Randy thanked her again for coming, and when she told him she'd driven all night to get there, he yelled "Praise God" in such a loud voice that other people looked at them.

Randy led the rescue personally and she saw how forceful he was as a leader. Over and over, she heard his voice on a bullhorn, giving them directions and assuring them that this was the right thing to do. When the police started to make arrests, she heard him yelling: "Go limp, go limp, and remember, you do not have a name until we tell you that you have a name." Although there were many arrests, Moira managed to escape, perhaps because she was only in the prayer column.

After hearing Terry speak again, she came back to Atlanta, if anything, even more imbued with his message than she had been when she met him in Washington five months earlier. "I thought that God talks, sometimes even in an audible voice. I thought I'd be willing to do this for a year. God is telling me to give a year of my life. I knew I would give up a lot to do it. I'd never liked Christians before because they weren't willing to stand up and give up anything. I hated Christians. I see real Christians as being willing to follow."

After New York, Moira poured herself into her work for Operation Rescue, spending all her spare time in the office and attending every rescue. The rescues seemed to come one right after another, especially during the summer of 1989 when Operation Rescue staged its biggest action to date outside the Democratic National Convention. After that, they targeted several of Atlanta's clinics for ongoing protests. Moira, who became a regular fixture at the rescues, also was a regular at the Fulton County Jail. She was arrested repeatedly, and like all rescuers, claims not to remember how many times she has gone to jail.

Moira developed something of an expertise in sidewalk counseling, a kind of direct intervention whereby a rescuer works to dissuade women from entering a clinic to get an abortion. Sidewalk counseling has gone on since the first picketers appeared in front of abortion clinics, but Operation Rescue was the first group to incorporate it into its training manual so all rescuers could use the same techniques.

Chapter 5 of the Operation Rescue training manual, in fact, is devoted entirely to sidewalk counseling. From it Moira learned to tell the pregnant woman: "You're beautiful, and you've got a beautiful baby inside of you, one that will make you proud some day. If you had a little window over your womb, you wouldn't be here."

She learned to be aggressive when she did sidewalk counseling. The manual urged persistence: "If she tells you she doesn't want to talk, DON'T say 'OK' and walk away. Be politely persistent... Your second or third effort might wear down her defenses."

Counselors were given specific arguments to counter a woman's responses. If a woman said she could not afford a baby, Moira assured her that Operation Rescue would help her with food, clothing, and baby furniture, whatever she needed. Although Terry has said he does not believe in public aid, rescuers are taught to tell women they will help them apply for public aid.

A woman who was worried about finishing her education was told that she would "definitely be able to finish the term you are in, possibly the year. At that point, you can give birth, maybe miss a term or two and then return to school."

Sidewalk counselors were taught to reassure a woman who was worried about her career that it didn't have to end because she had a baby. Counselors were to say: "Many, many women have both a career and a baby and are happy with both. Others have done it, so can you." If all else fails, counselors were supposed to tell women that if they killed their child, their careers would become a bitter taste in their mouths.

Through Operation Rescue Moira learned something she had long suspected, namely, that no woman normally wanted to have an abortion, but that they were pressured into doing so by their boyfriends, husbands, or parents. She could empathize with that, since she had almost been pressured into having one by her own mother. "My mother still thinks I should have had an abortion," she said.

Moira liked doing sidewalk counseling because it gave her a chance to deliver Operation Rescue's message in a very direct way. She asked me if I'd ever seen Baby Choice, one of two 22-week old fetuses that Operation Rescue displays at press conferences and rallies. That Baby Choice is a female is of special significance to her, an ironic reminder that feminists are killing their own kind.

When Moira did not work as a sidewalk counselor, she joined the others in the trenches, crawling forward on her hands and knees, grasping the legs of a woman trying to enter the clinic to slow her down and calling out "Hail Mary" or "Praise you, Lord; praise you, Jesus" as she let herself be dragged by the woman trying to enter the clinic. Sometimes she sat in front of the door of an abortion clinic, her arms rigidly locked with those of other protestors, singing "Jesus Loves the Little Children" over and over again for hours.

Like most Operation Rescue people, Moira believes that most persons who are pro-choice hold that view only because they are ill-informed about abortion. "I believe a majority of people do not approve of abortion. People who support abortion only support the 2 percent that are done because of rape or incest. Most people don't get involved enough to find out that women are really asking for abortion on demand." Furthermore, Moira believes most women do not appreciate the dangers abortion poses. "A woman recently died in Macon of a botched abortion," she told me.

Moira is soft-spoken about her beliefs. She explains what she knows and believes about abortion with an air of quiet assurance that contrasts to the kind of angry, frenzied approach many pro-life people take. Her self-assurance eventually led

Operation Rescue to send her out on speaking engagements all over Georgia. Often Moira spoke at rescues. Whether she was sidewalk counseling or talking to a group of women, Moira also had another weapon she could use, one that few born-again women have at their disposal. Moira had actually had an abortion.

Three years ago Moira was raped. She was in Marietta, an Atlanta suburb, at a party one night. Her date drank too much, and when he stopped the car on the way home, she bolted. Alone on a dark road at night, she started walking, hoping she would come to a gas station so she could use a pay phone to call a friend to pick her up. A truck driver came along and offered her a ride, which she accepted. "He picked me up, and he raped me, and he left me," she recalled. "I found a phone and called a friend who picked me up and took me home. He offered to stay with me, but I wanted him to leave. I spent twelve hours sleeping, but then I had to get up and go get my daughter. So I got up and showered."

The next morning, when she realized what had happened to her, she called several police precincts in a vain attempt to get help. "The police wouldn't help. I didn't know exactly where I was when I was raped. They all listened to my story and wanted me to go find the area by myself and come back and tell them where I was raped. That man who raped me had a certain kind of truck. It was very unusual. I could have found him. They could have found him.

"The police were also mad at me because I took a shower. They said I was stupid not to go to a hospital. But I had bruises and scratches and I needed to take a shower to treat them. I wasn't thinking.

"I gave up on the police. I didn't go to any rape crisis center. I just went over to my babysitter's and got my daughter. As a single parent, you just have to go on, and I did."

Six weeks after the rape, Moira experienced some genital soreness. Realizing that something was wrong, she went to the health department to be tested, and soon got confirmation for what she suspected: she had gotten a venereal disease from the rapist. She doesn't remember what the disease was, but she says the person she talked to at the health department told her it would never go away. "I felt awful when I heard that. I thought, I'm trash."

Over the next few weeks, a bad situation got even worse as Moira gradually realized she was pregnant. "I was afraid to tell anyone in the church. I didn't know they would be there for me. I thought they would be like the Catholic Church. The woman already knows she messed up. She doesn't need the Church to tell her. I never did tell them. It wasn't obvious they'd be there. I got counseling from the cult people. They said get an abortion."

A friend gave Moira the name of a clinic where abortions were provided on a sliding fee scale. Moira had no money to pay for a private abortion. She made the appointment for three days hence, and then anguished about whether she really could go through with the operation. She hoped someone at the clinic would help her make up her mind.

"I kept the appointment at the clinic. They always assume you're there for an abortion. They don't really talk to you. The counselor didn't care about me."

Moira was confused and not thinking clearly. At the time, she only knew that she hated the man who had raped her, and she vowed that she would also hate the baby. The counselor she saw only reenforced her view, telling her: "That's how men are." "She wanted me to hate all men, but I only hated that man and that baby. I hated that child at that moment, but now I feel I would have gotten over that. I know I would have. I don't know how fast I would have gotten over it, but I would have. I would have forgiven the man, I would have more than forgiven the baby."

Moira said she expressed her misgivings about going through with the abortion to a clinic counselor but was told: "Just have the abortion. You're in such a state—rape, disease, now you're pregnant."

After the abortion, Moira was angry with herself for going through with it, and bitter that she had not received better counseling. "There was no counseling. They just described the technique. I said, I'm a Christian lady, and that should have meant something. I said I've got a little girl who was supposed to be aborted, and I love her."

Four years later, she still anguishes about her decision to go through with the abortion and the ill-treatment she believes she received at the clinic. "Clinics don't call later and ask the woman if they need counseling. Operation Rescue would be there definitely. I know those people, and they will help."

Moira often tells women she talks to about her own experience with abortion and its aftermath. She hasn't suffered any long-term psychological damage, although she believes that many women do.

Along with other rescuers, she cheered in July 1987, when the Administration asked Surgeon General C. Everett Koop to produce a report on the psychological side-effects of abortion, and she was equally disillusioned when after several months of stalling, Koop admitted he couldn't produce the report because he couldn't find any reliable evidence of damage.

Moira also worries that she might be sterile as a result of her abortion. Although she says the sterility rate is low, only about 3 percent, still she, like every other woman who's had an abortion, has to walk around wondering if she falls into that percentage.* Until she marries and tries to have a baby, she has no way of knowing. "Not knowing whether I can have another baby is bad," she said. It is a fear she expresses over and over again with the women she talks to.

Moira says that her life has turned around since she became involved in Operation Rescue. For the first time in her life, she feels stable and secure. Even her finances took a turn for the better after she began working with Operation Rescue. Moira found a new place to live, a three-bedroom house that rented for a near miraculous price of $200 per month, low even for Atlanta. "God has settled me down. I've bought a new car."

Her bills get paid, she said, even when she is in jail, as she was for thirty days after the huge Operation Rescue protest during the Democratic Convention in 1988. When I asked her if Operation Rescue had given her any money, the usually patient Moira finally showed some impatience as she firmly told me no, that wasn't how it worked. She just has faith that her bills will

---

*No medical evidence suggests that sterility is a side effect of abortion.

get paid, and somehow, they always do—or have since she began working with Operation Rescue.

Although becoming a born-again Christian and joining Operation Rescue has changed many of her views about the world, they haven't changed all of them. Moira is not sure, for example, that she sees eye-to-eye with Operation Rescue on such issues as feminism and birth control. She admits to being a "former feminist" and says that Operation Rescue's views on these topics are still a little confusing to her.

"A person can lean toward feminist views," Moira said. "I'm a breadwinner and would not be happy if someone got paid more than me. But I've got no desire to show up men anymore. I used to do that. I was a good car mechanic, better than most men, but I don't do that anymore. Some things men can do better. Little girls need a man to show them what they should be." Moira also gave up working as a carpenter as she came to understand more about her new religion. She doesn't really mind, she says, because "the language was too bad."

I asked her if she thinks Randall Terry would ever let a woman preach or, for that matter, climb very high in Operation Rescue. She said, "A woman can be a spiritual leader, but biblically, she should be under a man's authority. There's nothing we can do about the Truth. God made men responsible for women. It could be a boss or a husband. If a woman is married, it is always her husband. A man in the church could be assigned to be a spiritual leader to a woman. If a woman is honorable and doesn't abuse her authority, then it's good, but I've seen some women trying to push their own agenda through religion. That's not right."

She is at odds with Operation Rescue over its views on birth control. Terry hasn't gone out of his way to denounce birth control to his followers, but there is a sense that if he could eliminate abortion, birth control would be the next target. When I talked with him at his Binghamton headquarters, he pointed me toward Pride's book, which denounces all forms of birth control, telling me it was an accurate representation of his views on the subject. Sometimes Operation Rescue's opposition to birth control is couched in deliberately vague language so they do not alienate their own membership, many of whom use contraception to plan their families. But there is little room for misinterpretation when Jesse Lee, co-director of the Northeast office of Operation Rescue, observes:

"God has given us a natural means—those are the only good ones." Pressed on whether he and the leadership of Operation Rescue officially oppose all forms of birth control, Lee smiled and answered, "Artificial birth control, the pill, abortion, yes. To use pills, abortion, that's wrong."

Moira once heard a minister preach against it when she was in jail. She recalls that he said, "If God doesn't make mistakes, was He making a mistake when he made my daughter?"

Moira adds, "God creates all life. Christians don't agree, but they're leaning toward not using birth control."

Moira even got a new job a few months before the Democratic National Convention protests. She worked for a company that makes software systems for hospitals. "I was a secretary-receptionist. It was my first real job. I had benefits," she says. Aware that she might be arrested and jailed during the Democratic Convention protest, Moira followed Operation Rescue's instructions to ask for all her vacation time, all her sick leave. She even asked for her honeymoon time since she had recently become engaged to be married.

As the time drew nearer, Moira spent more and more of her time working for Operation Rescue, often on her employer's time. She spent hours stuffing envelopes with literature and information about the upcoming rescue. Her bosses were not pleased, she recalled: "They didn't like the fact that I was involved. I had a lot of free time at work, and I did my pro-life stuff then. I did it quietly, though. Still, people would come by and stare. They were nosy."

Moira did indeed go to jail as a result of the Democratic Convention rescue. She was jailed, as were many other protestors, from July 19 until August 15, 1988.

Moira said she made every effort to stay in touch with her employer while she was imprisoned, but it wasn't easy. Sometimes she stood in line for hours just to get to a telephone. When she finally got to the head of the line, she did not call her supervisor. She was more eager to speak to Jessie. And that, Moira said, caused her to lose her job. "I couldn't stay in touch. I wanted to keep the job, but Operation Rescue was more important. They said they didn't fire me. They had another word for it. Oh, yes, they said I resigned."

Before the end came, there was an exchange of letters. Tony, Moira's fiance at the time, brought every letter to her in jail and she answered every one. When the company wrote her a letter saying they believed she was resigning, she wrote back saying that was not her intention. Eventually they wrote her a letter informing her that she had resigned, and that was the end of that.

Apart from losing her job, the biggest hardship jail imposed on her was that she couldn't see Jessie for three and a half weeks. She didn't worry about her because Tony was taking care of her. But she would have liked to be able to talk to her and explain to her what she was doing.

She was also moved to three different jails. Each time Tony came to visit her at one facility, he discovered that she had been transferred to another. He had to plow through the bureaucracy to track her down.

Moira said there were also problems with the legal counsel. "Our first attorney wasn't very good. He didn't understand that we didn't want to get out." Like most rescuers she had not been wearing any identification when she was arrested, had refused to post bond, and would not take any overt steps to get herself out of jail. The whole point, as she and other rescuers understood it, was for the "system" to recognize the righteousness of Operation Rescue's mission and release them because of that.

Protestations aside, Moira was not above feeling some resentment when other demonstrators got out sooner than the Operation Rescue people. She blamed this situation on Margie Pitts Hames, the Atlanta lawyer and pro-choice activist who had argued *Doe v. Bolton*, the companion case to *Roe v. Wade*. In Atlanta, Margie Hames is a Class A enemy of Operation Rescue. She has gone into court on several occasions to testify against them. "We would have been out a lot sooner," Moira said, "if it hadn't been for Margie Hames. She's the reason we had to stay in jail longer. She convinced the judge not to let us out."

All in all, though, Moira found the "retreat" exhilarating. She whiled away her days listening to the men preach from a nearby cell and talking to the other women about her beliefs. Moira's admiration for Terry only increased while they were in jail together. "He's very charismatic. He's a born leader who takes what he's doing very seriously. He talks to you and asks you about your life."

She doesn't feel Terry has gotten a fair shake from either the justice system or the media. During her incarceration, she read in several papers that Terry was a used-car salesman, something she believes is a deliberate attempt on the part of the press to malign him. Couldn't they have called him an entrepreneur? "They would have called anyone else that," she observed mournfully.

Like most Terryites, she believes that not only her leader but many other rescuers have been maligned by the press. Another story that wasn't in the papers, she told me, was the rough time that rescuers had in a Pittsburgh jail. Women's clothes were ripped off, and prison officials threatened to throw them in with the men. This is the kind of story that never, Moira says, appears in the papers. If it weren't for the Operation Rescue grapevine she would never know about these incidents.

As I talked to other rescuers, I would hear this story repeated two more times, each time with an escalation of the violence. In the second version, the rescuers were beaten by the police; in the third version, the women were raped. Operation Rescue women were forced to submit to body searches in Pittsburgh, but nearly two years later, no evidence has been found to indicate that any of the other charges had any basis in fact.

Since fall 1989 much of Moira's time, like Terry's, is spent going to court to defend herself against the various charges she has accrued as a result of her rescue activities. "Usually I get booked and leave," she says in a blasé voice. "Operation Rescue always represents you. You show up for your court date, and you pay your own fines. Operation Rescue likes you to do that. They say that people need to pay the consequences of their actions."

Moira is currently on probation for one charge, and for the past two months, she has been doing community service for another charge. Assigned to work in the stables of Chastain Park, a large Atlanta public park, she was enthusiastic about her community service, and obviously would not have minded had the work turned into a full-time job. When she goes to court again next month on a third set of charges, she hopes she'll get a judge she knows and likes so she can ask him to let her work in the park again.

"I've also got a $275 fine hanging over my head right now, but I'm planning to call the judge and ask him if I can work it off. If I can't," she added resignedly, "I'll just have to pay it."

When she wasn't doing community service, Moira continued to work at the newly opened regional Operation Rescue office after she got out of jail in August. Eventually Joseph Foreman, who is the head of Operation Rescue in Florida, offered her a paying job as his personal assistant.

The pay was low, but Moira had no other prospects, and besides she was thrilled with the offer. She isn't allowed to tell me what she got paid because there's been "too much bias about that in the press, and they told me not to tell anyone." Low paying or not, she loved the job.

"I had a wonderful time working for Operation Rescue," Moira said. "There was no big-company junk." Apart from assisting Foreman, she helped to get out fundraising requests to the hefty mailing list of prospective donors and opened the responses when they came in. It was rewarding work. "Pro-Life people don't have money, and we're asking them to go to jail on top of giving money. But I think it's good for Christians to be confronted. I think it's real Christianity. God requires things that are hard to give."

And she got to see Terry, who was frequently in Atlanta for his court appearances. Always he was polite and stopped by her desk to talk with her for a few minutes. He remembered Jessie and usually asked how she was doing.

Moira's tenure at Operation Rescue proved to be short-lived. In May 1989, eight months after she started working in the Operation Rescue office, she was let go. Joseph Foreman told her the word came down from Terry. "Randy was concerned that I wasn't seeing my daughter enough. He's really concerned about the closeness of families. With all these parents going to jail, he's most burdened about the families. And they told me they had someone in the New York office who was going to do the work I was doing."

A month after being fired, Moira isn't bemoaning what had happened to her, nor is she blaming Operation Rescue, although she no longer feels quite so on top of the world as she had when she worked for Operation Rescue. She hasn't found any other work yet, but is optimistic that she will. Her plans to marry have fallen apart and with them her hopes, for the moment, that she will have another child. It is just she and her daughter alone with each other these days.

In between court appearances and community service, Moira spends her time job hunting. Her criminal record is not an issue as long as the employment questionnaire only asks about felonies and not misdemeanors. All the charges against her were misdemeanors.

She says that she and her daughter have lived through lean times before, and they can live through them again. Still, she would not like to lose her house or her new car, the first material signs that her life has taken a turn for the better. She misses her job at Operation Rescue, but feels grateful that Terry cared enough about her own situation to take so personal an interest in her. She hasn't picketed any clinics lately, but says she'll get back to it as soon as she gets her life in order again.

Moira was impressed that I was going to interview Terry in person, and she assured me I would be impressed, too. She asked me to say hello to him and to Jesse Lee in New York, whom she has also talked to at great length about her work in Operation Rescue. I delivered her greetings to both men. And both men drew complete blanks at the mention of her name.

6 | A Woman of Color

Vernice Miller

T HE FIRST TIME I saw Vernice Miller, she was doing one of the things she does best: handling people. It was an unseasonably sultry late April evening in New York City, and we were both at a pro-choice rally at Foley Square, across the street from the federal courthouse. Foley Square is one of those tiny triangles of land that passes for a public park in a place like Manhattan.

Miller was one of the rally's organizers. She had helped to get out the publicity and, more important, had lined up the impressive array of speakers. Heading the list was then mayoral candidate David Dinkins, soon to be New York City's first black mayor. He had bravely defended the abortion right for years, at a time when most other politicians would not touch the issue. The other politicians were New York state representative Jerry Nadler and New York City councilwoman Carolyn Maloney. Most of the young Wall Street workers gathering in the small park, however, weren't there to hear the politicians talk.

Word had spread through lower Manhattan earlier in the day that actress Elizabeth McGovern was going to speak at an abortion rally. That was why nearly 3,000 people were gathered here. It had been astute of Miller to line up a movie star, especially someone young who would draw in other youth.

Getting the attention of people who wouldn't otherwise bother to attend such an assembly was why this, and countless other similar gatherings, had been organized across the country on this April 26.

The date coincided, not at all coincidentally, with the oral arguments of the Webster case in the Supreme Court. The rallies were an attempt on the part of the pro-choice movement to rouse the American people to the need to once again become involved in abortion reform. Across the country, abortion activists from the first abortion reform movement were gearing up once again for activity. Many feared it was too late to stop the Court from using the Webster decision to overturn *Roe v. Wade*.

With just minutes to go before the program started, Miller had her hands full. Was the table going to withstand Nadler's weight? The state representative might most generously be described as rotund. Where could they find a stepstool so several of the smaller women, herself included, could step up to the table without an unflattering show of immodesty? What about the speaker who had not arrived yet? Worse, it seemed that every politician had another pressing commitment that necessitated that he or she go on next, which meant Vernice Miller was constantly juggling the speaking schedule she had so carefully lined up earlier. Along with the political heavyweights and the movie star were a host of lesser beings whose egos nevertheless required handling.

None of these problems fazed Miller in the slightest. An instinctively tactful woman, she put her not insignificant negotiating skills to work. If she asked you to step aside so a state representative or some other honcho could speak the moment he arrived, she made you feel as if you were the next most important person on the plaza.

And this petite, golden-colored African-American woman with the world's tiniest braids knew how to work a crowd, too. When the rally started late, and the jaded Wall St. crowd threatened to move on down to South Street Seaport for beer and pretzels, it was Miller who hopped up on the table, grabbed a microphone and persuaded them to stay. Too sophisticated to be the cheerleader type, she acted and sounded more like a professional politician. It was difficult to imagine that Miller had, only a few months ago, been a reluctant recruit to the pro-choice movement.

Miller was the kind of woman the movement needed to draw in if it was to save the abortion right. With her leadership potential, she would easily become a leader in the pro-choice movement. The well-known faces—Faye Wattleton, Kate Michelman, Molly Yard—were in their mid-forties or even older (Yard was in her sixties), and this was their second time around with abortion. They all had been activists in the 1960s and 1970s. Even the rank-and-file members liked to joke that they were menopausal now, and that it was time for a younger generation to take up their struggle.

Miller's involvement in abortion came about through her work. She is the developmental director of the Center for Constitutional Rights, a nonprofit group organized in the 1960s to provide legal defense to poor blacks and others arrested during the civil rights movement. Gradually, the group's interest broadened to support a variety of other progressive causes such as minors' rights and abortion. In 1980, the Center was involved in *Harris v. McRae*, a case that challenged the right of the federal government to deny women the use of federal funds to get abortions. The Center lost the case, which went to the Supreme Court, when the Court ruled 5–4 that the government was under no obligation to pay for poor women's abortions. Most pro-choice activists viewed *Harris v. McRae* as a minor setback.

But Rhonda Copelan, who argued the case, saw the loss as a major blow to the pro-choice cause, the beginning of the end for freedom of choice. Time would prove her right, and in 1989, when abortion was once again on the Supreme Court docket, there was real reason to fear that the Court was at last ready to undo Roe. The Center's staff wanted to do something to make clear its support for the pro-choice side in the Webster case. The obvious show of support for a legal center was to submit an *amicus curiae*, or friend of the court brief, and that was what they set about doing in January, 1989, when the Court announced that it would hear oral arguments in the case. Miller was asked to help out.

Although she was too young to have been personally involved, Miller was well aware that women of color, a term she uses to describe herself and other minority women, had bitterly sat out the first round of abortion reform.

Black women declined to join the first round of pro-choice activism because they felt the movement—particularly when its participants talked of using abortion to limit the number of births—smacked of racism. As far as black women were concerned, white women who talked about limiting births virtually never were referring to the births of middle-class, white babies. Their goal was to reduce the number of babies born to welfare mothers, to poor, black and Latina and Third World women.

The loose alliance between abortion reform and population control could be traced to the fact that many abortion reformers had cut their teeth in the late 1950s and early 1960s on another controversial issue, the population-control movement, spearheaded by groups such as Zero Population Growth and Planned Parenthood. This crusade was in essence a revival of an early twentieth-century eugenicist movement that swept the country in reaction to the great wave of immigration that was then sweeping the country. The large numbers of Eastern Europeans, Irish and Italians were seen as a threat to the white Anglo-Saxon stock.

Eugenicists have often been accused of racism, which is to say, they are not usually talking about limiting their own numbers, but rather, about controlling the population of specific others, be they the poor, white immigrants from Europe, African-Americans, or brown-skinned Latin and South Americans.

The population-control groups of the fifties and sixties were no exception. They paid lip service to controlling white births, but their primary focus—and fear—was Third World populations. As a result, many American blacks viewed the abortion-reform movement as being fueled at least in part by the population-control movement. Therefore, they also saw it as an attempt to limit the black population, and possibly even as a way to persuade poor black women—often against their wills—to have abortions instead of babies.

Some in the black community insisted it was a calculated form of race genocide. The passage of time has done little to diminish their suspicion, and women of color are as absent from today's fight to save the abortion right as they were from the fight to legalize abortion. "That community," Miller says, "comes out of a certain civil rights struggle that still holds to the race-genocide theory even today."

When the Center asked Miller to work on its amicus brief, it was not surprising, then, that she had some reservations. We met at the Center for Constitutional Rights one crisp fall day to talk about her feelings as a woman of color taking the step to become involved in what she still firmly believed was a middle-class, white woman's cause.

The Center for Constitutional Rights is poorly furnished even for a poor person's legal aid society. I sat waiting for Miller on a cheap armless black, foam-rubber sofa in the small reception room, from which vantage point I could not help but observe that the beige walls needed a coat of paint. Idealism papers the Center's walls, however, the way rock-band posters cover the walls of teen-agers' rooms.

Photographs of black Americans, depicting the strained times of the 1960s, hang on one wall. On another, a portrait of a black woman named Fanny Crumsley bears the caption: "I think that I have the right and privilege to sit on my porch, plant flowers in my yard, and visit my neighbors freely without any physical and mental abuse." A newer poster announces: "The right to a safe and legal abortion is now in jeopardy. Fortunately, you still have the right to free speech."

Born out of the civil rights struggles of the 1960s, the Center for Constitutional Rights was founded by four attorneys: Arthur Kinoy, William Kunstler, Morton Stavis, and Ben Smith. Nine staff attorneys—seven in New York and two in Mississippi where the Center has another full-time office—work on the one hundred-odd cases that the Center takes on every year.

Each year, the Center publishes its own docket of the cases and issues it has tackled over the past year. The brochure describes the Center as a place dedicated to the "creative use of law as a positive force for social change."

The Center for Constitutional Rights is often compared to its much larger and more broadly based sister organization, the American Civil Liberties Union. But where the ACLU, with its overriding interest in protecting constitutional rights, reaches out to anyone whose rights have been violated, the Center strives to help minorities and what its annual docket report calls "progressive movements."

Asked to describe the difference between CCR and the ACLU, Miller, who has probably answered this question hundreds of times, says the two groups are much alike but, she adds: "There is one profound difference. We would never, ever, defend the Klan or any racist group."

These days, Miller feels the same way about attempts to roll back women's reproductive rights. Two Operation Rescue people recently called Miller for information about what they believed were violations of their civil rights. It was a logical move on their part. They frequently have turned to and gotten help from local Civil Liberties Unions. Miller, however, had other thoughts about helping them and told them so: "If I were a good Christian, I'd help you. But damn it, I won't."

Miller repeated the anecdote in a calm tone of voice with a smile on her face, and I soon learned that even when her words are inflammatory, she is not—or at least she is too controlled to let it show. She is above all else a shrewd politician, one who sees abortion as a complex issue whose solution requires compromise not only between pro-life and pro-choice forces but among the various pro-choice factions.

The Center's decision to write an amicus brief in the Webster case was not its first involvement in the abortion issue. In addition to organizing the *Harris v. McRae* case, it had also worked on a series of cases involving minors' abortion rights. The cases involved the so-called "squeal rules" that several southwestern states had passed in the 1970s. Under the squeal rules, doctors and abortion clinics notified parents whenever a minor reported for medical services.

The Center won all its squeal rule cases, but soon realized that minors weren't being told that the laws had changed. To remedy this situation, the Center briefly published a newsletter, circulated mostly in the Southwest, to educate teen-agers about their constitutional rights and abortion.

In 1989, the Center was also in the forefront in taking action against Operation Rescue. They joined with the NOW Legal Defense and Education Fund to get a court-ordered injunction forbidding Operation Rescue to block women's access to clinics in New York. Miller was instrumental in fighting the few Operation Rescue actions staged in New York City. She worked as a clinic escort and helped to organize the telephone banks that rallied women to defend clinics when they were hit. On several occasions, she attended rescues armed with the injunction and worked to persuade police, who often didn't know about the court order, to enforce it.

While working at the rescues was a personal gesture, something she could do to help other women, the decision to help out with the brief was much more difficult to make. This would be a public statement, something she as a woman of color would do as a representative of other women of color. The decision required more thought, and to her surprise, provoked more internal turmoil, than the decision to help defend clinics did. Although Miller's name would never go on the brief because she was not a lawyer, she eventually became a whole-hearted participant in its creation, especially after it veered off in an unusual direction.

It seemed only fitting that the Center should prepare one of the amicus briefs in the Webster case. Around the country, groups of clergy, historians, physicians, scientists, social workers, and lawyers were gearing up to write amicuses. An amicus brief could be filed by any party with an interest in the case, and that definition was usually broadly stretched as the lawyers in charge of a major case like Webster routinely granted permission to anyone who asked to file one. Webster would in fact generate more amicus briefs—the Court estimated it received 78 in all—than any other Supreme Court case in history.

Most of the briefs for any Supreme Court case, by design, are written to represent the views of a specific constituency. A brief filed by the American Society of Obstetricians and Gynecologists, for example, described the reasons they believed that abortion should be kept legal. The numerous religious briefs, many filed by ad hoc groups formed only to oppose abortion, are notorious for interpreting the views of their constituencies as narrowly as possible. Only a few briefs have no special constituency.

Initially, the staff at the Center thought they would end up writing one of those general briefs, perhaps one that advanced the latest theoretical thinking around the subject of abortion. Gradually, though, they began to narrow their focus to another constituency, namely, that of young and poor women and women of color. This was done mostly at the urging of Pat Maher, the director of the Center in New York, who had worked for many years in a woman's health clinic.

"Pat had personally seen what happens to poor women, and she's seen how terrorizing Operation Rescue and the conservative right have become," Miller said. "She got us to focus on the constituency as no one else did."

The Center's brief was the only one devoted exclusively to young and poor women and women of color, and one of the few that had no self-serving purpose.

Miller was even more interested in working on the brief once it began to match her own interests so closely. "The brief was very special to me," she recalled. "It addressed the needs of women who choose to have abortions in great numbers and who are most often maimed or botched by abortion. They are the women most affected but least talked about."

Shortly before the brief was sent to the printer, she took it with her one weekend as she flew to Atlanta to visit a friend. Her friend, a professor at Morehouse College, put down the brief after reading it and said: "This is the strongest, most devastating thing I've ever read."

Miller herself has never been able to read the brief all the way through in one sitting. She finds the footnotes, devoid as they are of legal argument, especially poignant. They tell the story of minority and poor women's experiences with abortion.

The footnotes reveal, for example, that in 1972, when abortion was still illegal, 64 percent of all abortion deaths were among women of color. By 1975, two years after legalization, that figure had risen to 80 percent. In Georgia between 1965 and 1969, 88 percent of all abortion-related deaths occurred among African-American women.

Most shocking is the fact that women are still dying from illegal abortions. According to the brief, the absence of federal funding played a role in a third of all abortion-related deaths between 1975 and 1979. Even the death rate from legal abortion was nearly double that of white women for nonwhite women; 5.7 nonwhite women died as opposed to 2.4 white women for every 100,000 legal abortions.

When the Hyde Amendment, named after its sponsor Senator Henry Hyde of Illinois and intended to cut off federal funds for abortions, was passed in 1975, the Centers for Disease Control estimated that the restriction of publicly funded abortions in all states would result in 5 to 90 additional deaths each year. The Center also predicted that the two-week delay in obtaining abortions that would result from the new Medicaid restrictions would increase abortion-related deaths in Medicaid-eligible women by 60 percent. In the first year that federal funds were restricted, the number of abortion-related deaths from illegal surgery rose for the first time since 1973.

One study showed that only 63 percent of 144 poor women who sought abortions were able to pay for one out of their own funds. Those who managed to raise the money did so by not paying the rent or utility bills, selling belongings, using money set aside for food and clothing, or fraudulently using a relative's health insurance.

Footnote 43 tersely told the story, gleaned from the files of the Centers for Disease Control, of a Mexican-American woman's death from an illegal abortion in 1977, four years after abortion was legalized. The woman, who had undergone two previous Medicaid abortions, was denied a third as a result of the Hyde Amendment. Unable to raise $100 for a safe, legal abortion, she died from a botched illegal abortion.

The New York Times cited the Center's brief as being one that might possibly bring the justices around to a more sympathetic view of abortion, but Miller sadly notes that there was little evidence that the justices ever read the brief.

The effect of the Hyde Amendment on poor women was devastating. Not only did it cut off most funds for Medicaid abortions, but it also set a precedent that the states were free to follow. Only thirteen states continued to fund poor women's abortions. In some years, the Amendment was altered to permit abortions in cases of rape and incest, while in other years, federal funds were available only to save a woman's life.

In 1979, four years after the Hyde Amendment was passed, the federal government funded only 72 abortions involving rape or incest. In 1987, the federal government spent $160,000 to pay for 322 abortions nationwide. Since women of color who get abortions are disproportionately unemployed (31.9 percent), young (25.5 percent are under 19) and poor (a third earn less than $11,000), they are the ones most harmed by the restrictions on federal funds. These are the women who turn to illegal abortions.

In *Harris v. McRae*, the case that challenged the legality of the Hyde Amendment, the Supreme Court established the principle it has stood by ever since: While the government had no right to impede access to abortions, neither did it have to help provide them. The Court held that the government is entitled to take a stand in favor of life.

The irony of this position, as pro-choice people like Miller often point out, is that the federal government fully pays for sterilizations, which some poor women resort to as a means of abortion, and pays 90 percent of childbirth expenses at the same time that it provides a meager amount of support after birth.

While the Hyde Amendment has not stopped most poor women from getting abortions, it has forced large, unknown numbers of them to seek illegal procedures, a situation no one could have predicted when abortion was legalized and hopes were high that virtually no women would ever again have to die of unsafe abortions.

As work on the brief progressed, it seemed to take on a life of its own. Miller read each section as it was completed and offered her perspective as a woman of color. But her most important task was to persuade other organizations to sign the brief. The Center's brief was unusual in that it was signed by a remarkably broad range of groups and organizations, one hundred and sixteen in all, representing many strata of society. Among the brief's signers were abortion providers, rape crisis centers and women's shelters, several YWCAs, several AIDS groups, gay and lesbian groups, several Jewish and Protestant service groups, and of course a number of Asian, black and Latina professional and service groups.

The American Lawyers Guild joined the brief, as did the Cathedral of St. John the Divine, the seat of the Episcopalian archdiocese in New York City; The National Organization of Legal Social Workers; and the New York Gray Panthers. The major reproductive rights groups, NOW, NARAL, and Planned Parenthood, did not sign because they were preparing their own briefs.

Among the more unlikely signers were a number of labor groups—Union Local 1180, District 65, and the United Electrical, Radio and Machine Workers of America. Their presence on the brief was largely due to Miller's personal ties.

Like the politician she once hoped to become, Miller has learned to tell her life story in soundbites. She tells people that she is a child of Harlem, and she is, having lived there much of her life, but she is also, one soon discovers, a child of labor.

She was born in 1959 at Harlem Hospital, the same hospital where her mother Helen Lyles and her father Harold Miller spent their entire working lives. In the late fifties, Harold Miller was one of the organizers of Local 1199 of the Health and Hospital Workers at Harlem Hospital, and Helen Lyles is a lifelong member of District Council 37, the nurses' union.

Harold Miller was also active in Jephtha Lodge 89, a Harlem chapter of the Masons. Although it was the lodge of such prominent black leaders as Percy Sutton and Adam Clayton Powell, money and political power did not count for much in the lodge's hierarchy. Miller's father had neither, and he was lodge president from 1958 to 1959. Known for its political activism, the lodge sent thousands of men and women to Washington in 1963 for the largest civil rights march the nation has ever seen.

One of Miller's earliest memories is of her father rehearsing speeches in front of the mirror that he would later give in front of the lodge membership.

Miller was born when her mother was twenty-six and her father, well into his fifties. Her parents separated when she was five and divorced several years later. Although Miller has a half brother whom she has never seen and a half sister whom she rarely talks to, she was, for all practical purposes, an only child, one in whom both parents took an intense interest. She has always been close to her parents.

When they separated, they agreed she would live with her father, mostly because his life was more stable than her mother's. As a single, black woman who wasn't earning much money, Helen Lyles often had trouble finding decent, permanent housing. When Miller was thirteen she moved in with her mother, who was then living in Jamaica, Queens.

She had always seen a lot of both parents, though. Every day after school, she packed her schoolbag and headed straight for Harlem Hospital, where she spent several hours on the ward with her mother before her father came to take her home.

Helen Lyles is a fourth-generation nurse. "I grew up surrounded by a family of women on my mother's side. My grandmother has three sisters and one brother and six granddaughters and no grandson," Miller says with a note of unmistakable pride in her voice. Her Lyles aunts were her role models. Evelyn, sixteen years older than Vernice, taught school, and Brenda, nine years older, wrote books.

She also admired a cousin Edie Brown, the mother of seven children. Although Edie relied on public assistance to rear her children, Miller says: "You never would have known it. She brought those kids up carefully."

More important from Miller's point of view, Edie was involved in the black power movement of the 1960s, and it was she who exposed Miller to the idea of empowerment—for African-Americans, for minorities, for women. Brown lived near Black Panther headquarters in Queens and her home was always well stocked with their literature. Despite their later reputation for anti-white radicalism, at that time they ran a service to feed poor children and were considered a stabilizing element in the neighborhood.

"The women in my mother's family were strong, and they had

extraordinary expectations," Miller said. Everyone's expectations, it seemed were high for the little girl, who revealed herself to be exceptionally bright even before she started school. The Lyles' expectations for her, though high, were not, she believed, as single-minded as those of her father. "My father had really high academic expectations for me," she recalls, quickly adding that she reveled in them.

Her mother, while interested in her daughter's education, enriched her life more culturally, taking her to dance recitals at Lincoln Center and showing her a New York outside Harlem. When she was old enough to travel alone, Miller began spending summers with her father's family in the Bahamas.

Miller loved school and never balked at studying. Even in her free time, she usually had a book in her hand. "I wasn't involved in sports or anything like that," she recalls. "I liked being top in my class. It would have bothered me to be second."

From the time she entered school, they impressed upon her that getting an education was her only job, that they would take care of anything else in her life. She ruefully recalls that her mother wouldn't even let her make her own bed or do other work around the house for fear that it would take away from her schoolwork. "I wouldn't let a child get away with that, and maybe my mother has some second thoughts about it in retrospect," Miller says with a small chuckle.

Miller attended P.S.100 in Harlem, also known as the Matthew Henson Elementary School and named after the first black man to reach the North Pole.

Junior high was less stable. She and her mother moved several times while she was in seventh and eighth grades. Miller first attended a school near her home in Queens, then was bused to another school for an advanced program, and finally ended up at J.H.S. 145 in the south Bronx, a school that terrified her because, at the height of the gangs' power in Harlem, they dominated the school.

She also resented the fact that the school was academically inferior to her previous school. J.H.S. 145, named after Arturo Toscanini, did have a wonderful music program and it was there that Miller got a chance to develop her lovely soprano voice. She was also selected to attend an advanced studies program on Saturdays at Fieldston, a respected private school in the Bronx, and that led to a scholarship for high school at Fieldston.

As private schools went, Fieldston was one of the more liberal; it sought out minority students to round out its student body before it was fashionable to do so. But even in the Seventies, minority students in private schools and universities were still perceived as having come in through the back door—via programs designed to admit a limited number of students who might not otherwise qualify academically. Miller, however, was fully qualified to be at Fieldston. Still, as one of only ten black students in her class of 165, and a scholarship student to boot, she felt that the pressure was on her to prove she was up to the task.

It was at Fieldston that Miller encountered her first serious academic competition. An overachiever who wanted to be the best student, Miller had difficulty adjusting to the fact that she was, perhaps for the first time in her life, in a room full of students all equally as bright as she was.

Miller is proud of her Harlem roots. She mentions them in nearly every speech she gives, telling people that she grew up in Harlem, went to college in Harlem, and will live there always. It is left to the casual observer to note that as a young professional, she could easily afford to live elsewhere, but chooses to make her home in a brownstone at 150th Street and Broadway, where she and her mother share two floors of the building. Her eyes light up when she talks about the neighborhood and the sense of community she finds there. When she tells you it has been her home for the last thirty years and she expects it to be her home for the next thirty, you believe her.

Miller feels at least as strongly about her union roots, frequently telling groups she speaks to: "The unions paid for my braces, they paid my doctor's bills, and they paid for my outings so I saw there was a larger city out there."

And when she was fourteen and needed an abortion, it was the union that paid for that, too, she recalls. Miller may have been a bookish child who, as she puts it, "was always reading and was totally turned off to sports or even to what my peers were doing," but she was a typical teen-ager in at least one respect. "I was curious about boys." Her first sexual experience happened when she was thirteen, with a neighborhood boy who was seventeen. "He knew he was the first for me, and he was cautious. He always used prophylactics."

Her second experience a year later, with a fellow student at Fieldston, was different. "He didn't use anything, and I didn't either. I know it defies rational thought, but I really didn't think it could happen to me. I suppose a lot of teens feel that way."

The "it" that Miller didn't think could happen to her did. She got pregnant during her freshman year. At first, she denied her pregnancy, and even after she had to stop denying it to herself, she still tried to deny it to her mother, with whom she was living at the time. Since she knew the boy's family could afford to pay for an abortion, which had been legalized a year earlier, she asked him to get the money for one.

Almost from the minute she became pregnant, Miller suffered from morning sickness and began to gain weight, both symptoms that made her mother suspicious. One morning when Miller had morning sickness, Helen Lyles simply marched into the bathroom with a plastic cup and demanded a urine sample from her daughter.

Miller naively believed that mixing water with her urine would foil the laboratory test, but by noon her mother knew the results of her test, and by nightfall, word had spread throughout the Lyles family as well.

Miller felt disgraced. She was even more upset when word of her pregnancy spread at school as well. To her fury, she walked into the school cafeteria one day and overheard the young man who had gotten her pregnant discussing the situation with their fellow students. Already feeling herself under enormous pressure to perform not only personally but as far as she was concerned, in behalf of her entire race as well at Fieldston, she went, in her own words "berserk." Miller remembered; "There was a lot of racism at the school, and I felt there were people who expected this, who were just sitting around waiting for it to happen."

She and her mother quickly agreed that they would not tell her father, who does not to this day know about his daughter's only pregnancy. "My mother made the arrangements for my abortion. She didn't give me a choice, but it was what I wanted, too. She paid for it with her health plan. She and my two aunts went with me to the clinic, and afterward, they took me to my Aunt Evelyn's to recuperate."

"When we got back to my aunt's apartment, she was cold to me. I could feel it. Eventually, she started yelling at me. At the time I didn't understand her anger, but it came out years later that she had been so proud of me, and she was now so disappointed that I had gotten pregnant. Not that I was having sex, but that I would get pregnant. She felt I should have known better," Miller said.

Evelyn Risien-Owens had reveled in her niece's successes— her good grades, the awards and prizes, and the scholarship to Fieldston. Both she and Miller's mother feared that all this would be threatened by Miller's pregnancy.

With hindsight, even Miller thinks she should have been smart enough not to get pregnant. "I should have known enough to use birth control. My mother never talked to me about sex or birth control, but she brought home pamphlets, and she put them in my hands. She said, 'Here, look at these.' She started giving them to me in sixth grade, but I guess it never sunk in. I have to learn from experience, and I guess that had something to do with it, too."

Miller's story, including her need to "learn from experience," is typical of most teens, and this is part of the reason that over a million adolescent girls get pregnant every year in the United States. The plight of pregnant teens is the one issue where pro-choice and pro-life people have, at times, been most in agreement, possibly because the pregnant teens seem to represent for many a painful symbol of the deteriorated quality of our family life.

The solutions that have been proposed from both sides, however, have usually resulted in some degree of infringement on minors' rights. Laws restricting minors' rights to abortion, for example, usually take one of two forms. Either parental consent or parental notification is necessary before a minor can get an abortion.

Some of the laws are more stringent than others. In Minnesota for the past few years, teens have been required to notify and get the consent of both parents, even though the parents may be divorced and the teen may have had little or no contact with the noncustodial parent in the intervening years.

When such strict laws are in effect, the courts have generally held that teens also must be given an optional by-pass procedure, whereby a teen can plead her case with a judge. Few teens, however, have the sophistication or the emotional wherewithal to use by-pass procedures, and at this point many forego the idea of abortion or turn to illegal ones—or worst of all, attempt to abort themselves.

Polls show that most Americans on both sides of the abortion debate—between 55 and 70 percent—believe that teen-age girls should have to tell at least one parent when they are pregnant. When the question is put to us, we can only respond from our own personal experience. If this were our child, we say, we would want to know. But the issues aren't that simple.

Underlying the sense that parents should be informed about their minor child's impending abortion is a belief in the family's ability to nurture its members under any circumstances. Yet most people who work on the front lines counseling pregnant teens do not agree.

Judy Sova, director of counseling at Reproductive Health Services, says that the occasion of a teen-ager's pregnancy can be the worst of times for a family to try to pull together. Many parents have no idea their daughter is sexually active until the moment when she announces her pregnancy, she says. At that point, a teen's pregnancy often becomes a power struggle between the teen and her parents.

Judy Sova explains, "The teen has proven her power, has announced her adult status by getting pregnant. The mother, who is shocked to discover what her daughter has done, wants to regain some of the control she has suddenly lost. She says don't have the baby. The teen, who actually is a scared little girl who may want to have an abortion, says I will, and you can't stop me."

Sova's job as a counselor is to try to get the parents to recognize that their child has already taken an action that makes her more adult than child. She adds, "Parents need to see their child as an individual with her own feelings, and as the only one who ultimately can decide what is best for her," she says.

While Sova and most other providers believe that teens—with or without their parents—need counseling and support to handle a crisis pregnancy, they do not agree that laws restricting a teen's access to abortion are helpful. The overwhelming number of unmarried teens—92 percent according to one study—did not intend to get pregnant, and many do not want to become parents at such a young age. According to the Alan Guttmacher Institute, over half of all women obtaining abortions are under age twenty-five, and nearly a fifth are teenagers.

Practically speaking, experts also tell us there is little difference between requiring consent or notification. Both delay a teen-ager's abortion, often by several critical weeks. Some laws also impose a waiting period of anywhere from forty-eight hours to a week, still another delay for teens whose reactions to their pregnancies often involve weeks if not months of denial.

The notion that our children will come to us with their problems is mostly a pleasant fantasy, mental health experts tell us. The fact is, few of us come from the kind of happy home that exists in television sit-coms, and those of us who are lucky enough to have been brought up in such an environment must imagine what life is like for the pregnant teen who lacks this support system.

A teen-ager who refuses to tell her parents she is pregnant usually has a good reason for not doing so: She fears the anger of an alcoholic or drug-addicted parent; she fears physical violence; she may even fear for her life. Or she may be pregnant as the result of an incestuous relationship with the father whose consent she must seek. To require notification of both parents is to send a teen out to look for a parent whom she may not have laid eyes on in years and who in turn may have never shown the slightest interest in her welfare. That parent can now, however, assert his parental rights and make a decision for her that will affect the rest of her life.

In Minnesota one teen-ager sought permission for an abortion from a judge because she was pregnant by her brother.

Although still in high school, she told the court she had solved her "problem" by moving out of the family home before she learned she was pregnant. Under no circumstances could she tell her father she was pregnant. She believed he would kill her.

The bottom line is that laws restricting teens' access to abortion are intended to control the sexuality of young pregnant females as much as they are designed to help teens or their parents through a family crisis. And that ultimately may be an impossible task. Laws restricting teens will probably prove as ineffective as those limiting adult women's access to abortion— only teens have fewer contacts and less money than adults to buy a decent illegal abortion.

We can't control our children's sexuality, at least not through legislation. We may be able to do so through the judicious use of birth control and sex education, but in most instances these topics are, thus far, taboo in our society.

European teens are as sexually active as American ones, but have far fewer abortions. This is generally attributed to more comprehensive—and realistic—sex education. One thing is certain: The legislative-judicial route is too easy. It lets us pretend the real problems—divorce and broken homes, a reluctance to deal with our children's sexuality, and the lack of communication in many families—do not exist. Attempts to legislate sexuality will ultimately fail, and countless young women will be hurt in the process.

Last year, Vernice Miller's nineteen-year-old cousin got pregnant and over her mother's protests, had the baby. "The strange thing," Miller says, "is that after the babies are born, you almost feel bad that you ever considered abortion because they're so precious. But my cousin was exceptionally lucky. She got to go back to school. Her family offered support. She got prenatal care. And we love the baby. But those are really rare, exceptional circumstances. Most of the time, when a teen gets pregnant, she loses everything."

Miller was one of the lucky few who didn't. She graduated from Fieldston and in 1977 enrolled as a scholarship student, at Barnard College, an elite women's school located at the bottom end of Harlem on Manhattan's West Side.

In college, she studied prelaw and political science because they would prepare her for the life she had always wanted in public service. "I had no flirtation with any other career choice," Miller says, and she only viewed her plan to go to law school as additional training for this.

Never one to be "a straight-up academic," Miller threw herself into campus activities. She joined the Barnard Organization of Black Women (previously called Barnard Organization of Soul Sisters, or BOSS), the Black Students Organization, and the Charles Hamilton Houston Prelaw Society, named after the first African-American to argue before the Supreme Court. She founded and directed the Barnard College Gospel Choir.

"Academically Barnard was okay," she says, "but the racism was unfathomable." Of the 535 women in her class, only eleven were black and only five graduated. "That's pretty dismal," she said, also recalling that the Bakke case, settled in 1978 (a date she remembers to this day) at the end of her freshman year, was seen as a major educational setback for minority students, who had just begun to find their way in higher education. In *Regents of the University of California v. Bakke*, the Supreme Court ruled that quotas set aside to benefit minorities were illegal, although race could be one of the factors considered in admitting students to schools and programs. Miller and her fellow black classmates read the decision as the first sign of major slippage since the gains made during the civil rights movement.

Miller found herself driven to be an activist on a campus that was still recuperating from the student riots in 1969. The school administration visibly flinched every time Vernice Miller and her fellow students organized another rally or gave another statement to the school paper decrying the school's racism.

School officials were right in assuming that something dramatic was going on among the black students on campus. Miller's years at Barnard and later Columbia turned out to be the seminal radicalizing force in her life, serving to reenforce her belief that the world was a more racist place than anyone wanted to talk about. She also emerged from those years a committed feminist.

Miller attended every rally, impromptu or organized, and instigated many of them. It simply wasn't in her nature to sit back and do nothing. "I have to do something. I have to be political. I was reaching out, calling attention to the institutional racism. I protested the school's investments in South Africa before that kind of thing was done. The college didn't appreciate it."

During her junior year, when she and other black women at the university felt that the black men weren't active enough in behalf of minority causes, they took out a full-page ad in the *Spectator*, the Columbia University student newspaper, to air their grievances with them. It was a call to arms for the black men, and another negative mark on Miller's record.

School officials took a dim view of her involvements and did what they could to dissuade her from her activism. Her request for campus housing, for example, never quite seemed to make it to the top of the pile. Miller attended school on a Higher Education Opportunity Grant. Intended for academically and economically disadvantaged students, the rules had been bent a bit for Miller, who was only economically disadvantaged. The program's director, a black woman, called Miller into her office several times to talk to her about her activism. "The message was that since they'd made an exception for me, I should be on extra-good behavior," Miller says.

When she didn't take the hint, the pressure escalated. "I got exactly enough scholarship money to pay for my education and not a dime more. There were no funds for survival."

Eventually, the school told Miller "to take a leap." She had spent the summer between her sophomore and junior year in the Bay Area, working for a family friend who was registrar at Golden Gate University Law School. Miller took a few classes at Berkeley that summer, but mostly she loved being 3,000 miles away from the academic pressure cooker she felt she had been living in since her Fieldston days. She stayed through what would have been the fall semester of her junior year.

When she returned to Barnard in January 1980, school officials talked to her again, asking her once more to tone down her political activities. When she refused, the school declined to readmit her for the spring semester and told her she would have to reapply for the fall semester.

She found a job in the Parks Department, where she worked for the next year. Shocked at not having anything to study after so many years of intense effort, Miller prepared to settle into what she considered a bad situation. Soon, though, she found herself fascinated by her new job as administrative assistant to a high-level Parks Department official. Learning how a huge city agency worked only spurred her to return to school and get her degree in political science.

When she returned to school, it was to the less prestigious School of General Studies at Columbia University, partly because she was denied her grant. Although she worked summers and got social security after her father retired in 1975, money was a problem throughout college, so that Miller was forced to take off after her junior year to earn enough to continue school. She had dropped twenty pounds in one year from eating irregularly.

Barnard officials had also pressured her and other minority women about their choice of career. The associate dean, a white woman, strongly urged all the black women to become teachers. Today, Miller proudly notes that all the minority women with whom she attended college went on to become doctors or lawyers. "The fact that we had this shit in 1980 was awful. But I never paid it any mind."

Not paying irrelevant advice "any mind" is a trait that has served Miller well. By the mid-eighties, when she would have graduated from law school, most likely an Ivy League law school, she would have been welcome at any number of corporate doors as a bright, young, go-getter minority lawyer.

Instead, Miller chose to move even further to the left politically at a time when the rest of the country seemed to be heading in the opposite direction. When she realized that her political sensibilities were out of sync with many of her generation, she abandoned the idea of law school, which she only considered a training ground for public office in any event, and instead, after knocking around at a few jobs she didn't like, settled into a career in the then flagging field of civil rights. Her choice of employers, the Center for Constitutional Rights, was clearly and deliberately to the left of the mainstream.

Working on the Webster amicus brief transformed Miller's thinking about abortion and also gave her an expanded network of contacts among many kinds of organizations, from the labor unions to the reproductive rights groups. Unlike many black women, she no longer considered abortion to be race genocide.

She says, "Like most people, I hadn't realized that women were still dying of illegal abortion, and of course, for me the salient fact was that the overwhelming number of women who are dying are black and poor. The fact that black and poor women are still dying of abortion—that's race genocide."

Even before she finished her work on the brief, Miller began to think about using her contacts to help these women. Other legal groups and the reproductive rights groups had shown an interest in CCR's brief, and she had spoken to several of them. She noticed that the discussions that followed her speeches invariably turned to the more general theme of how to expand the reproductive rights agenda so that more women could be brought into the movement. The leaders were aware that a broader base of support was necessary to convince Congress and state legislators that women were serious about preserving the right to choose. Ironically, during the months when the Webster decision was working its way up to the Supreme Court and abortion was a hot news topic, the time when the pro-choice forces most needed a show of strength, the CCR supporters were at their lowest ebb in years. Since Roe, only the diehard activists had stayed with the cause while most of the others had turned their attention elsewhere.

To increase its numbers, the movement needed to engage, for example, right-wing women who might not support a feminist agenda but who felt strongly about preserving the abortion right. It needed to draft the tens of thousands of young women who could not remember when abortion had not been legal. The largest and most conspicuous groups they needed to enlist were the blacks and Latinas, women to whom abortion might not appeal as a single issue but who would lobby for it in the context of other reproductive rights. They would not be easy to attract since both black and Latina women had strong ties to their churches, and the former women were still bitter over the last round of abortion reform.

Despite these inherent problems, across the country, abortion-rights activists had begun building coalitions of various constituencies of women. Miller correctly sensed that the timing was right to press the case of minority women, and that she was in a unique position to do so. If the movement leaders showed a willingness to open up the discussion to the degree most minority women felt was necessary to engage them, she, in turn, would show them what they needed to do to bring women of color into the abortion-rights movement.

The vehicle she used to do this was the Reproductive Rights Coalition, which she began to organize in January of 1989, shortly after the Supreme Court announced it would hear oral arguments in the Webster case. Miller did successfully bring together several otherwise disparate organizations to discuss the unique problems of black and Latina women.

Among the Coalition's founding members were most of the reproductive rights groups, as well as civil rights and legal groups, and labor unions. Miller welcomed everyone from the militant gay and lesbian group ACT UP to the National Conference of Black Lawyers, the Center for Law and Social Justice, and the National Lawyer's Guild. The Communications Workers of America Local 1180, which included Planned Parenthood's clinic workers, and Local 1199 of the Health and Hospitals Workers sent representatives, as did the National Organization for Women (NOW) and the National Abortion Rights Action League (NARAL).

To her disappointment, Planned Parenthood declined to join, citing as a reason the fact that is was already doing enough in this area. Miller still doesn't understand their reluctance to participate, especially since they had been the target of some of the most pointed criticism from blacks who believed their birth control policies during the 1960s had been racist.

Miller said, "We weren't trying to replicate Planned Parenthood or other mainstream groups. What we wanted to do was develop a broad-based group that would focus directly on the special problems that women of color have with reproductive rights. We felt that mainstream groups needed to see the whole agenda, especially the fact that reproductive rights is more than abortion." Many women of color, she points out, are uncomfortable joining these groups because of their homogenous—white, middle-class—memberships.

Miller said, "Kate Michelman and Molly Yard say they speak for women of color, but they don't know what's important to poor women because they've never asked them. Whites are not reaching out to blacks. No one came to Harlem and asked or encouraged black women to become a presence at either the April or November marches in Washington."

For women of color, the "whole agenda" encompasses far more than abortion. They insist that abortion is inextricably bound up with such issues as women's and infants' mortality and morbidity, prenatal care, and day care. If women had better prenatal care, better child care, in short, more support from society for all their choices, then women would not have to resort to abortion. Miller observes, "We have to put abortion in perspective alongside the right to have a child. And when you have the child, you also have to have a place to put the child."

For poor women, the denial of Medicaid money to pay for abortions has never been the minor issue that mainstream reproductive rights groups let it become in the Seventies and Eighties. In order to minimize the losses that the movement suffered in the courts over the funding issue, the groups played down the importance of funding abortions with public monies. The result was that while a majority of Americans were pro-choice, 61 percent did not want the federal government to pay for abortions except to save a woman's life.

And even when the pro-choice groups were enjoying renewed strength after the Webster decision, rather than reopen the fight for public funding, they brushed off the issue one more time, hinting that this was a loss the movement might have to sustain in order to preserve the overall right. The reproductive rights organizations did this even though they knew that disproportionately high numbers of minority and poor women undergo abortion.

Miller and I talked about the funding issue one night over dinner. "The funding issue didn't just spring up after Webster," she said, the anger apparent in her voice. "We've been losing on funding all along, but no one was concerned because it didn't affect middle-class women.

"The pro-choice forces are shocked six years after the *Harris v. McRae* loss when a case like Webster comes along, and suddenly, the abortion right is really in jeopardy. But the signs were there all along that the abortion right could be—was being—eroded. All the funding losses had little impact before the Webster decision, but suddenly after that loss, the white, middle-class women woke up to what they were losing."

Women of color, Miller says, are bitter about the failure to support publicly funded abortions. Instead of marching on Washington for the second time in a year, as pro-choice women did in November of 1989 in a NOW-sponsored rally, she believes the movement's money and energy might better have been spent protesting the Hyde Amendment.

In April, at the first national pro-choice rally in two decades, Miller proudly marched with the National Black Women's Health Project, the only contingent made up solely of African-Americans (although women of color were sprinkled throughout other groups). In September, I listened to her exhort a group of black Hunter College students to go to the November march, telling them that for the first time ever not one, but two, buses would be leaving from Harlem.

On the day of the march, however, no buses left from Harlem, and Vernice Miller was not among the thousands of pro-choice activists who converged on the nation's capital. When I asked her why she had not gone, she told me, "I told myself I was too tired to go, but the truth is, I was too disillusioned."

As an example of her disappointment, Miller recalled how indignant she felt at a NOW meeting when she was asked to produce a list of the leading black women's organizations. "Can you believe that?" she asked. "After twenty years of existence, NOW doesn't have a list of the leading groups of black women."

Racism is an issue that has shaken the reproductive rights movement to its core. Black women charge that the mainstream reproductive rights groups are ignoring recent Supreme Court rulings that have signalled major reversals in civil rights. Miller, and other young minority women like her, suggest that it is time for the civil rights and reproductive rights movements to join forces. They point out that the woman's movement could not have come about had it not been for the civil rights movement. Thus far, in a move that has further alienated black women, the abortion-rights movement has resisted the idea of linking the two.

Even within the black community, abortion must compete with other, and some say more troubling, issues, most notably the plight of young black men, who suffer from few educational opportunities, even fewer jobs, and violence that makes homicide the leading cause of death for black men under age 35. The black community is irate over the government's failure to do something to stem the loss of life. The most militant African-Americans suggest that young, black men have been deliberately targeted, but even the least militant cannot avoid drawing the conclusion that young black men are obviously an expendable resource in our society.

The level of concern over this issue is now so intense that many are reluctant to focus on abortion for fear it will detract attention from this more pressing issue. In a community at war to save the lives of its young men, abortion seems a minor, if not contradictory, issue.

Miller is sympathetic, but like many young black women, she feels there must be room to advance both issues. Both, she reminds me, revolve around the same much neglected subject: black people's health.

Her own involvement in black people's health problems is fairly new, dating back to a spring weekend of 1989 when she traveled to Atlanta, Georgia, to address a task force meeting of the National Black Women's Health Project. She had been invited to address the group on the subject of abortion.

The Project was founded by Byllye Avery in 1983 in response to what she saw as a crisis in black women's health. Avery believes that black women are subject to greater stresses than any other group in our society. She advocates self-help and education, and to that end, has resuscitated the feminist consciousness-raising groups of the sixties, but with a twist: black women only, and the issue is health. Meetings of the Black Women's Health Project are emotional affairs, to say the least, heart-wrenching, soul-searching sessions where women talk about what it means to a black and a female in our society.

The stoic and self-possessed Miller opened up as a result of what she heard and saw that weekend. "I got a lot more than I gave," she recalled. "Black women are used to going until they drop, and we activist types really don't ever stop and take a moment for ourselves. Byllye Avery is telling us we don't have to do this."

Miller returned from Atlanta more determined than ever to expand the subject of abortion to include the broader issue of women's health. While she is sympathetic to—and angry about—what is happening to young black men, she thinks the black community's determination to focus exclusively on them ignores the mounting problems of young black women, who are themselves plagued with rising teen pregnancy and suicide rates.

Another issue that makes abortion more problematic for black women is the role that the churches play in their decisions to terminate pregnancies. The hold the churches have over their lives is a lively topic of discussion among black women these days. The minority experience, particularly women's, is solidly church-based, a fact that has been ignored by mainstream reproductive rights groups when they try to recruit black and Latina women. Their Roman Catholic roots are the reason for Latinas' ambivalence toward abortion, even though Catholic women undergo abortion at the same rate as other women.

Less widely known is the influence that black ministers wield over their congregants. Almost to the man, the black clergy opposes abortion. The reason, Miller told me, is the fundamentalist tradition in which most black ministers have been trained. "They read their Bibles literally, and as far as they're concerned, the commandment, 'Thou shall not kill,' applies to abortion. It's real simple—and real simplistic," she said. "But I tell you, I read the same Bible they all do, and I don't read the same thing."

Although Miller considers herself a born-again Christian, she started attending the nondenominational (and nonfundamentalist) Riverside Church on Manhattan's Upper West Side several years ago. But like most black women, this is a subject she still struggles with. Strongly attached to their community-based churches, the women do not want to leave, even to the extent that Miller has.

They hope that the struggle over abortion can somehow be resolved within the church. While ninety-nine percent of black ministers, deacons and church policy makers are men, women fill the pews every Sunday morning. It is their money that supports the churches. Miller has some words of advice for women who want to stay in the church: "We need to say, if I pay you, you deliver to me. We know the majority of sisters in those pews have had abortions. They may not talk about it in Bible School, but it's true. Well, it's time to communicate that."

The last time Miller and I talked, she was also disillusioned about the Reproductive Rights Coalition, which had taken off in directions even she had not foreseen. Over 400 women had shown up at the first meeting in January, so many that the meeting was moved at the last minute from the Constitutional Rights Center to the District 65's huge meeting room around the corner on Astor Street.

Even though the group was still in the early stages of formation, it was the only New York City reproductive rights group to react to the Webster decision. On July 3, the day of the decision, the Coalition had spawned a rally of several hundred angry women at the federal courthouse in New York City. Two days later, the Coalition gathered 7,000 people for what became the largest pro-choice rally in New York City in twenty years.

The Reproductive Rights Coalition provided a sense of community that New York women lacked. Pro-choice groups had been far more active in developing grass-roots support in every part of the country except the East Coast, where women had only belatedly begun to gear up for action when the Coalition was founded. The national offices of the major reproductive rights groups were based in New York and Washington, but in the months preceding Webster, these groups were more consumed with orchestrating national publicity around the case than with organizing grass-roots activism in their own back yard.

Miller's dissatisfaction with the Coalition stemmed from the fact that while the group was providing a home for many young pro-choice women who had not previously known where to direct their energies, it was not serving the purpose Miller had hoped it would, namely, to promote the agenda of women of color.

She was especially chagrined at recent events involving a coalition committee called the Women's Health Action Committee, or WHAM. It was the brainchild of a group of young radicals who were also active in ACT UP, a gay and lesbian group that sponsored provocative direct actions to draw attention to AIDS. WHAM was involved, for example, in the disruption of a Mass in St. Patrick's Cathedral in November of 1989.

Predictably, the action had offended the Latino community. Miller said, "They alienated the Latina women just as we were making progress with them. They don't understand how sensitive this issue is. Latina women were infuriated. They think the pro-choice movement is against the Church, but we're not. We only want them to change their position on abortion."

Miller is angry that the Coalition has been commandeered by young, white women unattuned to the needs of women of color, women who she believes are politically naive about the fine-tuned art of abortion diplomacy. She does not know what will happen to the Coalition, whether she can keep the organization on course with her vision or whether it will be taken over by the young militants.

Meanwhile, she has stood by, her hopes dashed, watching her chance to start a dialogue between middle-class white women and poor, minority women slip away. Miller senses that the euphoric camaraderie that existed among various factions of the reproductive rights movement in the days and months after the Webster decision will fade quickly, perhaps never to be recaptured.

She fervently believes that women of color would have brought—and still would bring—something valuable to the abortion discussion. Theirs would be a voice of mediation, a much-needed bridge between pro-choice and pro-life forces.

In the past few years, pro-life forces have co-opted the family as their special concern, and in doing so, have managed to make the much saner pro-choice forces look radical and anti-family. In response, the abortion-rights activists have painted themselves into a corner, from which they have been forced to portray abortion as a singularly simple, black-and-white issue.

Such a position is not only inflexible but risky in a society that governs by consensus. If the movement is going to round up the support it needs from mainstream America, let alone from minority women, it must begin to address the full range of issues related to abortion and reproductive rights. The ambivalence most Americans feel about abortion must be addressed, and we must begin to deal with the realization that abortion is, at best, a necessary evil that no one welcomes or supports except as a last resort.

The family may prove to be the one great area of common concern about which the two deeply divided movements can agree. This is the message that women of color would deliver, if given the chance. They want more choices in child care and prenatal care, more support for families, the freedom to make decisions that would result in fewer abortions. By listening to their black and Latina sisters' insistence on a fuller, more comprehensive agenda, the pro-choice forces, which have always been far more sensible and mainstream than the pro-life forces over family issues such as sex education and abortion for minors, could reclaim the family as their own issue and once again begin to shape the abortion debate.

7 | The Dissident

Frances Kissling

Frances Kissling, who is the executive director of a small but influential organization called Catholics for a Free Choice, may be the sanest voice in America on the subject of abortion. She believes there is room to compromise on this deeply divisive issue, which everyone from the highest placed public policy experts to the average person on the street have written off as irresolvable.

After twenty years in the pro-choice movement, Kissling says there is a new component to her thinking about abortion these days. It is very simple: Frances Kissling wants peace. She is not tired; she can easily fight on for another twenty years. But she is weary of what abortion has come to symbolize.

Although pro-choice forces have benefitted from the Webster decision, she dislikes the intense politicization it has brought to the issue. She does not want abortion to be a weapon that both sides use to browbeat politicians, nor does she want it to be a factor in the 1990 Congressional elections, or for that matter, in the 1992 presidential election as some in the pro-life and pro-choice forces are hoping it will be. Kissling does not like it that abortion has become a mother lode of donations for organizations on both sides of the debate. She does not think poor women and minors should be the political pawns of legislators and the pro-choice and pro-life movements, nor does she think women should have to continue to suffer over abortion.

230

Kissling believes there is a solution that will please most Americans, if not the most hard-line pro-life and pro-choice activists, and will require that individual women give up little of their hard-earned right to choice.

Frances Kissling has not always been judged so sane. She is a child of the Sixties and all the madness that decade stood for. If truth be told, she lived a little more than most of us during that infamous era, heading off at the drop of a hat to live in Malaysia for a year, where she did nothing but sunbathe and drape her apartment in batik fabrics she found in the local markets. On another whim, she and a man she was living with picked up and moved to Mill Valley, California, in the late Sixties to live with the Blues Project, a rock band on the rise. A year and a half later, Kissling was back in New York state immersing herself in the social movement of the moment, women's liberation.

A graduate of the New School for Social Research in New York City, Kissling was among the early ranks of Viet Nam war protesters, and like most of us who came of age in the 1960s, she blithely chose a useless major (English literature in her case) and gave no thought to what she might do to support herself. A sense of direction about anything—marriage, a career, life—was not something the children of the Sixties deigned to be bothered with, and for the past two decades, Kissling has been no different than the rest of us in letting life more or less have its way with her. Although she has not exactly led a directionless life, she has nevertheless been open to new ways, and that has led her down some interesting paths. It has all turned out well, though. Her mind has only sharpened with the years, and her theories, revised and refined since the 1960s, are now more relevant than ever before.

The most striking feature about Frances Kissling is her intelligence. Short and solidly built, with the pale hair and eyes of her Polish ancestors, she is physically unimposing. Most people who have met Kissling describe her as the smartest person they know and leave it at that. But such descriptions shortchange her powerful intellect. Kissling's mind is creative and iconoclastic, and fortunately she has found a way to organize her life so that she spends most of her time in the realm of the abstract. Which is not to say that Kissling is an impractical theorist of the type that tend to infest social movements. She isn't. Kissling is a very practical woman, and that makes her suggestions about resolving the abortion issue all the more valuable. Her practicality is the result of her early life.

Kissling's mother was the youngest of seven children of a Pennsylvania coal miner. Her father's family was also working class, but she knows far less about the Romanskis, her parents having ended their wartime marriage before Kissling was old enough to go to school.

That Florence's family was solidly Roman Catholic made her two marriages and two divorces that much harder for her family to bear. But Florence Kissling was the original role model for her daughter: A teen-age rebel, she broke with her family and moved alone to New York city at the age of seventeen, and married not one but two men not of her parents' choosing, all in an era when nice, young Polish women were not doing that sort of thing.

Charles Kissling, her mother's second husband, adopted Frances and her younger sister and took them to live in suburban Flushing, just outside New York City. A Protestant, he was the spoiled, charming only child of a rich family, their ne'er-do-well. Despite the obvious differences in their personalities, Charles got along well with his overachieving stepdaughter, and Frances was his frequent companion for tennis, golf and horseback riding during the years they were a family.

When Florence and Charles divorced after twelve years of marriage, however, the children were stunned when he disappeared, never bothering to pay child support or stay in touch with his two stepchildren and the son and daughter he had with Florence.

Despite having borne four children, whom she seemed destined to rear alone, Florence was not cut out for motherhood. It was from her mother that Frances got her quick and inquisitive mind, her curiosity about the world, and her eternal restlessness. Kissling remembers her mother as a "tough broad" who did not especially like children, her own included. She was not, Kissling recalls, emotionally well-equipped to be a parent.

She let her eldest daughter take over many of her responsibilities, including caring for the younger children and cooking for the family. Kissling says she didn't mind, but she does recall, however jovially, that when she ran away from home briefly at age twelve, she left behind a note saying she was tired of being the mommy. Most of the time, though, Kissling likes to take charge of situations and people, and unless a room is full of exceptionally qualified people, she is often the person best able to do so.

Her early assumption of her mother's role never ended, and Kissling offers up the information, with some pride, that she is "still the head of the family." But the pressure she felt at such an early age may have been a factor in her decision, reached when she was still in high school, never to marry. Kissling says she never had the dream of most little girls to grow up and get married and have lots of babies. She once asked Florence if she recalled ever hearing her express a desire for this kind of life, and Florence said no, she couldn't recall her ever fantasizing about those things.

Kissling also remembers receiving little encouragement from either of her parents to lead a traditional life. Charles, in fact, once told her that her needs were such that he did not believe she would marry early, if at all. Apart from these not insignificant departures from the usual parental expectations, Florence and Charles were supportive parents who recognized their eldest child's unusual academic abilities and did all they could to help her to develop them.

Kissling wears a button on her coat lapel that announces, "I'm a product of Catholic schools," and since she has made a career of taking on the Church, one assumes it is a sarcastic commentary on her past experience in parochial school, but this turns out not to be the case. Kissling is proud of her Catholic school education and feels it served her well. She believes it is the reason she is one of only two persons in her mostly blue-collar family who have graduated from college.

Her education during her teen years was a special time of growth for Kissling, who attended Bishop McDonnell Memorial High School. "I had extraordinary teachers, the nuns. In general I think Catholic education is wonderful. If you can't go to Dalton, or some other fancy private school, the next best thing is a Catholic school. My high school teachers were very bright, well-educated women, who recognized my intelligence and took the time to help me see it. They gave me many extras. They went out of their way to talk to me and gave me special books to read. St. John's, where I went to college for two years, was anti-intellectual after what I was exposed to in high school."

Although life was hard after Charles left the family, and Florence went to work for the New York Telephone company to support herself and the children, Frances had already been awarded a scholarship to St. John's University on Long Island. In 1962, Kissling thought she knew where she was headed next: She was going to be a nun.

Now it seems an anomaly that someone as outgoing and iconoclastic as Kissling would have chosen the cloistered religious life, but at the time it seemed like the natural thing to do, and it is a decision that still makes sense to Kissling in terms of who she was at the time.

"It's so far in the past," she says, "and seems so insignificant in terms of what has happened since, but it made sense then. I went to Catholic schools. I was taught by nuns, and they were my role models. Most of them had masters degrees, and many had their doctorates. And then you have to understand that the decision to be a nun meant I didn't have to decide to be anything else. That has a certain appeal for a seventeen-year-old. I just had to go to college for one year and then enter a religious community. And that's what I did.

"I was a religious kid. Now I have to qualify that by saying I was not a holy kid. There's a difference. I didn't walk around with rosary beads in my pocketbook. I didn't have religious pictures hanging over my bed. There were no special saints I liked. Even then, religion interested me from the intellectual perspective, the same way it does now. But I've always been interested in it.

"Besides you have to remember that at that time, there were only two directions the life of a good Catholic girl could take. She could get married, or she could remain single and become a nun. Of those two, the highest state was the religious life. You dedicated your life to service and to God, you strove to do what was best in life.

"There were few other models for what one could do. I wasn't interested in having children, even in high school, and I was uninterested in marriage. That was reinforced by my family. My mother had been married twice, and neither marriage had worked out. With the limited breadth of my experience at the time, being a nun looked like a pretty good option."

Kissling made plans to enter a convent of the Sisters of St. Joseph during her second year of study at St. John's University. Before assuming the cloistered life, she decided to look up her biological father, whom she had not seen since she was a toddler and had no memory of. She told her mother she wanted to meet him, and Florence produced Thomas Romanski's address and telephone number in Buffalo, New York.

Kissling's call was warmly received, and her father, who had remarried and had a second family, was eager to see her, even going so far as to send her a plane ticket to Buffalo.

"He was a nice, working class man, he managed garages. He was happy to see me and did everything to make my visit pleasant. He and his wife drove me to every shrine in the Buffalo area. Since I was entering the convent, they thought it was the best way to entertain me, I'm sure.

"But I felt nothing special for him, had no independent interest in him beyond the fact that he was my biological father. Because I was entering the convent, and postulates are cloistered and see virtually no one, there was no expectation that our relationship would continue, at least not in the next few years.

"When I left the convent, I never contacted him. I felt no need, and simply never wrote to him to tell him."

Kissling's life as a nun was short-lived, lasting only six months. She wasn't rebellious as one might expect, didn't get into any trouble, but as she became more deeply involved with religious philosophy, she realized that she was, not unexpectedly given her background, more and more at odds with the church on such issues as birth control and divorce.

"These things loomed larger as I studied them in more depth," she recalled, "and I found myself doubting the Church in its entirety. They became inhibiting factors to my remaining in the convent. I had no business being there. It lacked integrity to be a nun and not believe in the Church's teachings on these subjects."

Kissling's departure from the convent marked a break with the Catholic community in which she had grown up, and was also a break with her faith. She never returned to the Sunday Mass, and never fully returned to the Church. "I wasn't angry, but I wanted nothing to do with the Church. It had no relevance to my life in that period."

She went back to St. John's for a brief period, and then transferred to New York City to finish at the New School, an eye-opening experience at any time but especially so in the 1960s when the liberal university was in the forefront of the social upheaval that had beset American society.

"I became a typical person of the Sixties. I was single, I lived in New York City, I protested the war, and I was sexually active." She was not, she is quick to add, profligate. "I saw and see nothing wrong with sexual activity outside marriage, nothing wrong with the sexual act. It's a normal, natural act that should be engaged in with affection. I don't see it as a profoundly sacred event that requires vows of external commitment. But I was never promiscuous."

Kissling worked at a series of odd jobs while she was finishing school and for a few years after graduating in 1965. Her favorite was selling tickets at the Bleecker Street Cinema, a small art film moviehouse in Greenwich Village, because "I got to see all the movies, and I've always been crazy about movies. And I worked there because of the people. Such interesting people came to that theater."

She worked for the Girl Scouts, as an administrative assistant in a psychiatric clinic, in product marketing for Macmillan publishing company, and as a cook in a therapeutic community. The latter left her with a lifelong love of cooking; she considers it one of her most creative activities. In her spare time, she studied poetry with LeRoi Jones.

In 1970, she became involved with abortion, which had just been legalized in New York State. Through a chance meeting with some friends, she met two physicians who were opening an abortion clinic. They asked her to become the clinic's director, a job she eagerly accepted. Kissling had no qualms about accepting the position even though she was only twenty-five and had no special training for the work.

Her religion proved to be no barrier. Kissling recalls that she hadn't been indoctrinated one way or another on the subject of abortion; it was simply an unmentionable subject when she was growing up. "The Church influence was so strong when I was growing up that no one even talked about abortion. It was never even mentioned, so I had no negative indoctrination," Kissling recalls.

"I'd never known anyone who'd had an abortion, and I'd never had one. I had one pregnancy scare once, but that only lasted for three days, so it hardly qualified. I'd never approached what I might have done had the decision been before me."

Kissling became one of the first abortion care providers in the country. Between 1970 and 1973, she first ran a clinic in Pelham, New York, a northern suburb of New York City, and another one on East Sixtieth Street in Manhattan.

While Kissling's mother had expressed some misgivings about her daughter entering a convent, she had none about Frances working in an abortion clinic. Over time, in fact, Kissling brought several members of her family, including her mother, to work at the Pelham clinic.

Florence had found work commensurate with her abilities at last, and she was soon running her own clinic in Washington, D.C. Over the years Frances and her mother had become good friends, and Kissling's loss was all the greater when her mother died prematurely of lung cancer in 1983. Kissling took six months off work to nurse her mother during her final illness.

Kissling's work in the clinics was a baptism by fire for her as it was for most other clinic directors. She had daily, hands-on contact with women who were in the process of making the painful and, for some, the traumatic decision to terminate a pregnancy. She listened to the reasons that women wanted abortions, and rarely found them to be frivolous. She also observed that the women who came to her clinic weren't concerned with their reproductive "rights." This was something they needed for emotional, physical or economic reasons. There was no political satisfaction in the decision. Few of the women were feminists, and those who were could not have cared less about feminist principles at that particular moment in their lives.

Abortion was, she came to understand, an intensely individual experience. Women's reasons for wanting an abortion were as varied as the women themselves. Gradually, she came to understand that abortion was too complex to be discussed in strictly theoretical or philosophical terms.

Although she would not know it during her early years as a clinic director, with the exception of the occasional self-imposed sabbatical and the months when she nursed her mother, Kissling would be involved in one way or another with abortion for the next two decades of her life.

After three years of working in the clinics, though, Kissling found herself ready for her first break. She was tired. A few years earlier, she had met and fallen in love with a man named Carl Chanin, a Jewish "hippie accountant." They had been living together for several years in a small house she had bought in upstate New York when Chanin, who was thirteen years older than Kissling, underwent a midlife crisis. Convinced he needed to change careers, he sold his accounting business, and persuaded Kissling to move overseas with him. They traveled for a while, and eventually settled to live for a year in Penang, Malaysia.

It was a rare period of inactivity for her. "I did nothing during the time we lived there," Kissling recalled. "I played bridge, bought beautiful fabrics and scattered and hung them around our house, and went to the beach." Chanin and Kissling returned to the United States in the late summer of 1974, a few days before Richard Nixon resigned as President. In her absence abortion had become legal throughout the country as a result of the *Roe V. Wade* decision. There were now many more opportunities in abortion services, and Kissling decided she would look for another job in the field.

A director of a Planned Parenthood clinic in Pittsburgh had told her about a newly established family trust in Chapel Hill, North Carolina, whose mandate was to facilitate abortion worldwide. Still enthralled with the possibility of seeing the world, Kissling applied and got the job. For the next year and a half,

New York would be her home base while she traveled around the world setting up abortion clinics.

She spent a lot of time in Mexico, where abortion was illegal but widely available. There, she set up a clinic and arranged for the training of the physicians who would work in it. She smuggled a vacuum aspirator into Mexico by claiming that it was used for the treatment of asthma.

When Italian feminists began waging their own war to legalize abortion on the Vatican's turf (they were successful to the shock of the Catholic world), Kissling went to Rome to meet with a group of them. She offered money to establish an illegal clinic. "I had no problem helping women get illegal abortions," Kissling said. "Women will get them when they need them. The only question is whether they will get safe ones."

In the late 1960s the times were such that the Italian feminists felt they must turn down Kissling's offer of help out of fear that they were being offered CIA money. The women, who were leftist and communist, finally decided that even if the money was not coming from the CIA, they would still be accused of taking CIA money if they accepted any U.S. funding. Unable to take Kissling's money, they accepted her offer to work with them in setting up their clinic.

The hardest-fought battle was in Vienna, where abortion had been legalized in 1975. Kissling traveled there to offer her services and the funding of her foundation only to find that legalization had done little to change the firmly entrenched views of the conservative establishment in Austria. Despite legalization, it was still almost impossible to get an abortion in Austria. Kissling recalls sitting in one prominent physician's office and discussing the need to set up abortion clinics so women would have access to inexpensive, safe abortions.

In essence, he told her: "Now that we've won the battle for legalization, we don't want to jeopardize this victory by actually doing any abortions."

In time, Kissling did manage to set up Austria's first freestanding clinic, but getting doctors to staff it was another matter. To recruit them, she took to loitering in the halls of Vienna's medical school.

During this period, Kissling also become involved in helping to form the National Abortion Federation, a professional umbrella group for abortion-care providers. In 1975, two years after legalization, abortion services were provided mostly by freestanding clinics. From all external appearances, the clinics looked and appeared to operate alike. Internally, however, there were two distinctly different types of clinics, profit and nonprofit, each with its own operating philosophy.

The for-profit clinics were mostly owned by physicians, who at that time were predominantly male. They tended to operate their clinics as they did their offices—in the conservative, often paternalistic tradition of the medical establishment.

In contrast, the nonprofit clinics, far fewer in number, tended to be feminist-oriented, and as such, were committed to counseling and educating women as well as providing them with abortions. These clinics were run by women. Each group had its own fledgling professional organization.

NAF was the result of a merger between the two professional groups. It grew out of a 1976 providers' meeting in Knoxville, Tennessee, which Kissling attended even though she was no longer running a clinic. Someone posted a sign announcing a meeting to discuss the establishment of a new professional group, and Kissling went to see what was going on. Initially, the two groups were suspicious of each other, and for a while it looked as if a merger would be impossible. Kissling was asked by a group of feminist clinic operators to sit on a steering committee and see if she couldn't save the foundering organization.

Although even her negotiating skills were stretched to the limit, she worked steadily for six months, soothing egos and ironing out petty jealousies, and finally managing to bring about an agreement between the two naturally antagonistic groups. Her reward was to become the first president of the National Abortion Federation.

While Kissling traveled around the world setting up abortion clinics and around the country on behalf of NAF, Chanin stayed home reading and listening to music and sinking deeper into his midlife crisis. "All relationships have their good, their bad, and their neutral years," Kissling says. "What happened to us was too many neutral and bad years. We started to bore each other."

Kissling has never had much tolerance for being bored, and

after nine years of a relationship she considered a marriage, she reluctantly decided the time had come to end it. Their breakup began peacefully enough when they began to live apart. Two years later, though, Kissling found herself embroiled in a struggle to hang on to her house. She managed to salvage her home, which she still uses every chance she gets as her weekend and vacation retreat.

Since then there have been other serious relationships in her life, but no one permanent for the past few years. "That's okay," she says. "As I get older, I become an increasingly private person. I need an enormous amount of time to myself. It's part of doing public work that I need a lot of time alone so I can think. I'm comfortable with my time alone. My personal resources to amuse myself are adequate."

In her rare moments of leisure, Kissling devours books (fiction and nonfiction), watches television (which she loves almost as much as movies), and occasionally listens to rock music, although she confesses she "often forgets to turn it on." And she watches the exotic fish that populate the large aquarium that dominates one wall of her living room.

Even though she says love is not a high priority right now, she admits she would not be averse to falling in love again. "I know I'll have more loves in my life," she says.

In 1979 Kissling found the cause that had absorbed her energies for the past ten years and will, she expects, consume many more years of her professional life. She was approached to work on the board of an organization called Catholics for a Free Choice. That the name is an oxymoron seems too obvious to mention as Kissling and I each settle into her two deep, red-and-orange striped sofas on an unusually crisp December day in Washington, D. C., to discuss her emergence as the "cardinal of choice," as her friends, and occasionally her enemies, call her.

Kissling's vintage 1920s apartment reflects her comfort with herself and the course her life has taken. It is a large, cheerful place filled with books and mementos from her travels. A handsome brown-striped Afghan rug leads into her taupe-colored living room. The living and dining rooms are the stylish, sophisticated public areas, where she gives the frequent dinner parties, sometimes for as many as sixty people, for which she is justifiably famous.

The less stylish den and bedroom are more reminiscent of the Sixties radical. The bedroom, sparsely furnished with an old Pier One wicker chair and a bed that rests on the floor, brings to mind every woman's first apartment.

The old kitchen is painted bright red and filled with the smell of a turkey roasting. Tonight Kissling will entertain her staff at her annual Christmas party, but this afternoon, she is giving herself over to a survey of her past and present life.

"Catholics for a Free Choice approached me to go on their board. My job had ended with the foundation, and I was deeply involved in planning some grass-roots activities for a pro-choice group. I'm not sure how they knew my history, but they obviously did. I told them if they didn't mind the fact that I no longer considered myself a Catholic, then I would like to go on their board. I thought it would be intellectually interesting."

Kissling was ready to come back to the Church, but only on her own terms. When she left the convent nearly twenty years earlier, she not only had rejected the Catholic Church but had felt rejected by it. She had accepted the Church's view that she could no longer be a Catholic because of her views on sexuality.

Over the years, those views had not changed. She had lived with several men, obviously had enjoyed sexual relations with them, and even more obviously had practiced birth control, all of which were taboo in the Church's eyes. In the intervening years, however, Kissling had not completely closed out Catholicism. She had read a lot about her religion, including its history, and had over time developed a new perspective on the Church, specifically her relationship with it.

"I had let the institution define my membership, and by accepting their definition, I had believed I could not be a member of the Church. From my reading, I gradually came to the realization that if I want to be Catholic, if I willed it to be, I could be a Catholic," she said.

Kissling was saying that she would no longer let the Church—and by that she would soon come to mean the patriarchal and, to her mind, spiritually corrupt, male hierarchy that dominated it—determine whether or not she was a Catholic. If her conscience gave her no qualms about how she lived her life or her beliefs, then she was a Catholic and therefore free to practice her religion.

Kissling's experience as a board member of Catholics for a Free Choice, where she met other kindred spirits, helped redefine her sense of herself as a Catholic. "The board meetings were a good place to explore these issues," she recalled.

During the years she was on the board of CCFC, Kissling found herself increasingly fascinated with the ethical aspects of abortion, particularly as they existed in relation to the Catholic Church. CCFC takes the position that Catholics need not be opposed to choice in the matter of abortion, indeed, that the Church's most consistent teachings on abortion have been that the decision to end a pregnancy was a matter of individual conscience.

In the Catholic Church, Kissling observed, abortion has always been tied to the question of sexuality. Abortion was wrong because it diminished the value placed on human life, but also because it was evidence of sexual sin. In the Church, sex may not be separated from its procreative role. Early Church records of penances, which reveal that the sin of fornication was often punished more severely than the sin of abortion, are considered some indication that the Church has been at least as concerned that abortion would be used to hide and avoid punishment for sexual sins as over the value of the life that was destroyed.

Within the Church, the rightness or wrongness of abortion hinges on the religious issue of ensoulment, the moment when a soul is believed to enter a developing fetus. The early Church fathers differed over when ensoulment occurred, and there were three main schools of thought on this subject. Some believed that ensoulment occurred at the moment of fertilization, while others believed it did not occur until birth. The third view, which gradually came to be the most widely accepted, was that of delayed animation, which held that a human fetus became ensouled at some point after fertilization and before birth. Even those who believed in delayed animation, though, could not agree on its actual moment or that it was the same for both sexes. Some early Church fathers put the date for ensoulment at forty days for a male, eighty for a female, which meant that female could be aborted much later than a male.

In 1588, Pope Sixtus V decreed that abortion and contraception were homicide at any stage of pregnancy, but this papal ruling was more of an attempt to restrict prostitution in Rome than an attempt to regulate sexuality. Three years later, Pope Gregory XIV rescinded the harsh ruling, and recommended that where an inanimate fetus was involved, abortion be regarded as the minor offense it had been for fifteen hundred years in canon—and civil—law. In 1713, the Church ruled that inanimate fetuses could not be baptized.

Starting in the mid-nineteenth century, a period that corresponded with advances in biology (including for the first time an understanding of the process of fertilization), the Church began gradually to reverse its position on abortion. Now that scientists could see small sperm swimming under microscopes, a discovery that led to a false image of sperms and fetuses as miniature but fully formed human beings, the Church moved closer to the idea that ensoulment occurred at the moment of fertilization.

In 1864 for the first time, a theologian raised the issue of potential life as something to be considered apart from ensoulment. Theologian Jean Gury wrote that even though a fetus was not yet ensouled, it still was directed toward the formation of a human being, and as such could not be destroyed. Over the next 150 years, the idea that potential life was as valuable as realized life slowly gained credibility among the Church hierarchy, if not among the laity. Although the theory of delayed animation has never been rejected and is indeed still widely accepted and taught by many theologians, implicit in any belief that potential life is as valuable as realized life is an acceptance of the theory of immediate animation.

The final development of this view has been what the literature of CCFC describes as the "right to life" phase, a period when the Church hierarchy has become increasingly rigid in its view that abortion is not only a sin but the sin of homicide.

Although it must be presumed that the Church also has come around to the belief that animation is immediate, Catholics still do not practice fetal baptism for miscarried fetuses, and the Church rarely baptizes stillborn infants. A CCFC publication, *The History of Abortion in the Catholic Church: The Untold Story*, points out that "the Church makes a distinction, in every case except abortion, between the potential human being represented in the developing fetus and the actual human being which the fetus eventually becomes."

Kissling points out that no articles of faith have ever been presented to substantiate the Church's most recent stance on abortion. She views the Church's revised position as political in origin. It is, she said, an attempt to consolidate papal authority as well as a backlash against what the Church perceives as threats to its views on the family and sexuality. To bolster her argument, she pointed out that none of the Church's bulls issued over the years on abortion has ever been pronounced *ex cathedra*, or as an infallible statement.

Nor is the prohibition on abortion ever likely to become an infallible teaching. For a doctrine to be considered infallible, the Church must, among other requirements, have taught it as an article of faith, that is, as a consistent teaching since the Church's origins. About the only thing consistent about the Church's teaching on abortion, Kissling observed, are its inconsistencies. And in the absence of any consistency in its teachings about abortion, Kissling and Catholics for a Free choice believe that the decision to end a pregnancy must remain a matter of individual conscience.

In 1982, Kissling was asked to take over the presidency of Catholics for a Free Choice. She was interested in doing so, but as in her convent days, the old issue of integrity intervened once again. Was she a good-enough Catholic to become a spokesperson for a Catholic organization, even one the Church disapproved of? Many members of CCFC took communion with a free conscience every Sunday, but that wasn't the problem for Kissling. Kissling had to square her decison with her conscience.

She decided to take the job and use it as an emotional as well as an intellectual experiment. As she described the process she would use to do this, Kissling leaned forward with a new intensity. Her small bare feet hit the floor, and she pulled her denim dress primly around her knees.

"I decided that I would suspend my doubts about my faith. I would make a leap of faith, would will myself to believe just as people will themselves to fall in love. I would suspend suspicion about the unknowable—about the existence of God—and accept my faith in a willful way," she said. "I was curious to know whether it, this willful suspension of disbelief, would generate faith on my part."

The winter afternoon had gone gray, and the living room was so dark that we were shadows in it as Kissling described her decision to affirm willfully a faith she had rejected years earlier. It was a dangerously compelling idea, if something of a dance of the intellect. And had it worked? I asked.

"It's an ongoing experiment," she at first answered coyly, but then, her voice softer, she went on, "I have to admit that in the end, it will probably fail. But it has worked for the time. I have not felt that my behavior during my time as head of Catholics for a Free Choice has lacked integrity, and that is the essential question for me. I'm not pretending to be something I'm not for a political purpose. I do think the Church is wrong in its stand on abortion, and that I as a Catholic have a right to challenge it."

She believes the Church's view on sexuality and abortion is both rational and irrational, that is to say, it was at one point rational historically, but has since evolved into something irrational as it has been stretched to fit the Church's theology. Kissling believes the Church has entrenched itself over the abortion issue even beyond what can be supported by its own teachings. At this point, abortion has become primarily an issue of control. "It's about government, about a group of men maintaining power. It's not about theology any more," she observes.

Kissling says there are two criteria for holding power in the Catholic Church. The first is that the power holder must be a man, and the second is that he must have agreed not to use his own sexuality. These two standards qualify one to be in charge, and they also, she pointed out, lead to the conclusion that sex is not good.

As for the Church's curious attitude toward sexuality, Kissling speculated that the Catholic clergy, perhaps rightfully so, recognized early that the body was a serious rival with the soul in terms of the pleasures each was able to provide. At minimum, it became a rational necessity that priests renounce their sexuality, and that the laity use it only for the specific purpose of procreation.

What no one would have counted on was that in two thousand years of Church history, the hierarchy's convictions on sexuality would have become so skewed that the church leaders would shift from viewing sex as a necessary evil to seeing it a source of power. It is the sense of having renounced their sexuality that makes the Church's priests, and especially its hierarchy, feel superior to its congregants.

If sex is a source of power to the Churchmen, as Kissling suggests, it is easy to see why so much energy, emotion, rage, and power has been directed into preserving this negative image of sex. Abortion becomes a particular target because it is the clearest sign that one has rejected the Church's teaching on sexuality. That is why the hierarchy rails against abortion and birth control, Kissling said, but "doesn't get crazy over nuclear war."

If the Church altered its position on birth control or abortion, it would have to admit that all its teachings on sexuality were flawed, including its claim that the ability to renounce one's sexuality somehow makes one superior. Any substantial change in this position would weaken the claim of the hierarchy to its power, and perhaps lead to a complete reorganization of the Church. The laity could be given a true voice in Church government; priests might be able to marry; and women could become priests.

"This is what makes my work so exciting to me," Kissling said. "There's the importance of working on abortion, but there's also the challenge to the institutional church. Catholics for a Free Choice is one of the most viable threats to the Catholic Church today, to the institutional church, that is. The Church is corrupt. And it is worth changing. But I'm not your classic iconoclast who's out to destroy the institution in order to save it. I believe there's something of profound value to the world in Christianity. It's there in other religions, too, in Buddhism, for example, but also in Christianity. It makes the world a better place to live.

"We have to remember that the institution is merely a vehicle for good. It is presently, I believe, on a corrupt path, and our work touches the heart of that problem."

With this statement, Kissling leaned back against her colorful sofa, and folded her hands serenely in front of her before she spoke again: "The Church can be a very powerful vehicle for accomplishing many things, and I'm gratified to be a part of what is going on." With just the hint of a smile, she added: "I've spent years looking for a government I could overthrow without going to jail, and I've found it in the Church."

It was within the fold of Catholics for a Free Choice that Frances Kissling found her voice on the subject of abortion. Catholics for a Free Choice, founded in 1973, was a relatively small and ineffective organization until Kissling took over its leadership. Today it is still small, with a membership that numbers in the thousands, but it wields a considerable amount of clout for its size.

As nonprofit groups go, CCFC is a small one, with an annual budget of only a half million and a staff of eight, counting Kissling. Before she assumed the presidency, the group spent most of its energy and resources trying to persuade Catholic legislators to vote pro-choice. Kissling restructured the organization, turning it into a nonprofit corporation, something it could not be so long as it was lobbying elected officials. CCFC's primary purpose is now educational, and indeed Kissling runs the group like a think tank, generating new ideas and publishing material on Catholics and abortion.

About $400,000 of the group's annual funding comes from foundations; the Ford Foundation and the Sunnen Foundation are the largest donors. Another $100,000 is generated by what Kissling calls "our very, very loyal group" of core donors, who comprise about 3,000 individuals.

CCFC does not solicit funds by mail; instead it recalls its hard-core members once a year and asks them to renew their pledges. Most do, although this year, as every year, there have been some surprises. Donations from the West Coast dropped in 1989 when some members decided to divert their money to earthquake aid and into state pro-choice activities after the Webster decision made it obvious that the state legislatures would have a larger say about abortion in the future.

"I like to say that every year I get one nice surprise in the form of an unexpected big check, and I get one major disappointment. The disappointment is usually a small family foundation that looses interest and decides to put its money elsewhere," she said.

Foundations, especially family foundations, Kissling observed, can be whimsical. One of the nice surprises arrived even as we were talking. Kissling got a call from her office telling her of an unanticipated $10,000 check that had arrived in the day's mail.

One of Kissling's first projects as head of CCFC was to move the group into its present quarters, a bright cheery loft with raw brick and slate gray walls. Located in a gentrifying Washington neighborhood known as the Fourteenth Street Corridor, the area is still mostly black and was the scene of some of Washington's worst rioting after the death of Martin Luther King, Jr.

Foundations have a way of announcing their wealth (or lack thereof) through their office furnishings. Unlike most, CCFC looks neither rich nor poor but, rather, like the home of an interesting, well-traveled professor. An "open" space arrangement prevails. There are doorways but no doors in the offices of top staff members. The support staff sit in a large, open office. A contemporary painting and several colorful woven wall hangings adorn the gray walls. The space is sunny, and the office staff friendly and cheerful.

Kissling's modest, sunlit office is the only private room—that is, the only office with a proper door. Even so, her door is usually open, and she draws my attention to the fact that there are no draws in her desk, a sign, she says, of her preferred open style of management.

Her desk, a slab of cool green glass resting atop two fire-engine red metal sawhorses, is an appropriate metaphor for her personality, which paradoxically manages to combine the cool objectivity of the scholar with the religious fervor of a reformer. Four chairs surround a low glass coffee table, and it is in one of these chairs that Kissling chooses to sit when she is talking to a visitor.

Catholics for a Free Choice maintains an active publishing program, producing a bimonthly newsletter called *Conscience*. It is a lively report on the goings-on of the Church and CCFC in the area of reproductive rights. In recent years, the organization has also published an array of pamphlets on such subjects as the Church's attitudes about birth control, teen-age sexuality, and abortion.

Although CCFC has retreated from the lobbying business, it still maintains contact with legislators and strives to be an information resource for them. Most politicians consider CCFC a valuable resource, one they can rely on for a fairly unbiased view of the abortion-rights struggle. CCFC is far less political, for example, than the big reproductive rights groups. "We won't go into a Congressman's office and say we won't vote for him if he doesn't change his vote," Kissling tells me. "Instead, we take the idealistic position that we can change people's minds by disseminating the truth."

The truth, as Kissling sees it, and the polls confirm her thinking, is that most Catholics, at least most American Catholics, are pro-choice. About a third of all abortions involve Catholic women. This has led Kissling to divide CCFC's work into two spheres: the secular and the nonsecular.

Her secular work is an attempt to neutralize or counterbalance the Church's view by articulating a coherent Catholic pro-choice position. This she does through her contacts on Capitol Hill and a series of press briefings she instituted in 1982 for members of Congress.

Initially, only a handful of legislators showed up. Gradually the number grew to about fifty, where it hovered until 1989. It has soared since the Webster decision made abortion a hot political issue once again.

At the briefings, Kissling typically brings together a theologian, such as Daniel Maguire, who is professor of theology at Marquette University and an outspoken critic of the Church's position on sexuality and abortion; a media consultant who can offer legislators practical experience in dealing with this touchy issue; and a pollster, whose job is to reenforce with hard figures CCFC's claim that most Catholics are pro-choice.

In the nonsecular arena, Kissling is a frequent guest speaker at Catholic women's church groups and among theologians, where her constant theme is to push them to speak out as Catholics about their pro-choice views. Among such groups, said Maguire, "Kissling is a power. Many groups—church groups, ordination groups, and women's groups as well—consider her to be a leader, and include her in their deliberations on abortion and other subjects as well."

The material from the first Congressional briefing was published in book form in 1983, along with an introduction by then representative Geraldine Ferraro on the need to maintain legalized abortion in a pluralistic society. Ferraro's essay infuriated New York's Cardinal John O'Connor, and came back to haunt her during her 1984 campaign for vice-president when the cardinal suggested that Catholics could not in good conscience vote for Ferraro because of her published views on abortion.

Equally irate that the Church would politicize the abortion debate, Kissling rallied to Ferraro's support by taking out two ground-breaking ads in *The New York Times.* Both were signed by prominent Catholics, including nuns, theologians, and lay leaders. The Vatican was outraged enough by the first ad, which expressed its support of Ferraro, to threaten the nuns that signed it with dismissal if they didn't change their views and to attempt to discredit many of the theologians who signed. The second ad, printed a year later, expressed support for those who were chastised for signing the first ad and supported the rights of Catholics to dissent from the Church's teachings.

More than anything else Kissling has done, *The New York Times* ads made her a force to be reckoned with by the Catholic Church. Richard Doerflinger, assistant director of pro-life activities for the National Conference of Catholic Bishops, called her theology "a mixture of lies, innuendo, and misinformation," a statement the Washington press office of the Bishops' Conference recently told me it stands by.

Among other things Doerflinger has criticized CCFC for accepting *Playboy* money. Kissling doesn't hide the fact that the group took money from *Playboy* in the early 1980s. The last time they applied for or accepted a *Playboy* grant was in 1983, although the Catholic Bishops' Conference continues to insist this is an issue. "We took a lot of flak for that," Kissling admitted, adding that most of the other reproductive rights groups also took *Playboy* money.

"Our position was that we considered it reparations. Besides, we don't look behind the donor. Our acceptance of someone's money implies neither approval nor acceptance of his or her views. If you ask us, do we subscribe to *Playboy* Magazine, the answer is no. In the end, we stopped asking them for money. It wasn't worth it."

Another criticism frequently leveled against Kissling's group is that its membership is not primarily Catholic. Indeed CCFC's literature does have two categories of membership, one for "baptized Catholics" and another for "sponsors," or non-Catholic members.

Kissling denies that CCFC's membership is not Catholic. "We recognize that our constituency is not large," she said, "but it is Roman Catholic and it is growing as more and more Catholics learn of our existence."

This year for the first time, as a result of publicity from the Webster case, CCFC began to organize lay Catholic volunteer groups in twenty-four states, and it expects the number to grow next year. "This kind of growth is beyond my wildest dreams," Kissling said.

The Church's criticisms of Kissling are a sign that it has taken note of her presence. Most Catholic insiders think it has done more than that. "The Church considers Frances Kissling a considerable threat," said Maguire. "They were paying attention to her even before she became a force in the reproductive rights movement."

Kissling is aware that the Church watches her, keeps files on her, and even issues reports on her. When she traveled to the

Philippines in 1989, the bishop in Washington, D.C., sent a biographical memo to the Church and pro-life people there. (On a certain level, Kissling is tickled to be a thorn in the side of the bishops. For example, when the *Washington Post* magazine proclaimed her the "cardinal of choice" a few years ago, she relished the thought that the proclamation just might have given the bishop a touch of early Sunday-morning dyspepsia.)

Maguire thinks her threat is not only real but serious: "She hits the bishops in every vulnerable area. She's brilliant and she knows her Catholic theology, its weaknesses and its strengths. She has assaulted an issue that for no good reason the bishops have chosen to make the litmus test of Catholicism. She's right about everything she says about the bishops. Is she a threat? She's a woman, she's a feminist, she's theologically sophisticated. She's a major threat."

Adding to her might, he says, is the fact that the power has already shifted in the Church. "The press gives more weight to the bishops than Roman Catholics do. The power in the Church has already shifted, and some of it has gone to women. Kissling is one of their leaders."

Recently the Church has taken a new tack with its dissidents. Announcing that it would deny communion to Catholic pro-choice politicians, it made an example of Lucy Killea, a San Diego woman running for the California state senate. Killea, an underdog in her race before the Church stepped in, soared to victory.

That loss may be why the Church appears to be treading more gently with New York Governor Mario Cuomo, an outspoken advocate of free choice. Thus far, there have been no threats of retaliation other than the suggestion, made by Auxiliary Bishop Austin Vaughn and backed by Cardinal O'Connor, that the governor runs "a very serious risk of going straight to hell."

Kissling, who has watched the Church's recent actions with great interest, doesn't believe it will take any direct action against her. "The Church is too smart to make a scapegoat out of me. They know I'm expressing an opinion shared by many Catholics."

All the attention being paid to abortion has pushed Catholics for a Free Choice into a more visible role than it would ever have imagined for itself. Three years ago, when she became convinced that the Supreme Court could no longer be counted on to protect the abortion right, Kissling hired a new staff person, Mary Jean Collins, to work as a Congressional liaison on Capitol Hill. The new office in Uruguay is another response to growing interest worldwide in abortion reform.

CCFC's biggest project to date, however, was the amicus brief it produced for the Webster case. The brief eloquently outlined CCFC's position that, in the absence of any consistent position by the Church, abortion should remain a matter of individual choice for Catholics. CCFC reiterated its belief that such decisions can only be made freely if abortion is kept legal.

Kissling has committed herself to raising an extra $200,000 in 1990. It has not escaped her notice that now is the time, should she be so inclined, to grab some of the dollars flowing into the pro-choice movement and expand Catholics for a Free Choice into a larger, more influential group along the lines of Planned Parenthood or the National Abortion Rights Action League (NARAL). But she suspects she won't make the move to become what she wryly calls a "major player."

"I probably don't have the oomph for bigness. I like things the way they are. I won't turn this into a multimillion-dollar organization, although I want some added funds so we can do more in-depth serious work."

Because the foundation is small, Kissling's strategy has been to involve other groups whenever possible to work together on cooperative projects. Her forte is putting together coalitions that might not otherwise become involved with one another to work on abortion as a single issue. On December 20, I joined Kissling for an exploratory meeting with People for the American Way, a group organized by television mogul Norman Lear.

Active in the area of free speech, People for the American Way has never been involved in abortion before, but in light of the Church's recent repressive activities on college campuses, the organization had decided to take a pro-choice position. Kissling has suggested this meeting because she hopes to help shape that position. She also wants to explore the possibility of some kind of joint project.

The meeting, scheduled for 9 A.M. in the offices of People for the American Way, started late, probably because the unusually cold weather and the U.S. invasion of Panama the night before were keeping most Washingtonians glued to their televisions a little longer than usual. Kissling arrived fifteen minutes late wearing a cheery red dress and beige snow boots. She was accompanied by one staff member, Mary Jean Collins, in contrast to the eight people from People for the American Way who gradually filtered into their conference room. One woman hugged Kissling and greeted her saying, "It's the cardinal."

A few minutes were occupied with seemingly innocuous chitchat, which Kissling will later explain to me is invaluable to her. She uses this informal method to gather information from her carefully calibrated network of contacts—liberal, highly placed Catholics; Catholic legislators; and nuns and priests in various states of dissidence—who maintain contact or have access to the Church hierarchy and report back to her.

There was also chat about the hiring problems of the Bush Administration, especially at Health and Human Services, where the government was reportedly having a hard time finding any woman who wasn't pro-choice. "They're making it a litmus test," someone said, and everyone nodded in agreement.

Then the talk turned to the Church's attempts to squelch free debate about abortion on the campuses, a major concern among liberal Catholics these days. Several campus papers have been ordered not to publish any announcements for pro-choice groups, and there are fears that the blackout will soon extend to the editorial pages as well.

Rumors are rife that pro-choice professors have been fired at Marquette and Duquesne Universities, both Catholic schools, and there is alarm that new faculty members may be forced to face the same kind of litmus test the government is trying to impose. Kissling's contribution to the conversation is to observe that these actions have had a chilling effect on Catholic education, something no one in this room finds acceptable.

She tells the group she is also worried about the subtle pressure the bishops are putting on state and local legislators, the kinds of visits, she says, that don't get press coverage. There are many such one-on-one visits, enough so that when United

Press International recently asked its local correspondents to report on any knowledge they had of these meetings, they were overwhelmed at the results. Kissling would like to see more attention drawn to these lobbying efforts by the Church.

Even the mainstream Protestant churches seem to be waffling on their support for abortion rights. Many who staked out a pro-choice position over twenty years ago are now rethinking it, mostly due to pressure from their Catholic colleagues, Kissling suspects. She speculates that after working together so long to achieve some degree of ecumenicalism, the Protestants may not want to risk alienating the Church at this point.

Kissling notes in a more cherful tone that the Episcopalians are still making pro-choice efforts. "And they're good for our image," she chuckles. "They have good clothes, and they still dress up." The laughter produced by this statement quickly fades when Kissling adds that matters are far worse in the Lutheran Church, where jobs may be at stake over pro-choice support.

"Are there any collars on our side?" someone else asks, referring to support that might exist among the Catholic clergy.

"No, they'll take the collars away if they say they're pro-choice," Kissling answers. "There are folks, responsible laypersons, who can be brought to the forefront as spokespersons, but we won't get collars. Priests and nuns will speak privately, off the record. They will go to a legislator's office or some other meeting place if they are assured that no publicity will ensue from the meeting. The Catholic legislators are paying attention to what the bishops are doing, and the bishops have to go after defectors as a result."

Prominent Roman Catholics, such as New York's Governor Mario Cuomo, however, need to engage the Church in debate. Kissling suggests that Catholics for a Free Choice might work with People for the American Way to sponsor a forum that would permit such debate. The idea is well-received, and within minutes preliminary steps have been taken to explore the suggestion further.

As the meeting is drawing to a close, someone asks Kissling how she feels about the recent protest during a mass in St.

Patrick's Cathedral in New York City. Pro-choice activists interrupted a Sunday morning service that Cardinal O'Connor was leading.

Kissling doesn't hedge with her answer, even in a room full of people who might consider the protest a fair practice of free speech. "We refused to endorse that," she says firmly. "Our policy is to avoid church buildings and services. We can picket at the Church office, at the bishop's homes and when they make public appearances, but it was outrageous to disturb a religious service. People don't like it. They believe there is such a thing as sacred space. If you gave the activists who disrupted the service other examples—such as the vandalizing of a synagogue—they would not go along. Tactically, it was a disaster." On that note, the meeting ended.

Kissling's fierce opposition to the disorder in St. Patrick's Cathedral interested and surprised me. It was the opposite of what I expected from a Sixties anti-war rebel. I brought up the subject again when we got back to her office.

"I'm not opposed to confrontational tactics," she told me. "I'm opposed to civil disobedience *in* the Church, not civil disobedience against the Church. My argument with the Church is not over spiritual matters. It's over the Church's activism in the political arena. It's okay to lie down in front of the chancery door or at a bishops' conference. I'm not even sure I'm opposed to the Cathedral Project—where gays stood up silently in their pews as a form of AIDS protest during a service. That was acceptable—but marginal.

"I'm opposed to the Church's stand on abortion, but I'm not opposed to religious services. Now the weak point in my argument," Kissling said, playing her own devil's advocate, "is that since Cardinal O'Connor has already used the services to issue a public political statement about abortion, he has already violated the sacred space. And since he has, so can I. I can treat it the way he treats it.

"But my answer to that," she continued, "is that I only contribute to his violation of it if I further violate the sacred space with an aggravated action in the same spirit as his. And I couldn't do that to another human being."

Kissling is a respected voice in reproductive rights circles, although she is aware that her power waxes and wanes with the politics of the moment. She says, "Immediately after the Webster decision, I played a central role with other groups in helping to shape strategy. Now my influence is minimal because the major groups have set their policy and there is little discussion about what course of action to take. That's the current dynamic, and I don't buck it. Instead I concentrate on other aspects of the issue until it's time for my voice to be heard again."

By maintaining a stance of objectivity, Kissling thus far has successfully managed to keep Catholics for a Free Choice above the fray of politics that sometimes besets the major pro-choice organizations, all of whom must fight for the same sources of funding from foundations and individual donors.

"I haven't been a principal in the in-fighting that has gone on among the pro-choice groups. I am not on anyone's side, and I'm not against anyone. NARAL and Planned Parenthood are jockeying for position and as such have to act on occasion to protect their own interests. I'm not in that position. I genuinely want whatever is best for everyone, and I think I've acted with that intention. This isn't to say that I'm a peacemaker—I'm not—and I'm not a make-nice person. I am a negotiator, always looking at how we might settle this. I don't shy away from fights. In fact, I like conflict, but I do try to keep my eye on the overall big picture."

She paused to stare out the window and I imagined that she was comtemplating her fate. Kissling continued: "I've consciously decided not to be a national voice like Faye Wattleton or Kate Michelman. As soon as I decided I wanted something for myself, the vultures would rip me from end to end. You can't be a broker if you're central to the movement. I'm the pro-choice movement's most honest broker, so I'm not a contender for the limelight. But of course, I do want something from the movement."

What Kissling wants is peace. She would like both sides to begin to look for ways to work together to de-escalate the debate. She would like to see some compromises. She is also the first to admit this is unlikely to happen. With Congressional elections looming in 1990 and a presidential campaign in 1992, pro-choice activists and other liberals believe they have at last found an issue that will break the Republican Party's grip on American politics. As a result, they would not necessarily like to see the heated debate over abortion die out. Kissling thinks both sides will try to keep the debate hot for at least four more years, if possible.

Still, she believes compromise may be possible.

Kissling knows exactly where she would like to see the compromises made, and they aren't the usual areas that pro-choice activists suggest. She doesn't think either minors' rights or public funding have to be sacrificed.

As Kissling sees it, the American public is divided three ways over the abortion issue: "At most, 30 percent of Americans are staunchly pro-choice—that is, they have no qualms about pro-choice sentiments and believe that women should have unimpeded access to abortion at all stages of pregnancy. Ten to fifteen percent of the population is totally opposed to abortion and rejects all women's claims regarding the role they should play in the abortion decision. But 50 to 60 percent of the population say this isn't a terribly important issue and would more than anything else like to see it settled. They're predisposed to some kind of legality, but they have concerns regarding the quality of the discussions.

"We can't do anything to change the minds of the 10 or 15 percent solidly pro-life population. And we can't change the minds of the 30 percent who believe a woman has an unfettered right. And by the way, I'm in that 30 percent. The pro-life and pro-choice people need to accommodate the 50 to 60 percent who are in the middle. Call it compromise, call it consensus building, that's where public policy needs to be formulated." She believes that appealing to the middle majority with some common-sense thinking about abortion would also immobilize the 10-15 fringe minority that is pro-life.

What Kissling proposes, however, to capture the support of the majority is anathema to pro-choice people and even to many women who are not pro-choice activists. She wants to bring the federal government into the abortion decision. In fact, she not only wants the government to fund the abortions of poor women—something many pro-choice activists would also like to see—but she would give the government a role in the counseling process. If the government truly wanted to assert a position that valued human life, then spending money to help women make a wise decision would be one way to accomplish that. And the fact that women received counseling to help them make the decision would also, Kissling believes, appease the ambivalent majority who are not so much opposed to funding poor women's abortions as they are concerned about the quality of the decision.

She says, "Women are not well-served by the idea of getting government off our backs, as the pro-choice movement now says we must. We want the government involved. We want them to pay for poor women's abortions. And it's hard to tell the government to get out and then ask them to pay for abortions." Hesitantly she adds, "I would give up a lot to get money for poor women to have abortions."

The problem with Kissling's suggestion, as far as most women are concerned, is that they do not believe the government would stay out of the abortion decision, especially if it controlled the purse strings. Pro-choice women respond to Kissling's proposal by pointing out that they have spent much of their time since legalization fighting attempts to bring others—not only the government but also husbands, parents, and physicians—into the decision.

Kissling counters that this could be prevented by penalizing anyone—a government or an individual—who sought to coerce a woman's decision. The idea has some validity. Indeed, some women have occasionally reported feeling coerced into their decisions by clinic counselors or others who sought to impose their values. A penalty for coercion would not only keep the government out of the decision, but would keep everyone else out as well.

But even with a penalty it is difficult to imagine any government remaining disinterested in the abortion decision. The subject is rarely raised, although it did come up briefly, in the Supreme Court arguments for Webster. Justice Sandra Day O'Connor asked former Solicitor General Fried, the government's counselor, whether he thought the government, at some point in the future, due to a "serious overpopulation problem," might see itself as having "a right to require women to have abortions?"

A shocked Fried insisted he could not imagine such a turn of events. Claiming that right, he hastened to observe, would involve the government's "violently laying hands on a woman and submitting her to an operation." In contrast, forbidding a woman to undergo an abortion merely prevented her from taking an action. He noted that, in the interests of living together peaceably, we prevent people from taking many actions in our society all the time.

But Fried's disclaimer struck me as ingenuous. More than any other element of society, governments have a stake in controlling their birth rates. Much rests on that right: the ability to fight wars or maintain peace, the strength of the work force, the health of the economy, the preservation of the environment.

The world has recently been shocked by Romania's birth control policy, but it doesn't take a communist government to exercise a need to limit or expand a population. And to the extent that the government has any control over a woman's power to procreate, it will always seek to control it in two directions: by influencing (or ordering) a woman to forgo an abortion, and by influencing her to undergo one.

Faced with an overpopulation problem, in recent years China enforced a strict population policy that forces some women to choose between their jobs and abortion. Most of the time women are prevented from undergoing abortions.

The winds of democracy may have whipped through Eastern Europe in 1989, but in those traditionally patriarchic societies, democracy did nothing for women's rights. As of this writing, Hungary's new constitution contains an anti-abortion clause. Poland is about to pass an anti-abortion law that would imprison women and physicians for three years. Strong anti-abortion sentiment exists in Yugoslavia. To offset a falling birth rate, the Romanian government made abortion illegal in 1966. During the first year, the birth rate rose from 14.3 to 27.4 births per thousand. But it dropped back down to 26.7 the next year, and continued dropping until 1983, when it reached the pre-illegalization rate of 14.3 births per thousand.

Women had obviously found ways to abort themselves and to obtain illegal abortions, a fact that was soon supported by rising maternal death rates. In 1966 when abortion was still legal, the maternal death rate was 86 per 100,000 births. By 1983, it had doubled, rising to 170.1 deaths per 100,000 births, compared to 8.6 to 8.0 for England and Wales and the United States respectively.

In a perfect world, Kissling's suggestion that we bring the government into the process would work. And certainly pro-choice forces should not give up on the idea of federal funding for abortions. A woman who has a right to a Medicaid-paid sterilization certainly has a right to a federally funded abortion. But the notion of bringing the government into the decision-making process, even as a payoff for insisting that it fund abortions, seems too risky, certainly for these times, and possibly for all times.

Kissling's suggestion of how to handle minors' rights is far more viable. She believes, as do most Americans, that teens should be treated as special cases. She says, "I don't want a fourteen-year-old coming to my clinic alone for an abortion and walking out alone after she has it. What kind of provider am I if I permit this?"

But she doesn't agree with current attempts to restrict minors' access to abortion by making it nearly impossible for them to get one.

She proposes the following: "Let someone—an adult—be there to affirm the teen-ager's needs. Let's admit that teens have a right to get abortions, and let's also say we won't make them get their parents' permission if that is an impossibility, as it is for the approximately 50 percent of all teens who come from broken homes. But let's tell them they have to come to the clinic or doctor's office with an adult. A clergyperson, a teacher, an aunt, someone who can affirm their need and willingness to have an abortion." Kissling also believes teen-ages should be required to receive some kind of counseling to help them make the abortion decision.

Her suggestions make sense, but thus far, only one state, Maine, has adopted them. As of this writing the Supreme Court has two cases involving minors' rights before it, and everyone expects that the rulings will be used to further restrict minors' access to abortion.

Whatever policies the pro-choice movement chooses to advance, Kissling believes the movement must also find ways to reassure the public that it takes abortion seriously. "That's the piece that's been missing thus far from the debate," she says. "We haven't talked enough about how we should be implementing the abortion right. We need to reexamine what would be good public policy."

For Kissling it comes down to the faith she isn't sure she has— or will ever have. "I have found that reinvesting myself in the world of religion is very meaningful. It's personally rewarding in terms of its spiritually. I still don't pray. I don't say the rosary, there are no crucifixes in my house, but in a deeper sense, I'm a believer. I believe we're here for a reason. And I believe that people are basically good.

"I believe in the good side of human nature. We have original grace, as some people are putting it. As for how that relates to abortion, the question is whether you believe women can be trusted to control their own lives.

"What must the pro-life people think of women if they believe that women will go out and kill their own kids? What kind of horrifying notion of humanity is that? These people see humanity as totally, horrifyingly corrupted.

"Somehow we have to raise this issue with the middle-of-the-road people. We have to ask what is wrong with a world that makes women go out and have so many abortions. It is an inadequate explanation to say that women are selfish. That doesn't begin to explain the horror or the magnitude of the pro-life movement's objections to abortion. We need to challenge these folks to get on with it, to tell us what would drive a woman to do this thing they consider so awful? Why do so many women do it? We need to say to them, if you really see abortion as the mass murder of innocents, then understand that your approach to it, making it illegal, is only a drop in the bucket toward solving the problem. If this world is so corrupted, so desensitized as to murder its children, then the solution is nothing less than a radical transformation of society so that women won't feel they have to do this."

More than anything else, though, Frances Kissling would like for all of us to get on with it in the most practical sense, once and for all to settle the abortion issue, an issue she optimistically believes can be resolved.

8 | Epilogue

A Turning Point Revisited

Iɴ ᴀɴᴛɪᴄɪᴘᴀᴛɪᴏɴ of the Webster decision, pro-choice activists · braced for their first major loss in seventeen years, while pro-life forces prepared to savor their long-awaited victory. No one could have predicted what actually happened.

The decision shocked everyone. The Supreme Court reiterated its support for restrictions on publicly funded abortions and permitted doctors to test for fetal viability. The former was nothing new, while the latter was mostly ineffectual since physicians and clinics already test for fetal viability, often even earlier than the court ruling allows. But rather than stand firm against intrusions on the abortion right, as it had in past decisions, the Court had opened the door to allowing the states to pass some restrictive laws. The Court declined to overturn Roe, as anti-abortion forces had hoped, but even so, it was widely perceived as a victory for pro-life forces.

In the weeks and months following the decision, however, the anti-abortionists watched in bewilderment as their purported victory slipped through their fingers. Seemingly given a mandate to overturn Roe, they not only found themselves unable to round up much new support, but they lost ground.

And to their amazement, after years of waging what seemed to be a losing battle in the arena of public opinion, pro-choice forces were stunned to discover that they suddenly had enormous popular support.

The American public quickly made it known that they disapproved of the Webster ruling. They didn't want *Roe v. Wade* reversed or abortion made illegal. They criticized their government for interfering with a woman's right to privacy. Polls showed that even those who did not personally believe in abortion felt that the decision was up to the individual woman.

Abortion had finally become the political hot potato that activists on both sides of the debate had long sought to make it. A *Los Angeles Times* poll revealed that one out of four persons vowed to become politically active as a result of the decision. Thirty-five percent declared they would switch their votes to a political candidate who agreed with their position if necessary. Forty-six percent of those questioned in an NBC-*Wall St. Journal* poll said they would be more likely to vote for a pro-choice candidate, compared only to 28 percent who would vote for a pro-life candidate.

Within a week of the Webster decision, Kate Michelman, head of the National Abortion Rights Action League, held a press conference in New Jersey in which she announced her organization's intention to target the pro-life gubernatorial candidate for defeat. Pro-choice leaders had resisted the idea of targeting candidates over a single issue, although the pro-life movement had done so with notable success for nearly a decade. Now the pro-choice movement vowed to use every weapon at its disposal.

The pro-choice movement threw its support to candidates across the country, but it especially targeted three key races that were already the subject of national attention. In the New Jersey and Virginia gubernatorial and the New York mayoral campaigns, pro-choice candidates who had been underdogs soared to victory when they announced pro-choice allegiances. Just weeks earlier, most candidates had avoided the issue unless they were pro-life. Now pro-life candidates struggled to save their campaigns as the pro-life label became a handicap.

Anti-abortion forces' grip on the state legislatures crumbled. Within days of the Webster decision, in a show of pro-life strength, Florida's pro-life governor Bob Martinez called legislators into a special session to pass his state's lengthy list of abortion restrictions and discovered, to his shock, that he could pass none of them. Ten thousand pro-choice protesters descended on the statehouse the night before the special session to make their views known.

Hundreds of pro-life politicians changed their minds about abortion. For months, each new day brought news of another formerly pro-life politician who was now declaring himself to be pro-choice. Even Congress joined the bandwagon, voting 238-189 to ease restrictions on the use of federal funds to pay for abortions in the District of Columbia. Thirty pro-life, and mostly Republican, legislators switched sides in order to support the pro-choice cause.

In a move that divided the Republican Party, President George Bush vetoed the bill. So long as the pro-life forces had been winning the war, few moderate Republicans had gone out of their way to oppose the party's pro-life plank in its platform, but now that the pro-choice movement had taken the lead, middle-of-the road Republicans crawled out of the woodwork to declare themselves pro-choice.

When President Bush, a former Planned Parenthood Republican, stubbornly clung to his newer anti-abortion views, the schism within the party grew deeper. Some predicted the President would use abortion to disprove the claim that he waffled on important issues. If he did, abortion might become, as one Republican consultant nervously observed, the one issue that "could drive a stake through the heart of the Reagan coalition."

The threat of losing the right to choose moved even previously non-political Americans to action. In towns and cities across the country, tens of thousands of women rallied to show their disapproval of the decision. When Deb Morse in LaCrosse, Wisconsin, heard about the Webster decision, she decided it was time to join the National Organization for Women (NOW) again. Surprised to learn that her community no longer had a local chapter, she organized one. Hoping to draw at least ten people to the first meeting, she was thrilled when over a hundred showed up. New York NOW reported an increase from

17,500 to 24,000 members during the year of the Webster decision. Nationally, membership soared after the decision.

Although the Webster ruling did not affect any state except Missouri, one could see signs of what was in store for women if other states enacted restrictive legislation. In St. Louis, Truman Hospital, the one remaining hospital that still performed abortions, stopped doing them because it feared it would lose its public funding.

Pro-choice activists tried to mitigate the loss by pointing out that the hospital performed very few abortions anyway, charged as much as the clinics, and provided no financial support to poor women who needed abortions. Such protests missed the point. There was symbolism in the fact that abortions were available to poor women at a large city hospital. Besides, in other cities there would not always be clinics like Reproductive Health Services to provide backup when public hospitals stopped performing abortions.

Since most abortions are done in clinics and private physicians' offices, most of the Missouri women who needed abortions still managed to get them. But three women who were denied abortions offer shocking scenarios of what may happen when other states pass restrictive laws. One, a pregnant woman who was the victim of a gunshot wound that left her fetus with no chance for survival, was refused an abortion at a public hospital. Two other pregnant women, who wanted their babies, were denied abortions when amniocentesis and sonograms revealed that their fetuses were severely deformed and would not live long after birth. They subsequently had to travel out of state to get them.

With the door open to restrict abortion, other state legislatures are making renewed efforts in that direction. Over one hundred bills, most of them already declared unconstitutional based on Roe, were pending in state legislatures as of January 1990. Many will now see new life.

Since Webster, fourteen states have voted on pro-life legislation, but only three restrictive laws have been passed. A law banning most abortions was passed in the U.S. territory of Guam. It has since been stayed by a court order, as has restrictive legislation in Pennsylvania. South Carolina passed a law requiring parental consent for minors.

Other states provided the pro-choice movement with some interesting post-Webster surprises. In New Hampshire, a state where the public sentiment is pro-choice while the Republican governor is not, a bill that was mostly symbolic, in that it echoed the protections already offered by Roe, was written to insure that women would be able to get abortions up to the point of viability. In a gesture that many believed would damage his political career, the governor vetoed the bill. Pro-choice forces in the state, unsure whether they could garner the votes to override the veto, were nevertheless still optimistic that it or some other protective measure would be passed in that state.

In Michigan, one of the twenty or so states expected to be legislative battlegrounds in the 1990s, the pro-choice governor vetoed a bill passed by the anti-choice legislature that would have required parental consent for minors. Governor James J. Blanchard said he approved of parental involvement but believed a consent requirement would take a "woman's right to help herself away from her." In Ann Arbor, Michigan, voters supported a local referendum declaring their city a "zone of reproductive freedom." The referendum imposed a token $5 fine on abortion were it ever made illegal by state or federal law.

In Minnesota, a state that most experts considered likely to restrict abortion, the legislature rejected a measure that would have prohibited most abortions. In Indiana, another state with a powerful pro-life lobby, legislators refused to pass a proposed ban on abortions in public hospitals.

In late March of 1990, in Idaho, a state that no one had targeted for much action, pro-life forces moved in to write the nation's strictest abortion law to date, one that banned virtually all abortions. It was patterned after the National-Right-To-Life Committee's model law. Pro-lifers claim the law, which outlaws virtually all abortions, is moderate because it seeks to punish the doctor and not the woman. The model law prohibits abortion used as "birth control." Pro-life forces hope that such a law will also make the Pill and IUDs, which probably function as abortifacients, illegal as well.

Although the Idaho law supposedly permitted abortion in cases of rape, the victim had to report the crime within seven days to the police. The law also contained a provison permitting the "father of the unborn child" to obtain a court order stopping the abortion, a move that abortion-rights groups claimed was tantamount to granting rights to a rapist. It allowed abortion in cases of incest only for victims under the age of eighteen.

Abortion-rights groups organized to boycott Idaho potatoes and tourism, two of the state's biggest industries. Although they were criticized for their threat ("Potatoes don't vote," retorted one pundit), it proved effective, and the state's anti-abortion governor Cecil D. Andrus vetoed the restrictive measure. Before his veto, he had consulted with costitutional law experts who informed him that the bill would likely be found unconstitutional. Pro-life activists refused to accept any compromises in the measure, though, and thus played a role in its defeat. Furious at Andrus's perceived betrayal, they announced they would target him for defeat.

Whatever else the Supreme Court does to restrict the abortion right, Webster will stand alone as the decision that changed the scene of conflict. No longer can either side expect to fight its battles in the courts.

The pro-choice movement cannot count on the U.S. Supreme Court to protect the abortion right from serious erosion as it has done for nearly two decades. And while pro-lifers are optimistic about their chances of overturning Roe in a future Supreme Court ruling, the Court still seems reluctant to take this final step.

Most constitutional law experts, such as New York University law professor Norman Dorsen, who regularly argues cases before the Supreme Court, predict that the Supreme Court will not overturn Roe outright. Even former Solicitor General Charles Fried, who argued the federal government's case in Webster, has said he does not see enough votes to overturn Roe.

In the future, activists will have to wage war on two new fronts: one legal, as both sides scramble to pass new abortion laws in the state legislatures, and one political, as pro-choicers and pro-lifers struggle for the sympathy—and votes—of the American people.

In many ways moving the debate to the states is a realization of the pro-choice movement's worst fear. Difficult as it may have been to hold the line in the Supreme Court, the movement will find it harder still to wage war on fifty separate fronts, and that potentially is what they now have to do. Yet the pro-choice movement also had not counted on the massive outpouring of support it received in the days and months following the Webster decision, support that will prove invaluable in their struggle.

Still, it is difficult to imagine that many states are the best place for the next round of battle. True, the issue is probably winnable in many state legislatures, but ceaseless vigilance will be required to protect each victory. At worst, pro-choice forces may only be able to achieve a stalemate in which abortion will remain legal in some states while becoming illegal in others.

Meanwhile, women, especially the poor, young, and minority who undergo most of the abortions, will suffer from this patchwork approach. The Alan Guttmacher Institute believes that for all women a twenty-year trend toward earlier, safer abortions will be reversed if the states are permitted to pass restrictive legislation. Among the constraints the states are likely to impose are waiting periods, residency standards, requirements that abortions be done in hospitals, spousal consent, and, in the case of minors, parental notification or consent.

All these actions result in delays, often of several weeks, in the woman's decision to terminate a pregnancy. Since the timing of an abortion is known to be one of the most important factors in its safety, most restrictive legislation will have an adverse impact on women's health. While the statistics probably won't soar to the pre-legalization highs, there is little doubt that legislation restricting abortions will increase the rate of complications as well as the maternal death rate for women. Many women who would formerly have gotten a first-trimester abortion will be forced into a later one, when the risks are greater.

Since legalization, abortion has become one of the safest surgeries done in the United States. Between 1965, when abortion was still illegal except to save a woman's life, and 1974, when it was legal throughout the country as a result of the Roe decision, the death rate declined from 193 recorded deaths to 7.

In fact, the number of deaths from illegal abortion was probably much higher, since many were attributed to other causes or never reported so long as abortion was illegal.

Other factors that affect the safety of abortion are the method used, the type of anesthesia, and the kind of facility in which it is performed. Repeated studies have shown that the safest abortions are those done by vacuum aspiration, the method used during the first three months of pregnancy. Women undergoing early abortions normally do not receive any anesthesia, whereas women undergoing later abortions are more likely to have it, and thus are at greater risk. Finally, studies have shown that clinics are as safe as hospitals for first-trimester and early second-trimester abortions.

For most persons on both sides of the debate, the biggest unanswered question is what lies ahead. At the moment, the tide seems to have turned against the pro-life forces, but it remains to be seen whether this is temporary or a permanent shift, and of course, much depends upon the strategy pro-life forces mount to counter their losses. Since the Webster ruling, pro-lifers have stood by idly. In a new post-Webster tack, they have begun to push for legislation to restrict abortions in two areas they believe are especially controversial, those done to use fetal tissue for medical use and those done for sex selection. The notion that abortions might be done for these purposes troubles many people, even those who approve of abortion under other circumstances.

Pro-choice forces believe these are weak areas to target. Information gathered about women's reasons for abortion indicates that only in the rarest of circumstances are they done for sex selection. Statistical evidence suggesting that women would become pregnant simply to abort fetuses in order to sell the tissue for a profit does not exist, perhaps because the idea is still too new, or because it is too ludicrous.

Experts point out that even if laws were passed to prohibit abortion for these reasons, they would be almost impossible to enforce. Women could easily deceive abortion providers about their reasons for wanting an abortion. Amniocentesis, the most common test to determine fetal abnormalities, also reveals the sex of the fetus, so a woman could claim she needed an abortion because of a fetal abnormality when in fact she wanted to choose the sex of her child. Laws could be passed forbidding physicians to tell patients the sex of their fetuses, but they would create more problems than they resolved. If doctors were forbidden to tell patients the sex of their fetuses, for example, they could be accused of withholding information, and when a woman subsequently delivered a baby with a sex-linked deformity, she could sue the physician for malpractice.

Laws forbidding the sale of human organs already exist in many states, and they will probably be extended or interpreted to cover fetal tissue. But to the extent that organ-selling laws are occasionally breached, so too would be the laws banning the sale of fetal tissue.

Pro-lifers also have renewed their campaign to ban late abortions. Yet only half of one percent of all abortions are done after twenty weeks. According to the Alan Guttmacher Institute, only 100 to 200 abortions each year are performed after twenty-four weeks. Of these, virtually all involve severe fetal deformities. Eight in ten Americans support this reason for abortion.

The Guttmacher Institute also reports that of the 4 percent of abortions performed after the fifteenth week, most are done for one of four reasons. Seventy-one percent of women did not recognize that they were pregnant or miscalculated the stage of pregnancy. Forty-eight percent found it difficult to make arrangements for an abortion, a number that will only increase with additional restrictive legislation. Thirty-three percent were minors afraid to tell their parents. And finally, 24 percent were women who needed the extra time to make the decision.*

Despite plans to continue the battle, it is difficult to imagine that the anti-abortionists could ultimately win, even with the weight of the Webster ruling behind them. With its refusal to recognize the complexity of the abortion issue, the pro-life movement has increasingly allowed itself to be put in the same kind of intransigent position that pro-choicers found themselves in only two years ago.

---

*Women gave multiple reasons.

view is radical and has only become more so in
egardless of whether the group is the militant
cue or the more mainstream right to-life organi-
by the Catholic Church. The pro-life movement
ne denial to women of access to liberties they have
enjoyed for thousands of years. Many women view this as a
rejection of the advances they have made in the past thirty
years.

After years of trying to evade the issue, the pro-life movement
has also revealed itself to be anti-birth control as well as anti-
abortion (to say nothing of anti-science). It is most threatened
by RU 486, an abortion pill that is taken to prevent implanta-
tion in the earliest possible stage of pregnancy. RU 486 was
developed in 1980 by Dr. Etienne-Emile Baulieu, since awarded
the prestigious Albert Lasker Clinical Medical Research Award
for his discovery. In 1982 clinical trials were begun on French
women, and in spring of 1988, the French government licensed
the pill for distribution.

The significance of RU 486 is that it will truly make abortion
a private decision, one that a woman will not even have to leave
home to act on. Such a pill would in the words of Werner
Fornos, president of the Population Institute, "make the entire
issue moot. It will take the judgmental community out of play."

Pro-lifers are betting, however, that they can prevent the
licensing of RU 486 in the United States and worldwide. To this
end, they organized a group called the RCR Alliance for the
specific purpose of fighting the new abortifacient. Thus far
their efforts have been more successful than anyone would have
predicted.

In 1988, when RU 486 was first approved for use, the RCR
Alliance, actually a coalition of the National Right-to-Life
Committee, the Catholic Church's anti-abortion lay group; the
Moral Majority (at that time still in existence); and Operation
Rescue swung into action.

Under pressure of a threatened boycott, Rousell-Uclaf, the
French manufacturer of the drug, on October 26, 1988, announced its decision to suspend distribution of RU 486. The
news provoked a storm of protest, including a petition signed by

over 1,000 physicians attending the World Conference of Gynecology and Obstetrics in Rio de Janeiro, Brazil.

The French government, which owns 36 percent of Rousell-Uclaf, ordered the company to put the drug back on the market. French Minister of Health Claude Evin called RU 486 the "moral property of women, not just the property of the drug company." In December the company agreed to distribute the drug, but only in France.

China, where the drug had been clinically tested, would not be able to distribute it as planned, nor would it be licensed as expected in early 1989 in The Netherlands, Great Britain, or Sweden. The World Health Organization, an arm of the United Nations, which had a contract to distribute it in developing nations, found itself in limbo over the delay in distribution. Feminist groups around the world set out to persuade Hoechst and Roussel to reconsider.

Angry at that prospect and also at the announcement that the drug would be sold in France, the RCR Alliance took an unusual step. Using an anonymous donation, it invested thousands of dollars and computer hours in researching a detailed financial profile of Hoechst and its financial dealings around the world. It then sent a courier to West Germany to hand deliver its message to the chairman of Hoechst. The memo outlined the actions the RCR Alliance would instigate if RU 486 were licensed in the U.S.

First, the group threatened a boycott of any U.S. financial firm holding Hoechst stock in international funds. (Hoechst is the most widely held and traded West German stock.)

Second, the Alliance threatened to use Operation Rescue to picket Hoechst's New York headquarters and other offices. It also announced its plan to release a blitz of publicity informing people that the drug company had holdings in South Africa and that its predecessor, I.G. Farben, had manufactured cyanide gas for the concentration camps.

Finally, the Alliance threatened to find and fund plaintiffs who would claim they were harmed by the drug. To show their seriousness, the Alliance retained the services of a French law firm.

Hoechst claimed it was not intimidated by the financial threat of losing its $5 billion U.S. market, which totalled one-fifth of its market worldwide. It said it simply didn't want the image of a company that manufactured an abortion drug.

Fearful of similar actions against them, no American drug company has agreed to manufacture RU 486. The National Organization for Women announced that it was exploring the possibility of forming a company to manufacture RU 486, but given the difficulties even established pharmaceutical companies encounter in getting drugs approved by the Food and Drug Administration, this seems unlikely to happen.

In October 1989, a year after the suspension of the drug outside France, 45,000 French women have used RU 486 with a 96 percent success rate. The pill still is not available outside France, although no one thinks the ban will last long. Women's groups insist that the drug will either be manufactured legally, or it will be smuggled into the country illegally, at increased physical risk and financial cost for women. The pill's discoverer, Dr. Baulieu, says it has the potential to save the lives of 200,000 women around the world who die each year from botched abortions.

In 1970, thirteen American drug companies were engaged in birth control research. Now only one, Ortho Pharmaceutical, is conducting such research. A recent article in *The New York Times* revealed that the United States has fallen decades behind Western Europe in the research and development of birth control devices, a loss to American business as well as to women. Most experts attribute the decline to the chilling effect of the pro-life movement.

The Catholic Church, perhaps the most substantial and powerful opponent of abortion, is increasingly taking an unbending, and some say self-destructive, position on abortion. Where pro-choice women once had their backs pinned to the wall over the issue, now it is the bishops who find themselves in this position. Their attempts to censor Catholic politicians for their abortion positions have mostly won disapproval from Catholics and non-Catholics alike, who believe it is inappropriate for a church to meddle in affairs of state.

New York Governor Mario Cuomo, in mid-March of 1990, issued a 3000-word letter reiterating his support for abortion rights. Abortion, the governor said, "must be a matter of a woman's conscience." He criticized the bishops for their politicalization of the issue, noting: "We shouldn't and don't expect bishops to be politicians. But I don't think we can exempt them from the demands of prudence in the political arena. When the public perception is that they are not simply exercising their teaching role for Catholics, but trying to influence the outcome of an election, there will be publicity."

An announcement by the Bishop's Pro-Life Committee of the U.S. Catholic Conference in April that they had hired a public relations firm and a polling firm to help them shape the public's attitudes toward abortion was met with astonishment and more disapproval, especially when the bishops said they expected to spend $3 to $5 million on their anti-abortion campaign.

Internal conflict was reported at Hill and Knowlton, the public relations firm hired by the church. Its new account was viewed by some as a conflict of interest, since the firm also represented *Playboy* Magazine, an abortion-rights advocate, and Wyeth-Ayerst, a contraceptive manufacturer. One anonymous staffer told the New York newspaper *Newsday* that "80 to 90 percent of the staff" opposed taking on the Church as client for the sole purpose of opposing abortion.

New York's Cardinal John O'Connor strongly supported the move, saying: "Given the stakes—life itself—we can do no less." Critics responded by observing that the bishops also opposed the death penalty, but were not taking any similar action on it.

All this comes at a time when the pro-choice movement is presented with its first real opportunity in several years to advance its cause. The movement has been accused of failing to conduct as rigorous a dialogue as it might, or as the ambivalent mass of people might want. In the late Seventies, pro-lifers forced the pro-choice movement into a defensive position, from which it had to react to the debate rather than control it. In an attempt to preserve the overall right, it refused to debate issues such as minors' rights or late abortions. At one time, pro-choice women even denied the complexity of the abortion decision, although they recognized that it was never simple or painless for any woman to make.

The movement now has a golden opportunity to recoup its past mistakes. Shocked over the loss in Webster and still ambivalent over abortion, Americans are at last eager for an honest dialogue over abortion.

As for concrete strategies to protect the abortion right, among the suggestions that have been made since the Webster decision are a federal constitutional amendment, state and federal laws mandating legal abortion, and renewed pressure on the Supreme Court and other courts.

Although Faye Wattleton, director of Planned Parenthood, has talked to Congress about a constitutional amendment, that is the least likely scenario. Mounting a campaign for such an amendment is a huge undertaking of the kind that is rarely successful even where less inflammatory issues are involved.

Passing pro-choice legislation in the individual states would be as difficult as fighting the sea of restrictive legislation that will follow in Webster's wake. Either one alone would be a full-time occupation, and the work would be overwhelming. Political pundits also say that however much support has shifted to the pro-choice cause, a federal law is not in the offing, either.

Pro-choice forces can no longer look to the Supreme Court for protection, either. Although they will undoubtedly be forced back into Court to fight pro-life lawsuits, they will not be actively taking their causes into the Court in the future. After President Reagan changed the face of the federal judiciary by appointing one-third of its new judges, civil rights groups learned they could no longer rely on the federal bench. Now it is the reproductive rights groups who are learning, in the face of a conservative Supreme Court, that they cannot rely on the high court for protection.

Some experts say the best hope for a permanent solution is to add privacy clauses to state constitutions, and to write them in such a way as to include abortion. Admittedly, this, too, would be a massive undertaking, one that would not be successful in every state. Still, it would be less cumbersome than spending the next decade fighting every single piece of restrictive legislation.

A few months ago, some constitutional scholars would have sought to dissuade pro-choice forces from following this course of action. They would have argued that the privacy right itself stood on shaky ground, that as the invention of a liberal Court, it has never been as widely established as the rights, for example, that are explicitly mentioned in the Constitution. These days that argument falls on deaf ears.

If the abortion debate has resolved nothing else, it appears to have settled the issue, at least in the minds of most Americans, of whether the privacy rights exists. Where people's thinking about abortion was once hazy and ambivalent, it now seems to have become clearer, at least in one respect. Americans have come to think of abortion as part of the privacy right, and of the privacy right as one of their more cherished freedoms. So long as the abortion right is seen as falling under the rubric of privacy, it will be entitled to special protection in the minds of those who count most in the debate: the voters.

The pro-choice movement has also revamped its ideological strategy. It is attempting to broaden the area of debate to include not only abortion but other related women's issues such as prenatal and poor women's health care. Even day care has worked its way into the abortion debate as pro-choice activists point out that more money spent to support mothers and children would help to reduce the number of abortions.

In an attempt to reframe the debate, pro-choice activists are also asking new questions. In the Eighties, their rallying cry was the "woman's right to choose," which offended some middle-of-the-road Americans who feared that a few women were exercising their right to choose in a cavalier fashion.

Now the movement asks, "Whose right to choose—the woman's or the government's?" Put in such clear terms, most Americans, loath to restrict individual liberties, see that the decision, however poorly or well it is made, ultimately belongs with the individual.

| Index

Marian Faux is the author of the widely acclaimed books *Roe v. Wade* and *Childless by Choice: The Challenge of Parenthood.* She is deeply engaged in writing about the basic personal issues of our time. She lives in New York City.